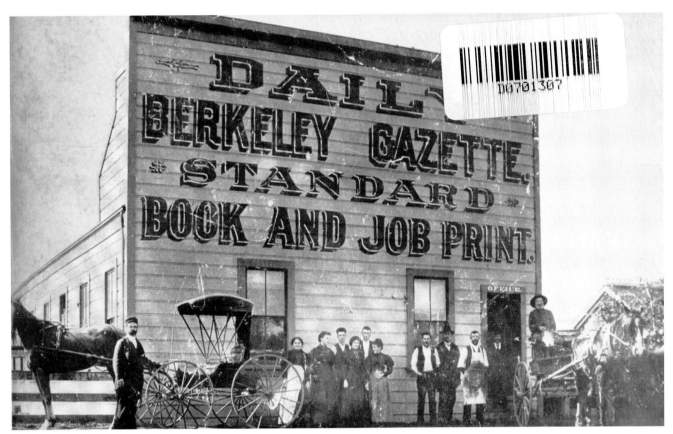

The Berkeley Daily Gazette offices at 2145 Center Street. Circa 1904. Courtesy of the Berkeley Firefighters Association.

Design by Elysium/San Francisco

Edited by Sauda Burch

Production by Diana Nankin

Technical assistance by Steven J. Brett, Computer Consulting, Berkeley, California

Printed in the United States of America on recycled paper.

05 04 03 02 01 00   10 9 8 7 6 5 4 3 2

ISBN: 0-9678204-0-5

Cover photograph: *Looking northeast towards the Berkeley hills from McGee Avenue. George Kidd (Captain
Kidd) in goat cart. Jim Donovan leading cow.* Courtesy of the Berkeley Firefighters Association.

RSB Books

telephone and fax: 510.524.1683

email: AMRSB@worldnet.att.net

STATEMENT OF CONDITION OF MATERIALS PRESENTED

The newspaper articles in this book are from copies of the *Berkeley Daily Gazette* that
are all about one hundred years old. They came to me in various stages of damage,decomposition and preservation. Some were half pages with no dating possible.
Some were torn off losing half an article. The articles are presented here in their
existing condition as I found them, complete with typographical and printing
errors, misspellings, etc., just as the Berkeleyans of 1900 saw them.

The photographs in this book are images of Berkeley, the Bay and related topics.
They too are all about one hundred years old. In both the newspapers and the
photos I was working with, there were amazing stories and vistas to be shared, many
in less than optimal condition. My choice in this book was to publish photos that
may be of mediocre resolution, but of fantastic views or topics. Also, it was my
choice to share many articles that I was sure would be of interest but were damaged
or partially presented. The alternative would be to let them decay unshared and
this seemed a sad fate for such a fine bunch of stories. I hope you understand and
enjoy the results of the passage of time on these magnificent resources.

Berkeley 1900

Daily Life at the Turn of the Century

RICHARD SCHWARTZ

Courtesy of the Berkeley Firefighters Association.

Table of Contents

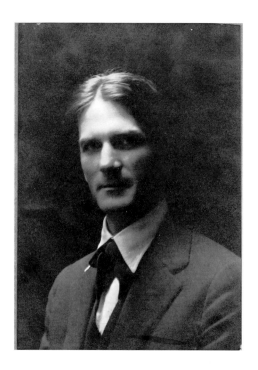

"Taking it all in all, if I had the choice of all the cities of the earth for a permanent dwelling place I should select Berkeley. I should make this choice because, despite the lack of developed civic pride, there are assembled here some of the finest types of men and women that our American culture has produced; because its site is the most significant, the most picturesque, the most charged with promise and expectancy of any commonwealth in our land. Let us all work together to bring out the best to enhance the natural beauty by municipal adornment, to make our city as fair as Athens of old, and as fruitful, that its name may typify the idealism of the Bishop who sang:

'Westward the star of empire takes its way.'"

—Charles Keeler, *Berkeley Reporter*, December 1906

Introduction

For almost two decades I have worked as a building contractor in Berkeley, California. Over the years, having worked on and visited hundreds of houses, I have often blurred my eyes and imagined the crews constructing each house—especially those of the 1800s and of the early 1900s: the carpenters arriving early each day to sharpen their hand saws, their conversation on lunch breaks, the laborers staking barrels of plaster and, finally, Berkeley families of yesterday moving into completed homes with their clothing, toys, photographs and often a goat or goose. Today as I work on these houses, I feel a connection to the builders, their occupants and the times.

In 1976 I worked for the U.S. Forest Service in the Sierra fighting fires. We were often in areas that were littered with artifacts from old logging camps or Native American summer villages. As I worked I sensed the lives of the people who lived there. I returned many times to reexperience the stirrings of the past.

In 1986 I visited a sixty-five-foot circle of roughly piled stones that had originally been in Stampede Valley, north of Truckee, California. The mystery of who built it and why clung to me. I took a year off to research the stone circle's origin. It became my first book, *The Circle of Stones*.

Almost a decade and a half later, I was led by my curiosity again. At the suggestion of my friend Steve Brett, I visited the Berkeley Historical Society to see a turn-of-the-century film of a streetcar in Berkeley. I was riveted. Later as I perused the Society's collection of photographs of old Berkeley, I saw fields where there are now entire neighborhoods. The university was rolling grassland crossed by the willows of Strawberry Creek. Through these pictures I experienced the past of my adopted home.

On my third visit to the Berkeley Historical Society, docent Burl Willes mentioned that someone had donated a two-foot stack of old *Berkeley Daily Gazette* newspapers from about 1900 to 1909. The Society could not keep them because of the risk of mold spreading to their

"It is said that the ardent patriotism of the Swiss people is due to their matchless mountains. If this be true then Berkeley and particularly North Berkeley should be the home of liberty loving, independent, high minded men and women."

—Victor J. Robertson, *Berkeley Reporter*, December 1906

other collections. I couldn't imagine these papers being thrown away, so I offered to take them. Though I didn't know it, that was the beginning of *Berkeley 1900*.

In these pages you will learn of much more than just Berkeley's people. Whales still roamed the Bay in 1900. Bears and rattlesnakes could turn up anytime. For the first time horses were having to share Shattuck Avenue with automobiles. Horses caused many more injuries and deaths than the occasional automobiles.

Telephones, electric lights, indoor plumbing and automobiles were marching into Berkeley and the nation.

The news articles in the *Gazette* detailed lives of average Berkeley citizens and their world at the turn of the century. Though the newspapers are now crumbling, this book and all of us might pass their stories on.

It was out of respect for these Berkeley predecessors, the people whose footprints are still under ours somewhere, that I was moved to write this book.

" Some well-intentioned critics say: 'It is not good for professors to live too closely together, and to stick to their Berkeley, like oysters to their rock.'"

—Robert Duponey, *Berkeley Reporter*, December 1906

I.   Origins of Berkeley

Though this book focuses on the daily life of everyday people in Berkeley at the turn of the last century, countless human footprints had already been pressed into the ground. The land on which Berkeley now sits had nursed small villages of Native Americans in many creek drainages for thousands of years.

Archeologists have recently hypothesized about a large drop in population 700-1100 years ago. Whether it was a big climate change or another culture moving here is not yet known.

"The only way to continue is to tell a story and there is no other way. Your children will not survive unless you tell something about them—how they were born, how they came to this certain place, how they continued."

—Simon Ortiz, *A Good Journey*

Another huge change in Native American culture occurred in the late 1700s when the Spanish arrived and established missions and presidios. By love, force, charm and punishment many Native Americans were enticed to join the missions, but some fled to the interior, beyond the Spanish soldiers' reach. Native peoples were killed by strange and powerful new technologies like horse-mounted soldiers with rifles and *riatas* (the deadly accurate Spanish whip).

The Native openness to these strangers perhaps contributed to their undoing. They had little defense against the Spanish resolve of making them into images of the Spanish Empire and culture.

By 1810 the original Native American villages of the East Bay were all abandoned. In 1817 Mission Dolores began using what would become Berkeley to graze sheep. Four years later retired Spanish soldier Luis Peralta received a private land grant from Spain that encompassed the area from San Leandro to El Cerrito.

By 1822 Mexico freed itself from Spain's rule. But Mexico was occupied by its own internal upheavals and had little attention and even less money to direct to this rough frontier.

The Alta California culture and economy was left on its own and became distinctive. Residents were trading longhorn hides and tallow for manufactured goods with foreign merchant vessels using tally sheets instead of currency.

In 1841, twenty years after his grant, Luis Peralta divided his rancho amongst his four sons. Domingo Peralta, his second oldest son, received the northernmost section, what we today call Berkeley. Domingo grazed longhorn cattle as his father had done.

Several years after Mexico's loss of the Mexican American War and the discovery of gold at Sutter's Mill, Yankee squatters began to light on Domingo's land like sand flies. By 1852 Domingo's herds were decimated by poachers and his land grabbed by squatters. At the same time, he was forced to sell much of his land to pay taxes and the land attorneys who were hired to protect his interests.

Land Domingo actually sold to pioneer developers in 1853 eventually became sites of the state college, Berkeley's first freight wharf at the foot of Delaware Street and numerous farms. Industry first came to Berkeley in the form of a starch mill. Fresh water, a bucolic setting and opportunity beckoned visitors to settle here.

The Civil War found the East Bay squarely on the side of the Union, and many local towns mustered volunteers. Bay Area soldiers were sent to the Southwest to patrol and fight Native tribes resisting American domination of the area. They also patrolled for invading Confederate troops.

In 1873 growth accelerated rapidly with the arrival in Berkeley of the transcontinental railroad. Supplies and commodities flowed with new vigor both east and west. More people kept arriving and by 1900 houses were squeezing out farms. There were now 15,000 people living in Berkeley versus only twelve souls counted in the census of Domingo Peralta's time.

Let's join these 15,000 citizens.

Description of Beautiful Berkeley

Sketch of Its Educational Advantages and Environments.

Location and Topography
Berkeley is situated on the east side of San Francisco Bay, adjoining and north of Oakland. It extends from the shore line easterly a distance of three and one-eighth miles to the crest of the foot hills and from north to south it measures, on the average, two and one-half miles, the south boundary line being irregular. The rise from the bay is gradual and uniform—the elevation reached at the base of the hills being about 500 feet, thus affording an excellent drainage and presenting every advantage for a perfect system of sewers and street improvements, as well as giving to almost every lot a charming outlook covering the San Francisco harbor, the Golden Gate entrance, and the mountain ranges along the coast.

Streets and Sewers
The streets are laid out with comparative regularity and in length embrace a total distance of 200 miles. Forty miles are already graded, macadamzied and sidewalked, and 90 miles of sewers have been laid. The small pipe system has been adopted and is so perfect in its working that the city is remarkably healthful and wholly free from epidemics of zymotic diseases. The death rate is as low as any place in the State.

University of California
Berkeley is the seat of the State University which has already attained an enviable position among the best in this country and is now enjoying a period of progress and development that is attracting the attention of the world.
Through the liberality of Mrs. Phœbe Hearst, an eminent French architect is preparing plans for laying out the grounds of the University, and the location of all the buildings that will be required for years to come, and will furnish general designs for the structures, thus presenting the best architectural features for this seat of learning the world can give, and in perfect harmony with each other and their environment. Large donations for carrying out this comprehensive scheme have been assured and the initial steps will be taken this year.

History
The location of the University of California on its present site gave the first impulse towards the growth of Berkeley. This was in 1858. In 1866 the name of "Berkeley" by a happy inspiration was chosen. In 1872 the first college building was erected. The city was incorporated, as the Town of Berkeley, in 1878, under a special charter, which continued in force till 1895, when the present freeholders charter was adopted.

Public Schools
Berkeley schools are abreast of the best in the State, and the town in consequence of its literary atmosphere has become the residence of a class of citizens who have been influenced largely in its selection by the educational advantages which it possesses over any other city on the coast. There are eleven public grammar and primary schools so located that each section of the place is well and conveniently served, and a High School centrally located, is easily accessible from all quarters. Sixty-six teachers and a Superintendent are employed.

High School
The High School is accredited by the University, and its pupils enter the college without examination. Children may therefore pass from the receiving class to the end of the college course, and the only expense is that for books and the usual outlay for maintenance. Berkeley spends each year upon her public schools, $75,000 for maintenance. Three new grammar schools and a new high school will be built this year at a cost of $100,000.

Commercial School
A very promising Commercial School has been made a part of the public school system, giving free of tuition an excellent preparation for a business life.

Private Schools
There are also four private Kindergarten schools, and six secondary and grammar schools of high standing.

D. D. and B. Institute
The California Institute for the education of the deaf, dumb and blind, located here, has no superior anywhere, and in many respects stands ahead of all similar colleges.

Public Libraries
Public Libraries are a feature of prominence in Berkeley. The large central library located in the Bank Block, is one of the largest and best equipped in the State. Branch Auxiliaries are located in the southern and western portions of the city, and all are well managed and liberally patronized.

Churches
Eighteen churches, representing nearly all the denominations, testify to the religious tendencies of the Berkeley citizens, and afford to every center of the town convenient opportunity for attending divine service. These organizations are all flourishing and the congregations are large, often taxing the accommodations to the utmost.

Population
In 1890 the population of Berkeley was 5,100, in 1900 the census will show the number of its inhabitants to be not far either way from 14,000.

A careful census taken under the supervision of Professor Plehn, in April of 1899, gave a population of 13,219. The increase has been remarkably steady throughout the decade, the business depression of 1892 to 1898 affecting the progress of the town but little. Present population about 15,000.

Societies
Besides the ordinary benevolent societies and orders, all are well represented, there are numerous social and literary clubs, imparting a delightful and cultivated character to the community, and affording the best opportunities for mental improvement. Lectures, musicales and entertainments of high order are frequent.

Assessment Values and Tax Rate
The last assessment rolls of the town showed a total valuation of real and personal property of $8,933,000. The tax rate for the year was $1 on $100 of valuation, and the money was approportioned as follows: General Fund, 31 cents; Street Fund, 14 cents; High School Fund, 17 cents; Grammar and Primary School Fund, 13 cents; Library Fund, 8 cents, and Redemption Fund, 17 cents.

Indebtedness
The Bonded indebtedness is as follows: School Bonds, 1892, $30,000; School Bonds, 1900, $100,000; Electric Light, $13,500, the sewer Bonds $14,800, total, $158,300.

Fire Protection
Berkeley has a volunteer fire department very effective and well equipped, as the very low percentage of losses from fire amply demonstrates. There are seven organizations, one located in each of the thickly settled neighborhoods.

Health Department
The health department is very energetically and efficiently administered by the health officer and sanitary inspector, who are ever watchful for menacing conditions, and prompt in abating them.

Electric Light and Gas
The town is lighted with 112 2,000 candle power arc lamps, on all dark nights, from dusk to 1-30 A.M., and from 5 A.M. to sunrise. An incondescent system is operated in connection with gas works, the rates for either of which being very reasonable.

Water Supply
The water supply of Berkeley, by the recent consolidation of companies, is assured to be ample and of good quality. The supply comes from flowing wells, tunnels and Lake Chabot, located in the hills to the east, and 250 feet above sealevel, being by filtration free from impurities and contaminations. The gravity force is sufficient for all purposes, including fire protection.

Means of Communication
Between San Francisco and Berkeley half hour trains run on the Southern Pacific Ferry System, leaving each terminus from 5:30 to 10 o'clock A.M. and from 3:30 to 7 P.M., and hourly trips from 10 o'clock A.M. to 3 P.M. and from 7:30 to 1 A.M. By the California and Nevada Narrow Guage Railroad communication is had with Contra Costa County. The Overland and Mainline tracks of the Southern Pacific, Santa Fe and Central Pacific Railroads skirt the west end of the town affording with the water front the best of facilities for transportation and making that section an ideal location for manufacturing purposes and giving ample accommodations for cheap movement of products to distributing centers.

Street Car Service
Berkeley is connected with Oakland, Alameda, Haywards, Fruitvale, San Leandro, etc., by car lines of two companies systems, the Oakland Transit Co. and the Oakland R. R. Co. Between East and West Berkeley and Peralta Park the horsecar lines of the C. U. & F. R. R. Co. are operated half hourly. The usual five-cent fares prevail, with transfers to most connections. Extensions of electric lines are under way.

Business Houses, Banks, Hotels, Etc.
Berkeley is well supplied with the usual lines of business houses, almost every retail trade being represented. One well-officered bank of $100,000 paid up capital, the First National Bank. Hotels and boarding houses, of moderate capacity.

Factories and Shipping
While Berkeley is pre-eminently a residence town, it possesses also excellent advantages for the location of manufacturing establishments. The west end of the town borders upon San Francisco Bay, and is distant by direct water communication from the metropolis of the State, only seven miles. Products from all parts of the world may be landed at its wharves and its wares shipped direct to their best market. The main lines of the Southern Pacific Company skirt its shores, thus affording perfect facilities for transportation of goods and materials by rail. Sites for factories may be had on most advantageous terms, and the energetic citizens of the shore district are eager to extend every inducement for the location of new industries. There are already in operation a planing mill, the largest in the State, the largest soap factory west of the Rockies, a match factory, broom factory, two oil works for producing linseed and cocoa nut oil, two tanneries and leather furnishing establishments, a soda water factory, an organ factory, shoe factory, factory for making silk cloth, chemical works and fuse works, lumber yard, wood pulp mill, brewery, starch factory, flour and grist mill, steam laundry, etc.

2. Gypsies

GYPSIES QUARREL IN CAMP

Bad blood between two hostile gypsy camps in West Berkeley has sprung up over the retention of two gypsy maidens, who, in addition to their beauty, are successful fortune tellers and, hence, greatly desirable members of a well-conducted gypsy band.

The rival clans are captained by Artante Immo and Pietro Marina, respectively, and the trouble over the two girls originated in the successful stratagem, whereby Marina's camp won the pair of charming gypsies over to his side. Whatever of romance may be mingled in the transfer of allegiance cannot be ascertained, as both sides are maintaining a sullen silence about the trouble, and the difficulty would be unknown at present had not the warring factions, now camped side by side on the Grayson tract, reached such a high tension that firearms have been brought into play. Sunday night the residents in the neighborhood heard pistol shots accompanying a great disturbance, and fears of bloodshed and general rioting among the strangers have brought the Town Marshal's force to the scene, where a close watch will be kept over the sulky foreigners to prevent any serious consequences of the quarrel.

August 15, 1905

GYPSY GIRLS PLEAD NOT GUILTY AND CASES ARE SET

Marie Mitchell and Rosa Marceloni, the gypsy girls who were arrested recently for stealing wood, appeared before Justice Edgar this morning and pleaded not guilty of the charge. Rosa's trial was set for September 14, and Marie's for September 19. Both, through their attorney, J. Graber, have demanded trial by jury.

In 1900 gypsies from Europe lived in several Berkeley encampments. Working-class neighbors often complained that the all-night parties at the gypsy encampments ruined their sleep. According to the *Gazette*, life in the gypsy camps appeared unhappy and chaotic despite constant celebrations.

Many residents urged the police to take action. Marshal Volmer of the Berkeley Police was mindful of the gypsies' rights. Since the gypsies held valid property leases, Volmer refused to run them out of town as he was encouraged to do by some residents.

None of the *Gazette* articles are written by gypsies and the *Gazette* reporting offers only negative views of gypsy life. We do not know how the gypsies perceived their dealings with neighbors and law enforcement.

WOULD RUN OUT GYPSIES

A petition signed by seventy-six residents of the West End and especially in the vicinity of the Pardee Tract, complaining against the presence in that tract of a camp of gypsies, caused quite a discussion at last night's meeting of the Trustees. The protest reads as follows:

"We, the undersigned residents and property owners of West Berkeley, desire to call the attention of your honorable body to the fact of a nuisance existing near Sixth street in the Pardee tract.

"Said nuisance being the encampment of the large number of gypsies in that section. Though in a sanitary district, there are not any sanitary facilities. We fear an epidemic of disease may arise therefrom, there being sixteen tents and a population of 65 or 70 people with horses, dogs, etc.

"Night is made hideous by their orgies, property destroyed, fences burned and hen coops looted nightly.

"We therefore ask your honorable body to have this nuisance abated at your earliest convenience.

W. R. Dickeson, F. Simon and others addressed the board on the matter, complaining vigorously against the gypsy camp. Trustee Ferrier was in favor of instructing the Marshal to give the gypsies twenty-four hours in which to get out of town and a motion to that effect was made by Olsen. Trustee Staats said he was of the opinion that such a move would not prove effectual. He believed that other methods could be resorted to in order to rid the town of these objectionable people. He said that the behavior of occupants of the camp would warrant their arrest on a great variety of charges, and if several of them could be taken up and prosecuted, it would result in driving the camp from town.

Other members of the board maintained, however, that the nomads should be ordered away immediately. At this juncture Marshal Vollmer stated that he had already attempted to drive the gypsies away, but found that they held a lease on the property, which does not expire until September 8. Although they pay but $4 a month for the use of the property, it would, nevertheless, be difficult to drive them off until the lease expires. Regarding the behavior of the gypsies, Marshal Vollmer said that both himself and his men had tried repeatedly to catch them in order to drive the camp away, but that the gypsies always conducted themselves quietly when policemen were in the neighborhood. A resident of the West End, one of the protestants, informed the board that the gypsies had been engaged in holding a celebration all that day. More than half the occupants of the camp were intoxicated, he said, and it was a good time to go after them.

It was finally decided to refer the matter to the Marshal and Town Attorney for immediate action.

August 29, 1905

Gypsies Seeking a Location.

Marshal Vollmer reports that he has not ceased in his efforts to oust the big band of gypsies camped in West Berkeley, who have become a great nuisance to the people residing in the vicinity. The gypsy leader stated yesterday that as soon as he could secure a satisfactory lease of land elsewhere, he would immediately move to another town.

August 31, 1905

Gypsy Girl Dismissed.

On account of her age, Mary Mitchell, the 14-year-old gypsy, who was arrested last month and accused of stealing wood, was dismissed to-day. The other girl who is more than 18 years old, will have to stand trial.

POLICEMAN ARRESTS GYPSY GIRLS AND IS ALMOST MOBBED

Policeman Atchison had a close call from serious injury at an early hour this morning when he arrested two gypsy girls whom he caught in the act of stealing wood from the grounds of an old distillery at the foot of Grayson street. When captured by the policeman the girls struggled to escape and the younger, who is but thirteen years old, screamed and fought the officer. The cries of the girl brought some twenty of the men from the gypsy camp, and in a few minutes the policeman and his captive were surrounded by a mob of angry gypsies. At this juncture Atchison, although he feared an attack at any moment, ordered the men about him to clear the way. The gypsies moved sullenly out of the way, but followed close behind the policeman and the girls he had captured. Fearing that he might be attacked any moment, Atchison went to the nearest telephone and called Detective Jamison to assist in taking the girls to the Marshal's office.

Something of a sensation was caused on the streets when Policeman Atchison and Detective Jamison marched the girls to the Marshal's office. Both the gypsies were scantily attired, the older one being in her barefeet. Both had apparently been out of bed only a short time and had probably been ordered to get wood to cook the morning meal.

Upon arriving at the police station the girls gave their names as Mary Mitchell and Rosa Marceloni. They were followed in half an hour by four male members of the camp. As Justice Edgar was not in town, Marshal Vollmer informed Police Justice Smith of Oakland of the occurrence, and he set the bail of the two women at $25 each. This amount the gypsies secured within a short time and the women were released. When the younger girl saw that it would be necessary to pay to secure her release, she wept and tore her hair.

Marshal Vollmer has had the gypsies watched carefully for the last few days, as their presence in the West End has been the source of considerable complaint. The Town Trustees at their last meeting, and acting on a petition from residents of the West End complaining of the gypsy camp, instructed the Marshal to get the nomads out of town as soon as possible. The girls accused of stealing wood, will appear before Justice Edgar to-morrow morning.

Arrested Here.

On information furnished from Fresno, Harry Gardner, a plumber, was arrested here yesterday on a charge of defrauding an innkeeper. The man claimed to be in Berkeley for the purpose of securing work. He was identified by the police through a description furnished by the Fresno police. Gardner deposited $50 bail.

Foley in Trouble Again.

Dan Foley of West Berkeley, who was arrested some time ago an suspicion of having had a hand in several burglaries, was arrested again last night by Deputy Constable William Atchison who charged him with being drunk and disturbing the peace. He was lodged in the County Jail.

September 1, 1905

GYPSIES HAVE NEW LEADER

The question that is puzzling the heads of the police and health departments at the present time is—What is to be done with the gypsy camp in the West End? Marshal Vollmer has resorted to numerous plans to rid the town of the objectionable persons; Health Officer G. F. Reinhardt has visited the gypsies and forced them to clean the camp thoroughly, but the nomads say they will not go. Yesterday Alexander Adams, who claims leadership of the gypsy band, arrived here from the East, armed with plenty of money, a good command of the English language and lots of indifference for the police. Yesterday and last night was devoted to feasting in honor of the chief, and to-day, it is claimed the camp will be moved—but not out of Berkeley.

It is understood that the gypsies have secured a lease of a tract of land on University near San Pablo avenue, where they propose to establish themselves at once, despite the objections of persons residing in that neighborhood. The lease on the land they now occupy on Grayson street, near Third, expires to-day, and they will in all probability move to-night.

Although the camp lost a few of its number when Mitchell Demetrio, the former leader departed recently, it still includes some 75 or 80 persons, and it is claimed more than 100 babies, ranging in age from two days to two years. Aside from these there is a large assortment of youngsters of a walking age, together with many dogs and horses.

Should this motely band settle on the University-avenue property, where it is understood they have secured a lease the residents of that vicinity will complain with even more force than have those in the neighborhood where the gypsies now reside.

WANTS GYPSY TAKEN INTO CUSTODY FOR BEATING HIS WIFE

Residents in the vicinity of Grayson and Third streets, were aroused at an early hour this morning by the screaming of a woman occupant of the gypsy camp in the Pardee Tract. John Mains, who resides at 470 Grayson, rushed from his home fearing that some one was being murdered. As he left the house a gypsy woman ran into the yard begging him to protect her from her husband. Prostrating herself on the ground the woman between sobs said that her husband had tried to kill her. While the women was still begging Mains to protect her, a number of other women from the camp rushed into the yard and dragged her away, almost tearing her clothes in their haste to get her out of sight.

Fearing that the woman might meet with injury Mains followed. He went to the chief of the camp and while explaining the case, the cries of the woman were renewed. Running in the direction from which the sound came, Mains saw the woman trying to get away from her husband, who had grabbed her by the dress. "While I was watching them," said Mains, "the man struck the woman in the face, knocking her to the ground. He then proceeded to pound her unmercifully about the face with his clenched fist. I called to him to stop and threatened to have him arrested."

Mains reported the case to the police and Justice Edgar, asking that a warrant be issued for the gypsy on a charge of wife-beating. He was informed that it would be best for the woman to swear to the warrant and he left in search of her, promising to bring her before the Justice to make the necessary charges.

Accused of Beating Sister.

Joseph White, a machinist residing at 640 Howard street, San Francisco, was taken into custody yesterday by Detective Jamison upon the complaint of Mrs. Fred Munday, sister of the accused man, who claimed that he had dragged her about by her hair and strucks her several times in the face. The disturbance was the outcome of a dispute between Mrs. Munday and her brother over the custody of her nephews, aged 12 and 14 years respectively. White was removed to the county jail, and this morning Mrs. Munday announced that she would not swear to a warrant against him and he was dismissed from custody.

Reports Girls Lost.

Efforts to discover the identity of the two young girls who were reported Saturday from Coulterville to have been lost in the Hetch Hetchy valley have failed, although Berkeley was well canvassed yesterday. Many prominent members of the Sierra Club, to which the party near Coulterville is believed to belong, were seen, but could throw no light on the matter.

Professor A. C. Lawson of the department of geology of the University of California, and an enthusiastic member of the Sierra Club, and Professor Joseph Le Conte, who is in close touch with expeditions into the high Sierras, were both asked if they knew of any party there at present from Berkeley. Neither of them could give any information, and until more information comes from the authorities at Coulterville it is not probable that the identity of the young women can be determined. At a late hour today Marshall Vollmer had no further news. The telegram follows:

"Coulterville, Sept. 16.

"Chief of Police, Berkeley, Cal.:

"Report here two Berkeley girls lost from camping party. One seen in Hetch Hetchy Valley; ran away; wild. Can you send any information? (Signed) "THOMAS COLLINS,

"Constable."

September 18, 1905

GYPSY WOMAN FINED IN THE METROPOLIS

The conduct of the female contingent of the band of gypsies which infests West Berkeley has bent the forbearing courtesy of the Key Route officials to the breaking point, and recourse to the Police Courts was sought Wednesday, when Rosa Carmeletta was taken before Police Judge Conlan of San Francisco, for expectorating on one of the boats, and she was fined $50 off-hand by the disgusted Judge.

A. A. Knox, representing the company, testifi,ed that every day about two dozen women of the tribe cross to San Francisco, disperse over every portion of the boat to which passengers have access, and by their disgusting conduct and insulting remarks make the lives of the passengers miserable.

September 22, 1905

MUIR ILL WITH GRIEF FOR WIFE

John Muir, the venerable naturalist and geologist and discoverer of the Muir glacier in Alaska, is seriously ill in Arizona. His condition—a complete nervous breakdown—is due to the sad death of his beloved wife at Martinez two weeks ago and the sudden and serious illness of his daughter Helen, whose removal to Arizona just prior to the death of Mrs. Muir was necessitated as the only means of restoring her to health.

As soon as the physicians attending his daughter informed the famous naturalist that the cold from which she had been suffering had settled on her lungs and that her removal to Arizona was imperative, he at once prepared for the journey. Mrs. Muir was then ill at the country home of the Muirs in the hills just outside of Martinez. She had been suffering for several months, but her death was not expected. The aged naturalist had no sooner arrived at Adamana, in Arizona, where friends of the family reside, than he was hastily recalled to the bedside of his wife at Martinez. While he was hastening home Mrs. Muir passed away peacefully on the morning of Sunday, August 9. Her oldest daughter, Wanda Muir, and near relatives were with her when the end came.

The shock of the sad news that awaited his home coming was all that John Muir could stand. After the funeral he returned to join his daughter in Arizona. Now Miss Wanda Muir has joined her father and sister in Arizona and is striving to bring them back to health. She is a student at the University of California in the senior class and a member of the Gamma Phi Beta Sorority, but has had to give up her studies in order to minister to her sister and father. She was accompanied to Arizona by Miss Safford of 2401 Le Conte avenue, and it has only been with the return of Miss Safford to her Berkeley home that news of the sorrow in the Muir family has become known.

John Muir knows the flora of North America as perhaps no other living scientist knows it. He has been in communion with the great forces of nature nearly all his life and has traveled on foot through the forests and plains of nearly every part of America from frozen Alaska to the torrid Isthmus. His books on the glaciers and forests of America have attracted attention among scientists and nature lovers the world ov...

Because of his kindly and lovable nature, which was akin to that of the late and well beloved Joseph Le Conte, he has hosts of friends and admirers who will hear with sorrow of his illness.

August 24, 1905

John Muir is an icon, especially in California. Although known best for his tenacious struggles to preserve wild spaces, the *Berkeley Gazette* reveals his personal life during some very rough times in August 1905.

Muir and his family lived in Martinez north of Berkeley. His daughter, Helen, had been ill and doctors recommended she be moved to Arizona. Mrs. Louie Muir, also suffering from ill health, remained behind.

When Muir arrived in Arizona, he was immediately summoned back to Martinez. His wife's health had deteriorated and Mrs. Muir died before John reached home. The *Gazette* reported that John Muir was near a nervous breakdown.

Muir would soon contract pneumonia and die from his travels in the rain to tend to his daughter's health.

John Muir, his wife Louie, and their two daughters, Wanda and Helen, at home on the porch at their Martinez, California, ranch in 1901. Courtesy of the Contra Costa County Historical Society.

4. Environment

"After having crossed the continent, after the agitation, the excitement, the noise and turmoil of the great cities, after the deserts discouragingly melancholy; after the majestic awe-inspiring mountains, I arrive in this delightful Berkeley, at the end of a world, opposite that Golden Gate which opens into another immensity, more beautiful, more strange, more mysterious also and more alluring, and a desire comes to me, to spread my wings once more, and resume my flight, to go on and on, in order to know what is beyond that marvelous gate, behind which the sun disappears every evening with an ever new majesty and splendor.

"But something holds me back, something indescribable, which fills my whole being. I love Berkeley; I love its wooden houses whose color harmonizes with that of the earth; I love the undulation of its hills and its pretty canyons; I love the bay and its constantly changing surface, now sunny and bright like a beautiful blue lake whose outlines are clearly distinguished, now lightly veiled by a haze whose transparency delicately softens the lines of the hills that skirt it. I love its moonlight nights, its university, its campus, its Greek Theatre and, seeing so much beauty, so many marvels, it seems strange to me that all its inhabitants are not poets or artists. But I will admit that I am asking too much—Berkeley people appreciate beautiful things, and that is a great deal."

—Jeanne Harouel Greenleaf, *Berkeley Reporter*, December 1906

Strawberry Creek on University of California campus. Courtesy of the Berkeley Firefighters Association.

FEARFUL STORM THIS MORINING.

Buildings Wrecked in Terrific Gale.

St. Matthew's Episcopal Mission Demolished ---- Residences Wrecked and Judson Factory Damaged.

In one of the most violent storms which has ever been recorded in the history of Alameda county, property to the value of several thousand dollars was destroyed in the space of a few minutes this morning. A terrific gale from the southwest swept through the southern portion of the city about 10:30 o'clock. The miniature cyclone stopped before it reached the business portion of the town, and then retraced its course, completing the work of demolition.

The climax of this morning's storm followed a burst of thunder and lightening. It came without a warning and swept along at an exceedingly high rate of speed. Persons who were out in the streets during the progress of the windstorm hurridly sought shelter. Fences, lines of telegraph and tele-

phone wires, windmills and trees, were blown down. Large buildings were totally destroyed and damaged in the storm's fury.

The St. Matthew's Episcopal Mission at the corner of Grove and Russell streets was totally demolished as was a dwelling being erected by Contractor John Rodgers on Woolsey street. Along the bay line small crafts were sunk, the Judson Iron Works buildings damaged and the semaphores at the Oakland mole blown over, causing considerable delay in the operating of trains.

ST. MATTHEW'S CHURCH WRECKED.

One of the most striking evidences of the fury of the gale is portrayed in the total demolition of the St. Matthew's Episcopal Church Mission building at the corner of Russell and Grove streets. The little house of worship, which was moved to its present location from Alcatraz avenue and Calais street but a few weeks ago, was struck broadside by the wind. After the walls had been partially blown over the northern half of the roof was lifted high into the air, carried a distance of a hundred feet and dropped on Russell street.

Had the catastrophe occurred while the congregation was in the building the loss of life would have been very great. Save a few twisted sections, the once pretty little church is now a mass of kindling wood. A remarkable incident in the destruction of the church consisted of the

fact that the furniture in the building was left intact. The lighting fixtures, however, were twisted and broken.

CHURCH DEBT JUST PAID.

Many of the members of the congregation quickly hastened to the scene of the wreck and several of the ladies could not refrain from crying as they saw the little church, the debt from which had just been lifted, in ruins. Under the direction of its pastor, Rev. T. L. Randolph, the church had just entered upon a particularly successful career.

The building was valued at about $1000 and the furniture and fixtures $500.

NEW HOUSE BLOWN DOWN.

The storm seemed to strike heavier in some spots than in others. One of these was on Woolsey street where contractor John Rodgers is erecting a number of residences. A dwelling, which was in the course of construction. The house was blown over and damaged to the extent of $500.

At Dwight way station the storm played pranks with many signs. Those of Frank B. Thompson, H. S. Howard and Mrs. Hartley were carried away. The tops of the rows of big eucalyptis trees on Parker street were broken off and carried to Blake street.

At 2128 Telegraph avenue the windmill of Mrs. Pidgeon was blown over, the machinery crashing into a roof.

A tree which was thrown across the track on Dwight way near Fulton street, stopped the running of electric cars until it was removed.

Trains were run irregularly during the morning on account of the damage done to the block system of signals at the Oakland pier. There the telegraph and telephone wires were snapped by the falling of lines of poles. Until late this afternoon no telephone communication could be had with San Francisco and telegrams were sent via San Jose. The entire forces of the companies whose property was damaged were sent out to make repairs.

JUDSON WORKS DAMAGED.

The immense strength of the baby cyclone may be estimated from the damage done to the Judson Iron Works property at Emeryville. There a huge chimney was blown over and the roof carried off one of the shops.

A number of workmen narrowly escaped death and serious injury by the falling of debris.

DWELLING TWISTED BY STORM.

The house of O. M. Jones at 1533 Julia street, near Calais, was badly wrenched by the wind. The top of the house was thrown two feet out of plumb and much damage done to the entire frame work.

There were ten men in the basement at work making leather belts when the storm struck the house. A rush was made for the door, but the twisting of the building made it impossible for the men to open the door. Had the wind continued an instant longer at the same furious rate the house would have been blown down and the men crushed.

A vacant house, owned by M. W. Davis, on Delaware street near West, was blown off its foundation a distance of four feet. The structure, which is badly strained, will cost $500 to repair.

December 14, 1900

Strawberry Creek above the University of California campus. Courtesy of the Berkeley Firefighters Association.

Nell and Blanche Morse in Strawberry Canyon.
Courtesy of the Berkeley Firefighters Association.

Old Terra Firma Moved.

A strong earthquake wave at about 2 o'clock yesterday afternoon shook the buildings of Berkeley and startled the few citizens left in town. The shock did very little damage, but was accompanied by an unusually great displacement of the earth's crust.

The actual disturbance lasted nearly forty seconds. The shock began at a few minutes before 2 o'clock with a slight tremor which increased in intensity until the principal tremblor made itself felt at 2:01 o'clock, then dying away in a series of lessening vibrations.

The shock was recorded by the instruments of the Students' Observatory of the University of California, the records being among the best that were secured.

The tracings, as read by Professor A. O. Leuschner, who is in charge, show that the shock proceeded from west to east, the preliminary oscillations beginning at 1:57:32½, Pacific standard time, as registered by the Ewing seismograph. Oscillations lasting for about thirty-eight minutes can be distinctly traced upon the smoked-glass plate of the instrument. Several pronounced shocks took place during that time.

The principal one was strongly felt, and was accompanied by a displacement of the earth's crust amounting to one-twenty-fourth of an inch. As the majority of shocks ordinarily felt are caused by a displacement ranging from 1-100 to 1-1000 of an inch, the temblor of this afternoon was an important one. The fact that the wave traveled in a direct line with an entire absence of twisting motion, accounts for the mildness with which the shock was felt.

September 11, 1900

Heavy Midnight Shock.

Last Night's Earthquake Lasted Twelve Minutes.

One of the severest earthquakes that has ever been recorded occurred shortly before midnight. According to the observations of Dr. Townley of the University of California, the shock commenced at 11:54 o'clock.

The data given by the instrument of Professor Leuschner at his home was almost the same being 11:53:58. It has been partially computed that the vibration continued twelve minutes, one shock being plainly felt.

The motion was from east to west the exact figures attending. The disturbance are being calculated at the Students' Observatory of the University of California.

August 20, 1900

A Heavy Shock.

About 11:30 o'clock this morning there was a heavy shock which caused considerable consternation. Books were thrown from the shelves in the school houses, and many other large buildings shaken.

December 7, 1900

RECORD OF THE 'QUAKES

The scientists in the University of California astronomical department are greatly interested in the seismographic study of earthquakes. Professor John Milne of Shide, Isles of Wales, may be rightly described as the leader of the new seismology. The new science of earthquake study began its work with the invention of the seismograph, which is an instrument used for analyzing earthquake motion and recording it in conjunction with a time scale. By means of these instruments it became possible to inaugurate an entirely new series of investigations of the nature of earthquakes, and ultimately to create a new branch of science.

Professor Milne was not the first designer of the seismograph. The honor of its first design is due, perhaps, to Professor Ewing, of the Universities of Tokio and Cambridge, but in the new line of research a leader was necessary—one who was well versed in physical science, having a high faculty of initiative, and willing to make the study a life work. Such a leader was found in John Milne.

In the earliest stages of the new science, when it was furnishing more questions that answers, he had the field mostly to himself; but when the results began to appear and multiply, chiefly through his patience and industry, new workers entered the field. At present they are numerous, and Japan, Germany, Austria and Italy, as well as the United States and England, have many learned.

The earliest form of seismoscope was, of course, one which signalled a tremor in the ground; but in order to gain a more instructive idea of the movement we need an instrument which will trace the whole motion automatically from the beginning of the quake to the end, showing at every instate the direction, the amplitude, and the frequency or periods of the vibraions. Such an instrument is called a "seismograph."

There is an intermediate class of instruments which give continuous records of the movements of the ground, and also show the directions and amplitudes, but do not unravel the various complicted motions. These are called seismometers. A seismograph is a far more complex insrument. Its first problem was, and is, to devise a "steady point"—that is to say, a mass which shall always remain at rest, while everything around it and even the support that upholds it is in a constant state of vibratory motion.

To attain it is far from easy; but if it can be attained, then we can imagine a plate attacher to it with a prepared surface, capable of receiving and recording the movements of a pencil or point. And we can imagine a tracing pencil attaches to the supports which vibrate with the earth, and the other end resting lightly on the smoked (or surfaced) plate. Or we can imagine the thing reversed, and the tracing point attacher to our unmoving, numovable mass, and the smoked plate attached to the supports that vibrate with the earth.

In either case the movements of the earth will cause a tricel line to be drawn on the plate, showing the motion of the earth, and the support, relative to them "steady point." In this way, though this is but a rough sketch of the theory of a very ingenious instrument, with many complexities and improvements for magnifying the extent of the motion, or rectifying the direction of the moving point, earthquakes are measurer; and this is the principle of the beautiful "seismograph," which Milne and Ewing and Gray have perfected.

Professor Milne has mapped out the earthquake centers of origin of the world into eighteen great districts; and he regards the great earthquake of Northern India as having had its origin in the nearest of these great districts, the Himalayan seismic ellipse.

All this is made possible by the earthly rigidity due to the enormous pressure existing throughout its interior. It is a law of physics that in any concentric spherical surface the resistance of the closed nucleus must be just equal the pressure of the surrounding she resting upon it, and thus the strain upon the matter of the globe increases toward the center.

This pressure is sustained by the increasing density and rising temperature of the matter in the earth's interior, which is thus under an inconceivable strain, for surpassing the strength of any known substance. As the matter is above the critical temperature of every element, it is essentially a gas reduced by pressure to a hardness greater than that of steel, and with an elasticity and rigidity infinitely near to perfection.

The result is that the explosive strain upon the matter of our globe from within, which is everywhere just equal to the pressure sustained by the enclosed nucleus, renders the interior matter more rigid than any known substanse; and even the outer layers, which are but slightly compressed, yield so little under the action of external forces that the glob as a whole is more rigid than steel.

It is this extreme rigidity which causes vibrations of any shock, external or within the earth, to be transmitted throughout its whole bulk.

August 18, 1905

Native American grinding hole site north of Solano Avenue. Circa 1908. Exact site unknown. Courtesy of the Berkeley Firefighters Association. Photo from Berkeley Chamber of Commerce election pamphlet, 1908.

Cerrito Creek. Circa 1908. Courtesy of the Berkeley Firefighters Association. Photo from Berkeley Chamber of Commerce election pamphlet, 1908.

"Massive Boulders and live Oaks are found everywhere in Park." Caption from Chamber of Commerce election pamphlet for new city park north of Solano Avenue.
Courtesy of the Berkeley Firefighters Association. Photo from Chamber of Commerce election pamphlet, 1908.

5. Animals

Few things are more hidden from our view than the natural world as it was even one hundred years ago. These news articles reveal that in 1900 Berkeley was still home to wild animals.

The battle the area's animals fought and lost to humans (to the Spanish in their cruelty and domination, and to the Yankees in their numbers and their commodity view of nature) was nearly complete by the 1870s. The *Gazette* vividly describes the final interactions between humans and the area's larger mammals. By the first decade of the 1900s the last descendants of these animals' ancestral lines flickered and lurched towards local extinction.

Those remaining animals struggled to survive in the middle and at the edges of this frontier outpost that was quickly becoming a city.

As animals and humans competed for ever shrinking available land, residents strategized how to eliminate these wild and domesticated animals. Poisoning of unwanted animals was common. Stealing animals was also common. We are encouraged, however, to read that Berkeley residents made efforts to ensure that animals in its public shelters were treated decently. For wild animals, on balance, the tone of many of the news articles shows that residents were both fearful of and excited by their brushes with these "invaders."

"Those early days were fine for shooting. I mean before the coyotes were driven back howling beyond the hills and you could catch the quail by merely putting salt on its tail."

—"An Old Settler," *Berkeley Reporter*, December 1906

Looking northeast towards Berkeley hills from McGee Avenue. George Kidd (Captain Kidd) in goat cart. Jim Donovan leading cow. Courtesy of the Berkeley Firefighters Association.

Ironically, as residents worked to rid the city of undomesticated animals, circuses and trained animal shows were big events. As illustrated by advertisements in the *Gazette*, these shows were attended by enough people to keep Berkeley on their circuits.

Whaling ships Bowhead, Beluga *and* Thrasher *of the Oakland Star Fleet wintering in the Oakland Estuary. Note the auxiliary steam stacks. Circa 1900. Courtesy of the San Francisco Maritime National Historic Park, Robert Weinstein Collection, photo #B11.0,020n.*

WHALES SPORT IN BAY

Strange sights will be witnessed by those who daily cross and recross the bay during the next few days, for a frisky school of whales now infests San Francisco bay, keeping the nerves of the pilots of the ferries and other bay craft constantly on edge. One of Crowley's big launches was nearly overturned by one of the mammals and the government steamer General McDowell was caught between two of them, but fortunately they dived to the depths of the bay before the steamer collided.

There have been times when a whale has entered this harbor, but it has generally escaped to the open sea before another day passed. But at present there is undoubtedly a number of them in the bay. Late Thursday evening Harry Johnson, the boatman, was returned from Alcatraz Island and off Folsom-street wharf he was astonished to see a stream of water shoot up. Soon a monster whale was seen. He moved slowly through the water and when last seen he was heading for the Alameda shore.

Yesterday morning Crowley's big launch Sentry, with James Sennett in it, was running along smoothly when, without the least bit of warning the boat was lifted out of the water and just as quickly dropped back again. Sennett stopped the engines and ran aft to investigate and was just in time to see a whale. The boat being uninjured, the surprised boatman headed straight for the wharf.

While the steamer General McDowell was making the morning trip to Fort Baker, which is on the Marin county side, a whale was seen dead ahead. At the same time another came up a short distance from her stern. When it seemed that a collision was inevitable the whales became frightened and with mighty swishes of their tails they disappeared.

The pilots of the ferryboats and other bay craft scan every ripple on the water, thinking that it is a whale. At night they pull out of the slips and do not rest easy until the boat reaches the opposite side of the bay. If the whales continue to stay in the harbor Thomas Crowley, the launchman, will get up a party and go after the mammals.

The Whalers Having Luck.

San Francisco, Aug. 24.—Thirty-four whales caught in the north. This is the record that comes to-day by letter on the salmon packer Salvator. All the whaling fleet have struck it rich The leviathans have shown no partiality among the different whaling captains and have distributed their carcasses pretty equally. The Thrasher and Narwhal of the Pacific Steam Whaling Company head the list with seven each. The William Bayliss is a close second with six notches on her gun. The Alexander and the Charles Hansen have captured five each, and the Jeanette has four.

This is a remarkably good record.

August 24, 1905

A Whaling Record.

Whaling Steamer Balaena arrived last evening with the largest season catch on record. Captain Williams and all the men of the crew are happy over the fact that the bone from twenty-seven big bowhead whales, amounting to 48,000 pounds, was brought back to port, for it means a small fortune to the hale skipper and a neat sum for each of the men who went into the Far North on the Balaena. In addition to the great quantity of whalebone valued at $150,000, the steamer brought back 180 barrels of oil. It is worth something, but bone is the thing that counts with Captain Williams and his men. The Balaena was eighteen months in the Arctic ocean, spending the winter at Cape Kellett, on Banks Land.

October 9, 1900

The ferry San Rafael *on San Francisco Bay. Built in 1877 it was the little queen of ferries on the Bay. On November 30, 1901, in a heavy fog near Alcatraz Island and under "slow bell," she was rammed by the ferry* Sausalito *and sunk thirty minutes later.* Courtesy of the San Francisco Maritime National Historical Park, J. Porter Shaw Photographic Collection, photo #B7.4819n.

The San Rafael Struck a Whale.

Yesterday afternoon the ferryboat San Rafael ran onto a whale. After leaving Sausalito at one o'clock the form of a whale rose above the surface of the water dead ahead, and the ferryboat bumped against it with considerable force. The keel of the vessel slid over the whale, which had apparently been pressed down by the weight, and a moment later it arose at the stern of the boat. Blowing up a column of water, the monster disappeared. Everybody on board the San Rafael felt the shock, and the engineer and firemen rushed on deck to learn the cause.

1900

MONSTER SNAKE KILLED

A large snake, feeding for months on valuable birds and the eggs in their nests at the aviary of Henry Rowe at his home in the hills of Berkeley, was killed Saturday by the owner and the mystery of many deaths among his feathered pets was cleared. For the past three months Mr. Rowe has found the eggs in the birds' nests broken and the contents devoured. At frequent intervals the dead and bloodless body of a valuable foreign canary or finch would be found and the perplexity was only made the deeper.

Saturday when Mr. Rowe went to feed the birds a great crawling rattler slipped across the ground, interrupted in the midst of a feast on a new-born bird. Immediately Rowe was called and he shot the snake. It developed that this lone intruder had lived and fattened on the eggs and the young in the nests. A cavity was found in a rock where the snake had been living. Rowe estimates his loss to the snake at some $3000. He has imported dozens of beautiful French and Australian birds and is an extravagant enthusiast. He now has some 200 feathered occupants of his aviary. Among this number have the horrible tragedies of bird life taken place almost daily. The death-dealing enemy measured about four feet in length.

July 8, 1905

MONSTER GOPHER SNAKE KILLED IN CENTER OF TOWN

Otto Putzker, the well known bicycle and automobile expert, has on display in the window of his store, 2142 Shattuck avenue, a large gopher snake about four and a half feet long. The snake was caught and killed in a barn near the corner of Durant and Shattuck avenues.

August 1905

TAIL OF RATTLER

On Saturday afternoon S. N. Wyckoff Jr. took his dog and shotgun and wandered up into the Grizzly heights in search of cottontails. As he walked leisurely along an old cattle train, densely overgrown with wild oats, he heard the ominous buzz of a rattlesnake. One bound placed him at a safe distance from the threatened danger, and he turned to take a look. His dog stood calmly in the trail unaware of his peril, while at his side completely concealed from sight by the high grass, the angry snake was sounding his dread warning. Instantly the boy raised his gun and fired in the direction from which the sound came. The report of the gun was followed by instant silence. A careful and cautious examination of the spot resulted in finding about four inches of the tail of the snake, with eight rattles attached, which the charge of shot had completely severed from the body but no other trace of his serpentine majesty could be found.

Young Wyckoff believes, and he bases his opinion on the diameter of the tail, the size and number of the rattles and the extent and quality of the fright he experienced, when he heard the crotalus lucifer's malignant salutation, that the serpent must have been thirteen feet long and that he weighed seventy-five pounds.

August 1905

"CINNAMON" IS IN HILLS

Eli Crocker of San Francisco reports an encounter Saturday with a cinnamon bear near the reservoir at North Berkeley, less than a quarter of a mile from town. The bear was about the size of a full-grown Newfoundland dog, and showed no fear of Crocker, allowing him to come within a few rods of it before the animal turned about and disappeared in the bushes. The bear seemed fat and sleek and Crocker believes many a hen roost in the vicinity has contributed liberally to the support of the beast.

July 24, 1905

BALD EAGLE ATTACKS HUNTER.

Deprived of Lamb, Bird Shows Fight and Is Finally Shot.

Santa Rosa, Aug. 14.—Lowe Adler had a desperate fight yesterday in the hills north of Preston with a bald eagle. Adler was out hunting and noticed an immense eagle, the first seen in these parts in years sweep down upon a lamb on the Cox ranch. The cries of the lamb forced Adler to run to its rescue. He fired a shot and inflicted a slight wound on the big bird. The eagle dropped the sheep and when the man came to close quarters flew at him and made a savage attack. Adler was badly scratched before he was able to use his gun and kill the eagle, which measured seven feet from tip to tip.

August 14, 1905

ANTHRAX APPEARS IN NAPA.

Dread Cattle Disease Attacks Herds in Lowlands.

Napa, Aug. 29.—Anthrax, the dread disease among cattle, has broken out on several farms southwest of Napa. Last week A. Callan lost about ten head of cattle by this scourge, and J. Carney lost eight head of fine cows.

Dr. Charles Keane, the State Veterinarian, was here yesterday looking into the matter. He was assisted by Veterinarian L. C. Kennon of this city. Dr. Keane has established a strict quarintine of the stock of the two ranches mentioned, and a determined effort is being made to stamp out the malady.

Injections of serum are being made by Drs. Keane and Kennon into the cattle on the ranches southwest of Napa as a preventive against the spread of anthrax, which is supposed to be due to certain conditions in the lowlands where there is a great amount of moisture.

August 29, 1905

Dairyman Bygum Fined.

Carl Bygum, the Catherine street dairyman, who was convicted of violating the ordinance which prohibits the keeping of more than two cows on an acre, was fined $3 by Justice of the Peace Edgar this morning.

Bygum is to arrange his dairy so that he will not be in conflict with the law.

August 31, 1900

Two cows grazing in rural Berkeley. Courtesy of the Berkeley Firefighters Association.

Bygum Found Guilty

Of Keeping More Than Two Cows on One Acre.

Carl Bygum was found guilty this morning of violating the town ordinance which provides that no more than two cows shall be kept on an acre of land. W. M. Morris was the complaining witness.

Bygum's attorney admitted the facts of the case which showed that five cows had been kept on a lot 50x 135 feet. The point upon which he based his defense was that while the bovines had been kept on the land in question during the night, they had been pastured on a larger area of land during the day.

Sentence will be pronounced upon Bygum next Tuesday. The defendent conducts a dairy on Catherine street.

September 4, 1900

KILLS WEEDS AND ALSO COWS.

New Preparation Does Its Work Only Too Well.

Haywards, Cal., Aug. 5.—A few days ago the Ladies' Improvement club of this city hired a man named Gould and instructed him to do his best to kill off the growth of weeds so abundant on the public plaza in the center of the city. Gould was equipped with a new prepartion, guaranteed to do the work effectually, and he applied the liquid weed killer very liberally.

On Wednesday Joe Cardoza, a dairyman, found himself short two cows they having died suddenly and without apparent cause. Yesterday it transpired that Cardoza's children, who each cut grass enough to feed the cows from the vacant lots in the neighborhood, had secured their last supply from the corner of the plaza to which Gould had given his best attention, and the mystery of the cows' death is now disclosed.

Cardoza is in a quandary whether to sue the Ladies' Improvement club, from which he might be unable to recover, or show his loyal citizenship by pocketing his loss without protest.

August 5, 1905

MRS. COW COMMITS SUICIDE

Perhaps because she feared to undergo the dreaded tuberculin test or perhaps because her bovine lover no longer smiled at her, a cow of this city committed suicide a few days ago, by eating a can of green paint.

It remained for Berkeley, with its atmosphere of culture, learning and refinement, to product a cow—a four-legged, two-horned bovine ruminant—that would end its own life.

The distinguished quadruped, which will without doubt be given its proper place among the wonderful things produced by Berkeley, was owned by Mrs. Rose Stricker of 1509 Carlton street. The cow died under strange circumstances. If it had been the death of a man or woman, instead of a cow, bright journalism might have said the death was mysterious. Anyway the cow died.

Mrs. Stricker sought to find out the cause of death and employed a veterinary surgeon to perform an autopsy. Such things on dead humans are common, but the performing of an autopsy on a cow is original with Berkeley. Again may the college town be proud.

The autopsy, like many other operations, was a great success. It revealed that the cow was dead. Also, that the cow had died from the effects of eating a can of green paint, minus the can.

A coroner's jurp would say:

"We do find that Mrs. Cow, age unknown and nativity undersired, died from taking poison, to wit: green paint, with suicidal intent."

COW'S SUDDEN DEATH WILL BE INVESTIGATED

Mrs. W. Stricker of 1509 Carlton street reported to the police to-day that a cow owned by her died yesterday from poisoning which she believes was administered by persons who objected to the presence of the cow in the neighborhood. After the death of the cow, Mrs. Stricker, who suspected that the animal had not died a natural death, had the carcass examined by a veterinary. The examination disclosed the fact that the animal had died of paint poisoning.

Mrs. Stricker requested that the police investigate the case and the matter was placed in the hands of Detective Parker.

VALUABLE HERD OF CATTLE STILL IN THE TOWN POUND

Early yesterday morning nine cows were captured by the poundman in North Berkeley. Numerous complaints had been made against the animals by residents in the vicinity, where they were captured, as the cattle had been tramping over flowerbeds and lawns. Although the cattle are all in good shape and evidently of good stock, no one has as yet come forward to claim them. Unless they are claimed within a short time the poundman will have to dispose of them at public auction.

September 4, 1905

WANDERING CATTLE ARE REDEEMBED BY H. ORTMAN

H. Ortman, who resides at the corner of Hopkins and Josephine streets, called at the pound yesterday and claimed the nine head of cattle found wandering in North Berkeley several nights ago.

September 7, 1905

Fractious Animals Stampede.

The pupils of the Lorin Public school are constantly endangered by the frequent passing of the animals driven down Alcatraz avenue to the slaughter houses.

Yesterday, just at noon, a drove of 200 or more were passing along when they became unmanageable, and divided into three separate bands running rampant over the community. Mr. Wooley of Alcatraz avenue saw the impending danger and hastened to guard the entrance of the school building and warn the principal of the danger.

The stampeding steers were not corraled and controlled for sometime and would perhaps have caused much trouble to the children. The property owners are considerably worked up about the frequent capers cut by these animals and will ask to have them driven down some other street.

August 24, 1905

TOO MANY DOGS IN BERKELEY

Colonel George C. Edwards of the mathematics department of the University of California complained to the police department this morning about the prevalence of unlicensed canines in the Town of Berkeley. The Colonel stated that the campus and the streets of the city were overrun with mangy curs and he wanted the poundmaster to be instructed to eliminate as many of the stray dogs as he could during the next month or two. Edwards thought that not enough captures were made by Poundmaster Ryan and as a result the number of dogs in town was becoming uncomfortable. After making his plea against the larger size of the dog population, Colonel Edwards produced four dollars, the fines of two of his dogs who were at that moment in the pound.

July 5, 1905

Have to Pay Twice.

Marshal Vollmer reports that some confusion exists in the minds of the people regarding the dog license question. Poundmaster Ryan, who has been very active of late, has gathered in hundreds of dogs and many of the owners of these, who come to redeem them, fully expect that the $2 fee they pay to get their dog back, also pays for a license. This is not the case. Two dollars must be paid for the releasing of the animal and two dollars for the license, making $4 in all.

Dogs roaming on lot at the northwest corner of Center and Milvia Streets. Note Foss Lumber Company in the background. This is now the location of the City of Berkeley's Building Permit Center. Courtesy of the Berkeley Historical Society, catalog #1494.

Homo Homini Lupus.

EDITOR BERKELEY GAZETTE: Dear Sir—It seems to me that no dog's death could be more affecting than that of Nig, the black hound of Ellsworth street, who fell a victim to Berkeley's mysterious dog poisoner.

This Nig enjoyed the full happiness of living to a degree that few creatures, be they men or beast, ever do. Harmless, loving, intelligent, he was exhuberant with vitality and, as he bounded along the street ahead of the Spaulding horse, his bark had a ring which it was good to hear. And then he was the pet and playmate of the children.

Only one year old and dead, poor Nig! But that his demise should be an example of what the wanton wickedness of man can do and show to what degree of perversity he can go when he gets a free hand to do evil, that is the really sad side of the case. That man should be a wolf to men, nay to children, for in the death of this dog the children who loved him are the real sufferers, this is something to inspire misanthropy.

The wretch who has poisoned Nig has done worse than if he had inflicted bodily harm to the dog's little owners; he has put a sting into their sensitive young hearts which they will feel through life, he has initiated them to the disenchantments of life and to mistrust in men.			E. B. LAMARE.

February 2, 1900

Horse and Dog Missing.

W. H. Stewart of 1732 Virginia street, has reported to the police the loss of a horse valued at $125, which he believes was stolen. A. J. Goodfrend of 1727 Euclid avenue reports he has lost a yellow mastiff. He believed it was stolen last Saturday.

Brutal Bull Dog.

Yesterday afternoon a little girl was going down Center street with her dog, a peacable bird dog. When in front of Bowman's drug-store a big bull dog jumped on the bird dog and began to chew him. Half a dozen men came to the rescue and it was only after much kicking and pulling that they were able to get the brutal bull to loosen his hold. The little girl went crying down the street with her bleeding dog by her side. Detective Parker was present and saw the affair.

No one present know who owned the dog but Parker took the license number, which was 311. There is a town ordinance making it an offense to allow a vicious dog to run at large. This dog is a particularly vicious one and is the same one that a few months ago nearly killed a small dog at the corner of Center and Shattuck. The bystanders who saw the brutal attack were thoroughly aroused and demanded that the dog be shot. Today the police are looking for the owner of the dog. The tag was a last year's one and had evidently been taken from another dog as the 311 issue last year was for a collie dog. Marshal Vollmer has notified Poundmaster Coryell and if that official finds the dog loose without a 1905 tag he will go to the boneyard in short order. Detective Parker is anxious to swear to a complaint against the owner of the dog if he can apprehend him and the matter will not be dropped.

September 15, 1905

VALUABLE ST. BERNARD DOG IS POISONED

A valuable St. Bernard dog, owned by Professor C. H. Stone of 2624 Channing way, was poisoned this morning near the corner of Hearst avenue and Leroy street. The animal it seems had strayed from the Stone residence early this morning, and it is believed that it was deliberately poisoned. Strychnine was used. Professor Stone has announced that he will give $50 for the arrest and conviction of the person who gave the dog poison.

August 1905

Berkeley girl Bethany Westenberg with pets. Courtesy of the Berkeley Architectural Heritage Association, photo #27.

Dogs Poisoned.

Wholesale Slaughter of Innocents Takes Place Last Night.

Some ten or fifteen dogs of all sorts, styles and value were poisoned yesterday and last night within the radius of a block from the corner of Bancroft way and Ellsworth street

The slaughter of dogs was wholesale. The poison did its work quickly, so quickly in fact that all attempts to save their lives proved futile. Several of the dogs poisoned were valuable.

The poisoner is of course unknown. There has been no complaint about dogs in that part of town, at least so far as could be

found out. Although there is a possibility that the deaths were due to some accident in placing poison, yet from all appearances it would seem that someone with a grudge against dogs in general was working nights in Berkeley.

C. A. Pringle of the Chi Phi Fraternity, 2222 Bancroft way, lost a valuable dog. W. Kelley, 2239 Bancroft way, also lost a valuable animal. Two dogs belonging to the Lester house at the corner of Bancroft way and Ellsworth street were found dead, and one belonging to Mrs Spaulding on Ellsworth street. Several other people had their dogs poisoned, the number amounting to between ten and fifteen.

If the dog poisoner is caught he will undoubtedly have a great deal of excitement on his hands, and some to spare.

Dog Poisoner at Work.

Percy Schultze of 1940 Channing way recently lost his valuable fox terrier, the animal's death being caused by poisoning. Schultze took the dog out for exercise, during which time it must have picked up some poisoned food.

Everything possible was done to save the animal's life, but it died after lingering for several hours.

July 5, 1900

Mail Carrier Bitten by Dog.

Henry Wilson, a mail carrier in West Berkeley, reported that he had been severely bitten yesterday afternoon by a dog belonging to J. F. Sullivan on Delaware street, near West street. No complaint was sworn to.

A True Dog Story

Death of a Scotch Collie That Was a Veritable Canine Savant.

This is the story of a dog and a cur. The dog is dead, but the cur still lives—a painful reminder of the survival of the less fit.

Deputy Marshal Fred Rawson of West Berkeley mourns the loss of his pet Scotch collie, "Pedro," known far and wide as a veritable phenomenon in canine intelligence. "Pedro" did not die of old age, inasmuch as he had not yet reached his prime, nor yet of any slow, wasting disease peculiar to his kind. He succumbed to a very violent attack of strychnine poisoning administered in meat by the other subject of this little sketch, whose personality is, unfortunately, so far unknown.

"Pedro" was famous among "trained dog men" for an intelligence that amounted almost to reason, and for a training such as no other dog has been known to acquire. Experts in this particular line have declared him the best dog in the world, and his owner had a standing offer of $400 for him, but he would not have sold the canine for twice that sum. The dog not only performed all of the ordinary tricks known to trained dogs in general, but he was equal to feats ordinarily supposed to be hopelessly beyond the brute capacity. He was able to distinguish the primary colors, to perform operations in mathematics which were unbelievable except to those who saw the achievement and to execute other marvels of animal intelligence too numerous to mention. His taking off by a creature so greatly his inferior is truly deplorable. It is bad enough for a good dog to die. But to be murdered by a cur!

January 13, 1900

Berkeley mailman Henry Wilson. Courtesy of the Berkeley Firefighters Association.

CHICKENS BECAME THIRSTY

Because the chickens of John Finnie of Third street, between Harrison and Gilman, had no water to drink for three days, his West Berkeley neighbors came to the conclusion that the old recluse was dead. Accordingly Policeman Lestrange was notified. When the door of Finnie's hut was opened the single room was found to be absolutely empty with no trace as to the whereabouts of the occupant. And the mystery grew thicker.

It seems that Finnie who is an old bachelor living the life of a hermit in the tumble down old shack on 'i. street had never been known, during his twenty years' residence there to have left his abode for more than a few hours at a time. When he was not seen for three days and his chickens began suffering for want of water, the neighbors naturally scented a mystery with a probable tragedy. This morning the situation was relieved.

Early this forenoon Finnie returned from a three days' camping trip at Lake Chabot. It was the first vacation that he had taken in several years and in the anticipation of the recreation that was in store for him he had forgotten all about leaving water for his fowl.

July 18, 1905

Berkeley boy holds chicken. Picture found in the attic of the Berkeley Architectural Heritage Association by Anthony Bruce in 1999. Courtesy of the Berkeley Architectural Heritage Association.

Old man Fleming feeds his chickens on the Fleming Ranch at the mouth of Wildcat Creek. Circa 1900. Courtesy of the Berkeley Historical Society, catalog #1466.

Interior of Berkeley's Own
TRAINED ANIMAL SHOW.

WAIT TILL
APRIL 2d

Tell your friends Berkeley has a Trained Pony and Dog Show of its own,
with live performing Sea Lions, Goats, Monkeys and Donkeys.

Trained Animals Are Coming.

Norris & Rowe's Big Trained Animal Shows will exhibit in this city next Thursday afternoon and night, under their waterproof tents. The show is well known to the amusement lovers of this city from the excellence of the entertainments given in the past. Performances will be given at 3 and 8 p. m. A street parade will be given at 11 a. m. on the morning of the exhibition, at which time the entire company of 300 animal actors will be seen. The show has been greatly enlarged and improved since its last appearance in this city and many new and novel features have been introduced. All the old favorites are with the show, and all have learned new tricks to amuse the little ones, likewise the older ones.

March 16, 1900

The Animal Show

With Norris & Rowe's Big Trained Animal Shows, is exhibiting in this city this afternoon and night under their large tents, which are located near Town Hall, will be seen many new and novel animal acts. The show has been greatly enlarged since its last appearance here, and many new special features have been imported. The performance given by the clever animals is nothing short of marvelous. The funny clown dogs, the only trained Harlem goat, the wonderful little elephants, the only trained African zebra, the the seventy trained Shetland ponies, the comical monkeys, and the only trained Bos Indicus, in this country give a performance that cannot be excelled.

The night exhibition will be at 8 o'clock.

March 22, 1900

KINDNESS TO DUMB ANIMALS

Editor Gazette: So many of us live along in this world with the well springs of kindness either choked up or untouched; or our sympathies are so illformed in character, that a stray starving kitten in our yard might elicit unbounded sympathy, but the larger needs of the animal kingdom are to us a matter of indifference. Most of us are emotional without sanity, the kind of sanity that calls for kindness backed by judgment.

No matter if our processes of reasoning be inductive or deductive, the fact remains uncontroverted, that to live in a civilized community, we must employ civilized methods if we wish to be just and sane.

It makes no difference if we love one animal and are kind to all animals on account of it, or that we love animals generally and are in consequence kind to any particular one, or whether we love animals at all. The point is, that we must see and be responsible both for the individual and the class in order to live the effective civic life. Or if we place the proposition in this way, we have a domestic home and a municipal home, and our social responsibility is not cancelled until we make both of those homes as perfect as our thoughts and acts can make them.

So many of us think that to fulfill a well rounded home life we have cancelled our duty to the community: but, that is but a phase—in a country governed by the people to be responsible merely for the home life, is as if we left off school at the primary stage and trusted to luck for the rest of our education. We have a way of throwing a conservative cloak about us, we think we are exclusive, but we are not; we are simply pinched and narrow, our hearts are not full enough of love and our thoughts are unwholesome.

We have had a pound mismanaged animals were starved and beaten to death, we are shocked as we well might be; but as most of us are just emotional and nothing more the subject passes.

But there is a more—every one of us is responsible; every educated adult individual in the community is in somewise responsible, we have been neglecting our municipal home, we have been starving one class of our charges, we have been found wanting. We have been living in the segment of the circle instead of the circle itself. Most of us are too indolent to even look into a subject; we have not been taught responsibility, and we are previous careful not to assume it. If we live and progress, one interest must reach out for another, and so on ad infinitum. But not to have interest, not to reach out, not to love, not to help should constitute a real crime among people organized to be responsible.

The appeal is made to the Berkeley people to redress this wrong, either by individuals or the Town Board, to give the dumb animals a chance from the poor old horse turned out to die to the intelligent collie gnawing at his prison in ravening hunger.

The appeal is made to the people now, to subscribe for membership, life-membership or contributing membership in the Society for the Prevention of Cruelty to Animals, and subscribe just so far as righteous thought may go, to assist in rectifying this public wrong and to wipe out this horror from our midst.

September 7, 1905

INHUMANE METHODS WILL NO LONGER BE TOLERATED IN POUND

When the Berkeley branch of the Society for the Prevention of Cruelty to Animals petitioned the Town Trustees to appoint E. L. Coryell poundmaster, a great many persons were of the opinion that it was all a joke. They have since learned that the appointment of Coryell to that position was the first step in a well planned campaign against conditions that have existed in the local pound for many years; a plan that fits in with the general purpose of the society of which Coryell is the head in Berkeley. From the humane society to the pound may appear to some persons as an incongruity—and so it would be should the pound be conducted as it has been heretofore.

The appointment of Coryell as poundman of Berkeley was merely to place the pound under the jurisdiction of the Society for the Prevention of Cruelty to Animals. It places the responsibility of the pound on the shoulders of Coryell, who, in order to better conditions in the pound and conduct that institution in the humane manner it should be conducted, has taken that responsibility. What the new poundman intends to do is a long story; what he found to be the existing conditions at the pound upon assuming his official duties a week ago, is a still longer story, but a few facts concerning the past condition of the pound and the manner in which it was conducted, will tend to open the eyes of the people to the urgent need of the change that has been effected.

In the first place the pound, as Coryell found it, was a disgrace to any civilized community. How it was conducted can only be judged by evidence found in the pound. The pound consists of a pen surrounded by a high fence; a filthy office and a filthier barn in which are housed dogs, cattle and horses. The pound is located on the water's edge at the foot of University avenue, and so close to the water that at high tide one end of the pen is flooded. With the receding of the water at low tide waste matter is left in the pen and beneath one end of the stable, thereby producing an

unsanitary and disagreeable effect. The floor of the stable has almost rotted away, leaving the place in a dilapidated and unsafe condition.

As to the conditions of affairs prior to the appointment of Coryell, evidence of great cruelty can be seen on every side. Although the pound is supplied with an asphyxiation pen for the killing of unclaimed dogs, it is evident that the device has not been used for years. Instead of disposing of these homeless dogs in the most humane way (by asphyxiation) there is every reason to believe that they were pounded over the head with some heavy instrument, until either dead or supposedly so, after which the carcasses were thrown into the bay, and in many cases left lying in the lower end of the pen. That this was the method of killing dogs is proved by the condition of a half-dozen carcasses found lying about the pen. An examination of the carcasses found in the yard disclosed the broken skulls and even instances where the back and legs were broken in the effort to kill them. The decomposed carcasses were found within a hundred feet of the pound office and several under one end of the stable. Here they had been allowed to lie unburied, in direct violation of the sanitary laws and a menace to the health of the entire neighborhood. Another evidence that the unredeemed dogs were brutally clubbed to death is furnished by residents of the neighborhood who state that on certain occasions the entire section around the pound would be aroused by the yelps of pain from the dogs as they were being clubbed to death. These persons also state that, although the pound was generally well stocked with horses, cows and dogs, they never saw any feed or hay delivered at the place.

It is known that a hungry horse will gnaw wood; where the animal is being starved it will nibble great holes in a post—that was proved in the case of the Oakland pound. There is hardly a whole post in the Berkeley pound. The walls of the barn have been

Berkeley Pound master E. L. Coryell.
Courtesy of the Berkeley Firefighters Association; photo from *Berkeley Reporter*, December 1906.

gnawed through in many places, while the window-sills of the office building have been almost eaten away by hungry animals. On every side within the small inclosure are mute signs of the suffering of dumb brutes that have fallen into the hands of the poundman where they have been compelled to remain until redeemed or put out of their misery with an ax or club.

It was this shameful condition of affairs that caused the humane society and Mr. Coryell to take a hand in conducting the pound, and if a knowledge of animals and their treatment, together with a desire to humanely dispose of useless animals, counts for anything, the Berkeley pound will no longer be the scene of suffering it was in the past. The actual work of the poundman will be conducted by E. J. Rogers, who has had some ten or fifteen years' experience in that line. He will be under the direction of Coryell, who will be responsible and who will see that the business of the institution is conducted along strictly humane lines.

While making a tour of investigation about town one day last week Rogers, the deputy poundman, was approached by an Italian dairyman whose place is located on San Pablo avenue. The man informed Rogers that formerly he had arranged with the poundman to allow his cattle to feed along the roadside for several hours every day. He stated that he was in the habit of paying from one to two dollars a month for that privilege and wished to make a similar arrangement with Rogers. The deputy poundman also says that the town is overrun with dogs. This year he states that only some 338 dog licenses have been taken out, against between 900 and 1000 eight years ago, when he was poundman of Berkeley. This indicates that there are many hundreds of dogs in town on which no license is paid. "These dogs," saids Rogers, "should either be disposed of or the city should receive a revenue from their owners."

In speaking of the proposed manner of conducting the pound Rogers said: "I see no reason why a pound should not be conducted as Coryell is planning to operate this one. It is my intention to carry out all his plans and there is no good excuse for not doing so as they are all practical. I intend to use the rope in capturing only large dogs, while for the smaller ones I will use a net. The pound will be practically remodeled and made sanitary in every respect. The unredeemed dogs will be disposed of in the least painful way, which is by the use of gas. If this method is properly applied a dog will die in one minute and a cat in forty seconds. They do not suffer in the least and it is the least unpleasant way to dispose of them. Under Coryell's instruction every animal impounded will be well fed and properly cared for until claimed or sold to pay costs."

Coryell is now engaged in arranging improvements for the pound. The buildings will be cleaned throughout, new floors put in, the dog pens rearranged and every care will be taken for the comfort of all the unfortunate animals that are impounded in the future. All animals it is found necessary to kill, will be buried and not thrown into the bay as was formerly the custom. To accomplish all this will require considerable capital which will necessarily have to be supplied by either the Town Trustees, or the society interested in the new pound. In order to secure the necessary money new members are being solicited by the humane society and in view of the nature of the new work undertaken, it is expected that many persons will join to assist in the work.

A local rodeo. Courtesy of the Berkeley Firefighters Association.

6. Life on the Bay

ABANDON SINKING VESSEL

With their boat rapidly settling beneath their feet into the bay waters about a mile from the West Berkeley shore, in full view of an excited crowd gathered on the Berkeley wharf, the captain and his assistant, together with a pet dog, was forced to climb into a dory, leaving behind all their valuables in the flooder cabin, and row to the shore. The craft was the scow "Alaska," loaded with shakes, shingles and laths for San Francisco. The men were taken to Sweetman's Hotel, Third and Delaware streets, where they spent the night and left early this morning for the city to get a tug and recover the waterlogged scow.

Some men working on the wharf noticed the scow making its way down the bay, but paid little attention to it. After awhile they saw that it was acting very peculiarly, seeming to make no headway and wallowing in the trough of the sea. The two men on board could be seen running about and it was soon noticed that the scow was sinking. After endeavoring to stop th leak, the men apparently gave it up and the vessel settled in the water until only its deck-load of cargo could be seen above the water. The men now left the scow and rowed to the shore, where they were taken to the hotel and their wet clothing was dried.

They stated that they did not know what had started the scow to leaking, but they had not noticed it until they were nearly opposite West Berkeley. It was their belief that some plank must have broken, for the water came in so rapidly. Had it not been for the cargo of lumber, it would have sunk immediately.

The men refused to give their names and left the small boat in Sweetman's hands, stating they would return for it.

July 11, 1905

The following articles touch on aspects of traffic on Bay Area waterways, particularly the volume of debris that often floated on the Bay. Most of the refuse was generated by the logging industry. Log rafts made of millions of feet of timber were lashed together for transport. Much of the lumber originated in Puget Sound and water transportation was the only means of delivering such huge and heavy cargo. Sometimes these rafts tore apart in the churning waters and broadcast innumerable numbers of logs with the tides. The debris was a hazard to ships, wharves and people.

The *Gazette* articles reveal the types of ships traveling across the Bay as well as the human traffic carried by these transports. From barks to steamers, Bay waters were used for commerce and recreation.

"In the good time coming, when the ships of all the nations lie rocking on the tide at the fair port of Berkeley, when all the land between the sea wall and the center of town is filled with industrial institutions, and the homes of tens of thousands of happy, healthy, prosperous operatives; when the benign influences now at work have culminated in the recognition of Berkeley as the art, musical and educational center of the West; Then—with a population of 100,000 or more, people will come from the four corners of the globe to see the ideal city of the world—Berkeley."

—H. A. Sully, *Berkeley Reporter*, December 1906

Photo originally captioned as "A Scene on the Waterfront" in the December 1906 Berkeley Reporter. *It is not known if this scene was actually Berkeley's waterfront or a promotional view from somewhere else on the Bay.* Courtesy of the Berkeley Firefighters Association; photo from *Berkeley Reporter* 1906.

RETURN, BUT BOAT IS GONE

The scow-schooner Alaska, loaded with shingles and lumber, which became waterlogged off the West Berkeley shore late Monday afternoon and was abandoned by her crew temporarily, mysteriously disappeared from the bay Tuesday. Though the deckload of lumber slipped off into the bay, the hold was full of lumber and it would have been impossible for the vessel to sink. For two days launches have been searching for the missing boat, but so far has found no trace of her. The supposition of the captain, Pederson, is that there must be a gang of bay pirates operating in this neighborhood who made off with the schooner.

The Alaska has long been plying in the waters of the harbor, and a few weeks ago she was bought by Captain Pedersen, a young Norseman who had saved money, earned working on bay craft. He had paid a part of the purchase price and was struggling along as a skipper of the boat in an effort to earn enough to pay the balance. Then when clear of debt he intended to ship a mate to share his joys and sorrows for life, and the young lady was preparing for the event when the last payment was made on the schooner. Now the vessel is lost, but the debt did not go with it, and the young skipper's wedding may be long postponed.

The schooner had her hold filled with laths and shingles, and on the deck was piled a big load of lumber. There was a strong flood tide when the vessel started on the voyage, and it carried her over toward the Berkeley shore. She was well out in the bay when it was found that she was leaking, and as the water poured into her hold she listed to starboard under the weight of it. . . .

July 13, 1905

Berkeley pier looking east. Courtesy of the Berkeley Architectural Heritage Association, photo #198, and Dianna Beers.

"I expect to live long enough to see Berkeley one of the most important ports on San Francisco bay, and I hope the city will own and control its waterfront, operating for the benefit of the whole community, but one thing is certain, if we do not take hold of this matter—if we fold our hands in fatuous self-complacency and wait for something to turn up—the something will turn up in the shape of a grasping corporation, with nobody to kick and no soul to damn, that will charge 'all the traffic will bear,' and reap the reward of our idiotic apathy."

—H. A. Sully, *Berkeley Reporter*, December 1906

Engine Crashes Through Pier.

Part of the Point Richmond wharf gave way under the weight of an engine and tender yesterday morning, big locomotive and the three men it carried sank out of sight. Two of the men escaped with their lives. The third lies with the engine five fathoms deep in the muddy waters of the bay.

The engine was No. 203 of the Bakersfield run, and it had for its crew William Allen, engineer, and P. S. (or "Doc") Adams, fireman. It was Adams who was killed.

The train, with 203 pulling it, had just come in from Bakersfield and the passengers had gone onto the boat, which had left the slip. The track upon which the train runs in continues on past the station house and down along the slip, where it switches into the back track by which, up to two weeks ago, engines reached the yard, a mile up the road from the wharf. Two weeks ago, however, it came to the knowledge of the management that the wharf was not safe, and immediately an order forbidding engines to go down on the wharf was posted on the bulletin board in the yard.

Where the engine went through the water is thirty feet deep. There are no broked piles in sight, indicating that they were driven down by the weight. It is probable that the engine can be raised without much trouble. Attempts will be made to raise it at once, and to find the body of the fireman it carried down to his death.

A few Berkeley young men who had gone to Point Richmond to fish and spend the day were witnesses of the dreadful event, among which was Mr. G. Sampson, the young butcher:

September 24, 1900

Berkeley Lumber Wharf at the Bay looking east. Probably Jacob's Wharf at the foot of Delaware Street. Courtesy of the Berkeley Architectural Heritage Association, photo #204.

West Berkeley Lumber. Courtesy of the Berkeley Historical Society, catalog #1509.

Repairing the Wharf.

The West Berkeley Lumber Company has commenced the repair of its wharf. Over 500 new piles are to be put in the place of old ones at a cost of $5000.

Last week the steam schooners H. C. Merchant and Mary Bidwell discharged 150,000 and 100,000 feet of lumber respectively on the wharf.

The company has been let the contract for furnishing the lumber for President Wheeler's new house.

August 29, 1900

The San Francisco *was one of the larger wooden Key Route ferry boats. Built in 1905, its double compound engines endowed it with much power.* Courtesy of the Berkeley Firefighters Association; photo from *Berkeley Reporter,* December 1906.

OAKLAND CRASHES INTO LOGS

Frightened by a collision and the sudden stoppage of the ferryboat Oakland, that left San Francisco at 12:30 o'clock this morning, 500 passengers including a number of Berkeleyans, on board were thrown into a panic that for a few minutes threatened serious consequences.

The Oakland pulled out from San Francisco promptly on time, and when within a quarter of a mile of the Oakland pier, the bow of the vessel crashed into part of a raft of floating logs that have endangered traffic on the bay for a fortnight or more, and came to a sudden stop. Passengers were hurled forward from their seats to the floor and those standing were huddled into a solid mass of struggling humanity.

For a few moments all was silent, then women began to scream, men to swear, and there was a wild rush for the life preservers. Luckily no one was trampled upon in the struggle for the floaters.

While the passengers were thus busily engaged in preparing for a desperate fight against the cold waves into which they expected to be precipitated every moment, the captain ordered the man at the wheel to back up and then steam ahead.

With a few puffs and a jolt that almost upset the pasengers again the Oakland passed over the logs and landed at the pier only a few minutes late, with nobody hurt, but many trembling and pale from the scare and still clinging to their life-preservers.

September 8, 1905

LOG CAUGHT IN PROPELLER CAUSES PANIC

Only the presence of mind of the deckhands on the Key route ferry steamer San Francisco averted a panic Saturday night on the 11:30 trip from San Francisco. A floating log or some similar obstruction became entangled in the propeller and caused the boat to jerk and roll in a manner to make shipwreck apparently imminent. Women shrieked and several fainted, while men were at the point of seizing life preservers.

The trouble occurred just as the San Francisco was rounding Goat Island. The noise occasioned by striking the obstruction, together with a series of sharp shocks, created the belief that the vessel had been stove in, and the excitement was intense. The deckhands went among passengers, and assured them there was no danger.

August 10, 1905

Central Pacific's double-ended ferry Oakland *built from the old river queen* Chrysopolis *in 1875. She burned in 1940 while being stored at the Alameda Mole of the Southern Pacific. As seen in George Harlan's* San Francisco Bay Ferryboats.

First log raft to reach San Francisco Bay in 1898. Photo site is probably Stella, Washington, according to the Oregon Historical Society. This type of raft was called a Robertson raft, and was used before the period when rafts were chained and bound before launching. Courtesy of the Oregon Historical Society, negative #6378.

LOG RAFT IS ADRIFT IN BAY

San Francisco, Aug. 31.—The ten-million-foot raft which was towed into the harbor last week went adrift last night and scattered millions of feet of logs over the south end of the bay. Desperate efforts are being made to corral the logs before they scatter and compel a practical suspension of navigation in the harbor.

There were strange doings on the south shore, off the sugar refineries, about midnight. A high tide slipped in and lifted the huge raft from her soft bed in the mud. The monster from Columbia river stirred uneasily. "She lives, she moves, she seems to feel"—gay and restive in an elephantine sort of way.

"Whee-a-bang!" went the big cable with which she was moored to the shore. The monster was free and floated with the swift ebb tide.

"Quit your shovin'! I can't stand the pressure," groans the big boom chain that holds in check a vast herd of loose logs— twenty million feet of them. With the mighty raft setting her shoulder against the pack the logs piled over one another and snapped the chain like twine. Then they swarmed out of the boom like a flock of sheep. Mad pranks were played in the darkness. Smaller craft were crushed like egg shells. Fortunately not many were near. Lookouts on a few vessels saw the shapeless terror coming and there was hasty shifting of anchorage. One or two ship's cables were caught and snapped like the boom chain and the ships went adrift.

As for the big raft she ambled about the front in tragic sportiveness. Any ship she rode down would have been given short shrift. But she drifted on harmlessly and finally buried her nose in the mud flats off the Union Iron works. She might as well have caused havoc to life and property. Several tugs are vainly trying to dislodge her so that she may be towed back to her anchorage. She will probably have to be broken up where she lies.

The fast scattering logs are a more serious problem and already menace navigation. The captain of the schooner J. G. Higgins came in yesterday and reported a school of logs to the number of about 500 strong from Bolinas to Lime Point.

This many were caught in the main stream and hurried out toward the open sea. Broken propellers and paddle wheels await steamers which meet them. Some of the logs are six feet in diameter and 150 feet long. One such could inflict serious damage in a collision.

The end is not yet. Meantime south-end launches are netting a harvest in running the strays back to safety and the broken boom.

August 31, 1905

A Benson log raft being towed into San Diego Bay, California. Note the chaining or bindings wrapping width-wise around the raft about every ten feet throughout its length.
Courtesy of the San Francisco Maritime National Historical Park, Groeper Collection, photo #D11.20,935n.

FIRE AVERTED ON THE BAY.

By Presence of Mind Boatman Saves Lives of Chinese.

San Francisco, Aug. 24.—The coolness and daring of Captain Thomas Crowley saved the lives of a hundred Chinese he was bringing ashore from the bark Lucille early yesterday morning after fire broke out on the barge on which he was bringing them to the dock.

Crowley had his tow about half way to land when a dense cloud of smoke broke from the pile of baggage in the center of the barge. Panic seized the crowd of coolies and a rush for the side of the barge began. Crowle sprang among them and commande them to stand still where they were. After cowing the frightened Mongolians he set them to work to tear down the pile of baggage and to passing water in buckets. The fire was quickly subdued and the trip to the dock resumed. It was discovered that one of the Chinese had a bundle of matches in his trunk, and these were ignited when he threw the trunk from the deck of the ship onto the lighter. The smouldering flames did not break out until the barge was in midstream.

The ferry boat Resolve. Courtesy of the Berkeley Historical Society.

A paddle wheeler on the Bay. Courtesy of the Berkeley Historical Society.

One Thousand Feet In Mid-Air.

Berkeleyan's Watch The Big Rock Shattered.

Shag Rock No. 2, the last and most important of the treacherous hidden rocks near Alcatraz, went sailing into mid-air today about noon.

Scores of people on the higher elevations of Berkeley singled out the interesting object with field glasses.

Shag rock No. 2 is only 150 feet from where Shag rock No. 1 reared its head above the water at low tide before it was blown out of existence. No. 2 is below the water at all times and, though small craft sail over it without hindrance, ships that draw over eighteen feet of water must keep at a respectful distance. There was no drilling done this time, as surface explosion alone will be employed. Nearly 3000 cubic yards will have to be removed to comply with the terms of the contract. One hundred and fifty charges of nitro-gelatine, containing 90 percent of glycerine, have been distributed along the rock. These are anchored to wire cables, and each is supplied with an explosive connected with a battery stationed on a barge 4000 feet distant. No boat or other craft was permitted within one mile of the rock before the explosion.

September 5, 1900

Stuck in the Mud.

Berkeley Hunter Removed From the Bay by Means of a Lasso.

The bay shore along opposite Sixteenth Street station is a first-class place for duck hunters to lie in wait for mud hens. Many Berkeley sportsmen go there and charter box cars in which to bring their game home.

Dr. J. A. D Hutton spent a successful day there yesterday from a sportsman's view. He also spent a considerable length of time removing blue mud from his person.

Dr. Hutton had been hunting in a boat and after loading it down with ducks started to land. Denny Landregan, who was watching Hutton making for the shore, shouted for him to look out for the soft mud. The sportsman in the boat smiled, waived his hand, cried back "Ta, ta," and stepped over the bow of the boat.

There is probably bottom to that mud bank, some place, but Dr. Hutton didn't find it. At the first step he went to his knees, and on expressing his surprise, sank over the top of his high rubber boots, which rapidly filled with chunks of soft mud and misery. The duck hunter controlled his emotions until the mud commenced running into his northwest vest pocket, and then he ripped out a yell that stopped the clock in the ferry tower.

The commotion on the water front brought a crowd to the scene. There was no way to reach the rapidly sinking man, and the excited crowd could only stand and shout all sorts of advice to the disappearing sportsman. Some cool-headed person telephoned for a wrecking train, and another for a derrick.

Landregan rushed along the shore and secured a rope. Hutton was flourishing his arms in the air when the rope was adroitly thrown over them. The noose was drawn up under his arms with a sudden yank that bit off a piece of yell about the size of a canvasback duck

The men on the shore took the rope and gave way. When they pulled Dr. Hutton out of the mud it sounded like a young man kissing his girl on a still moonlight night.

For the sum of 50 cents a small boy removed the mud from the sportsman and took the clams out of the big pockets of his hunting coat. He also got the ducks from the boat.

Although Dr. Hutton is a very genial man and likes a hearty laugh, he didn't quite see why Denny Landregan laughed a long rippling "ha, ha."

7. Crime

At the beginning of the twentieth century, crime in Berkeley ranged from laughable matters to serious incidents. *Berkeley Gazette* reporting was represented by many writing styles, personal, tongue-in-cheek or crisp and professional.

A woman is arrested for failing to connect her plumbing to the sewer. A Chinese laundry owner is arrested for conducting business in a residential neighborhood. A school teacher is arrested for riding her bicycle on the sidewalks. These incidents were news in the small city of Berkeley. Events were reported in the *Gazette* that today wouldn't pass as gossip. A bundle of rope is stolen from a wagon. A woman's school pin is lost on the trolley. A plasterer leaves his street shoes at his work site where they were stolen by a newly arrived Irish immigrant who believed the shoes abandoned.

The art of burglary was as today—easy entry through an open back window or door or by jimmying a rear door lock. Shattuck Avenue merchants hired night watchmen to protect their goods. Some children were then, as now, involved in gangs and participated in vandalism and theft. The stage coach was still in use in the early 1900s, vulnerable to bandits on Bay Area back roads.

Marshal August Vollmer, head of the Berkeley Police Department. He was appointed in 1905. Courtesy of the Berkeley Police Department Historical Preservation Society.

"Until recently our police department has not been organized in any sense of the word, we having had only a marshal and three deputies. We now have a marshal and sixteen uniformed officers, and they are all doing their duty. In addition to this we have an up-to-date 'police alarm signal system' which would do credit to any city, and likewise a complaint and report record file, which is the only one on the coast, enabling us to keep track of notable criminals from all sections of the State."

—Mayor Thomas Rickard, *Berkeley Reporter*, December 1906

Alarm and call box system of the Berkeley Police Department. Circa 1908. Courtesy of the Berkeley Historical Society, catalog #1504.

It might disturb our view of these more "simple" times to read how prevalent crime was against friends and neighbors. The number of men and women pulling scams as gas inspectors and other confidence schemes was surprisingly high. Domestics had a fascinating class of articles. In one scenario, a domestic would disappear, leaving all her possessions. In another, a domestic and her employer are lovers and she disappears with his possessions. Wife beatings were common. Alcohol was implicated in many sad incidents and failed marriages.

Berkeley law enforcement addressed behaviors that were inconsistent with the mores held by the community, but also respected residents' rights. A government with the strength and resources to enforce its laws had replaced the lawlessness and corruption inherent in the latter part of the 1800s in the West.

Newcomers and foreigners were treated roughly, but for the most part protected by the law. However, that didn't mean they were protected from their fellow citizens who often scapegoated immigrants for the community's problems.

Marshal Vollmer was depicted as a formidable force. Ever vigilant, he was often at the scene of the crime, making arrests. He was also portrayed as compassionate but could become quite the interrogator to those he believed guilty.

The telephone makes its entry at the new century. When mob rule or other crimes were occurring some distance from the police station, or if an officer needed assistance, phones installed on the streets for police communication quickly brought the necessary response.

The Oaks. A remote spot on the University of California campus where Rockwood Flint might have walked.
Courtesy of the Berkeley Firefighters Association, photo #378.

ROBBED ON THE CAMPUS

Rockwood Flint, the 14-year-old son of Mr. and Mrs. G. L. Flint of 1911 Henry street, told a story yesterday afternoon to the local police of having been held up and chloroformed in broad daylight while crossing the University of California campus. According to Flint's story he was accosted by a tramp in a lonely and thickly wooded part of the campus about 11 o'clock yesterday chloroformed and robbed of a gold ring, which was the only thing of value he had on his person. When the lad recovered from the effects of the drug it was past 1 o'clock and he was lying in the bottom of a ravine about twenty feet from where the original assault took place.

The assault was reported to the Berkeley police and Deputy Marshal Moran was at once detailed on the case. One suspect was arrested last night, but was released, as young Flint was unable to identify him as his assailant. Flint is employed by J. D Jay, a Shattuck-avenue grocer. He was returning through the University grounds after having performed an errand.

"I was passing through the woods just below the University orchard," said Flint in telling his story to the police, "when I noticed a tall man with black hair and a Van Dyke beard sitting on the bank of a ravine. He had a roll of blankets lying on the ground beside him. He called to me and aske be where I was working. I told him and then he said, 'Sit down a while and talk to me.' I walked over to him and as I was about to sit down side him he clapped a handkerchief under my nose. That's all I remembered until I came to and found myself lying at the bottom of the ravine. My pockets were turned inside out and my gold ring was gone. I did not feel hurt except that my lips and nose felt swollen and pained. I hurried as fas. I could back to the store and told Mr Jay what had happened."

July 1905

The Chloroforming of 14-Year-Old Rockwood Flint

CHLOROFORM STORY PRONOUNCED A MYTH. MANY POLICE CASES

That Rockward Flint of 1911 Henry street, who told a heart-rending tale to the local police of having been chloroformed and robbed on the University of California campus last Wednesday, is a liar of the first water, beside whom Baron Munchausen was a mere tyro, is the unanimous opinion of Marshal Vollmer and his deputies. Though confronted with the evidence that not a word of his wonderful story, which made mother's throughout Berkeley terror stricken for the safety of their children's lives, was true, the youthful fictionist looked his questioners in the eyes and said, "It all happened as I told you." Nothing could shake this statement.

The entire Marshal's office spent all yesterday seeking for the bearded tramp whom young Flint declared used him so cruelly. Suspect after suspect was brought before the boy but he could identify none as his assailant. So innocently did the youth look at the officers and so straightforward was his oft-repeated story, that the policemen hated to suspect that he might not be telling the truth.

Late in the afternoon Marshal Vollmer took the boy aside and questioned him severely, causing him to make several admissions which showed that all the facts were not just as he claimed them to be. The deputies were immediately sent out to carefully trace his course Wednesday when he claimed to have been chloroformed and the result of their investigation showed that the boy's story was purely a myth.

It was found that the Flint boy left the store of his employer, J. D. Jay of Shattuck avenue near Hearst avenue, at 9:45 a. m., to deliver some goods at a house near the corner of Bancroft way and Telegraph avenue. He started to return to the store, but met a friend of his who drives for J. Bull,

the coffee man. The two boys spent nearly an hour driving about town and then went to Cain's blacksmith shop on Dwight way, alternating between that place and a fruit store, whene Flint lavishly treated a number of his boy friends. At 12:30 the left Dwight way and started for their respective employer's stores. Fearing that he would be punished for staying away so long, it is presumed that he concocted the famous chloroforming story, displaying a great skill and cleverness in regard to details.

Marshal Vollmer presented these facts to the parents of the boy and they were convinced that he was telling a huge falsehood, though the youthful narrator, struck stoutly to his tale.

July 28, 1905

Berkeley boy Frank Glaser on Sixth Street. Perhaps a Rockwood Flint look-alike. Courtesy of the Berkeley Architectural Heritage Association, photo #248.

CHLOROFORMING AND ROBBING OF JOHN BOYD

Editor GAZETTE: So many people are inquiring why the fountain has not been painted, that I wish to relate an unfortunate accident that happened to me. I went down to the Oakland trotting park on Thursday last to see the races. Meeting a gentleman there who inquired, "What plug are you betting on." I replied that I was not betting on any, when he inquired, "How much cash have you got?" I replied, "The fountain money given me by the citizens of Berkeley to paint and fix up that structure."

Then he said, "You ought to bet on Deadbeat. He's a 16 to 1 shot and you are sure to go home with $128 for the $8 that you bet." The gentleman was so sure that I—well, I went home after the races was over feeling pretty seedy and took a walk through the U. C. grounds. In a lonely and secluded spot I met a dark looking tramp with a Vandyke beard, who stopped me and said, "Hello, little boy; how much money have you got?" I told him that I didn't have a cent because I lost it all betting on—I mean I told him I had $8. Then he chloroformed me and when I awoke my money was gone. I lost it down at the Oakland race—I mean I had been robbed by this stranger who chloroformed me and took every cent. I at once reported the facts to Marshal Vollmer, but when I mentioned to resubscribe when I come around with another subscription paper and to donate liberally and help a poor youth who losts all his former subscribtion down at the Oak—I mean in the U. C. grounds.

JOHN EVERGREEN.

P S.—You might say the police have a clew; it reads better. E.

August 1, 1905

Bicycle Crimes

ARRESTED FOR RIDING ON THE SIDEWALKS

Bert Alway was arrested this morning by Policeman Farrar for riding on the sidewalk. Alway was taken to the police station, where he begged that he might be released as he had only resided in Berkeley two weeks and was not acquainted with the ordinances. He was released after being warned not to repeat the offense.

August 1, 1905

MOTT WANTS NO BICYCLES ON SIDEWALKS

OAKLAND, August 1.—Mayor Mott has given his reasons for vetoing the much-argued bicycle, ordinance, and has asked instead for a law prohibiting many of the points which were vague in the ordinance as passed by the Council.

One of the principal objections to the ordinance is that it requires bicyclists riding on the sidewalks to dismount when passing pedestrians. The Mayor's faith in human nature will not permit him to believe that the law would be obeyed. He suggests that instead of giving the rider cause from a bicyclist's standpoint, to violate the ordinance, that bicycles be considered vehicles, and therefore kept on the highways, keeping the sidewalks for pedestrians. The Mayor declares himself as opposed to any ordinance which will permit of the use of the sidewalks by any but pedestrians ,but fails to cover the possibility that during the rainy season half of the Oakland streets are impassable because of mud or defective paving.

August 1, 1905

The Bicycle Habit.

Miss E. M. Wilson Arrested For Riding in the Sidewalk.

Miss Ellen M. Wilson, a teacher in the Seventh street school, was arrested this morning by Deputy Marshal Preston for riding a bicycle on the sidewalk. She was releases on $5 bail and given until tomorrow to plead.

Miss Wilson had been told by the Town Marshal and all of his deputies not to ride on the sidewalks, but continued to do most of her scorching on them The arrest followed and Marshal Lloyd says more are to come. When Miss Wilson was taken before Justice Edgar she said she didn't know much about law. Judge Edgar said "What's that!" in a tone that nearly lifted Miss Wilson out of her chair. She explained that someone had been arrested about seven years ago here in Beautiful Berkeley for the same offense and it had amounted to nothing but a fine display of red tape, not even suitable for neck ribbon.

When putting in her appearance at the Town Hall this morning Miss Wilson rode her wheel on the sidewalk up to the portals of that edifice. On leaving she mounted her wheel and again started to ride on the pavement, but being hailed by part of the constabulary concluded to walk to the street.

The bridge at University and San Pablo avenues has caved in leaving a hole in the roadbed about two feet square. Work of repairing commenced this afternoon.

Work on the new car line along San Pablo avenue is progressing rapidly. The teams ploughing up the road for the track bed have reached University avenue.

Piano lessons Raif method; at pupil's residence at reasonable rates. 2527 Piedmont ave. Tel. Mason 1151.   *

August 2, 1900

IDENTIFY JAPANESE CYCLIST

As the result of injuries received through the reckless riding of a Japanese bicyclist, Robert Bush, the civil engineer, who was knocked down yesterday at the corner of Cedar street and Shattuck avenue, is in a precarious condition. Bush sustained internal injuries of a serious nature and is being constantly attended by a physician.

When the accident occurred, the Japanese, whose carelessness may result in the permanent injury of Bush, made his escape, leaving his bicycle lying in the street. All efforts to find him yesterday proved of no avail. The police however, having the bicycle in their possession, were confident of learning the identity of the owner. This morning I. Kaneko, who resides at 1514 Louisa street appeared at the police station to claim the wheel. As no warrant had been issued for his arrest, he was permitted to take his wheel and go.

It was at first thought that the Japanese was George Nagatoni who resides at the same address, but Nagatoni denies that he was the careless rider and states that Kaneko is the guilty person. Nagatoni was arrested on May 6 for riding on the sidewalk for which he was fined $5.

As yet Bush has taken no action against the Japanese responsible for his injuries, as the luckless engineer is still unable to leave his home. It is understood he will take some action in the matter as soon as he recovers.
. . .

Hermineme Ogden on her bicycle at Grove Street (now Martin Luther King, Jr. Way) and Rose Street. Circa 1909. Courtesy of the Berkeley Historical Society, catalog #1467.

Jack the Hugger.

Unknown Man Makes an Attack Upon Ladies.

Some man with an irresitible desire to hug women has caused such a fright among the gentler sex in this city that no one dares to venture out after dark witohut masculine protection. The strange individual has always contented himself with a mild embrace and then retreated as rapidly as the frightened woman.

On three or four occasions several young ladies together were accosted by the hugger. He caught one of them in his arms, but fled, frightened by their screams. His attacks are generally made between 7 and 10 o'clock in the neighborhood of Channing way, Bowditch and Ellsworth streets. The first appearance of this persistent hugger was made about two months ago on Bowditch street, when Mrs. Douglas Keith was attacked. Mrs. Keith succeeded in frightening the rascal away, but he has kept up his work from time to time ever since.

Great difficulty is found in getting a description of the man. The women hugged are generally too badly firghtened to notice what the man looks like. Others object to the notoriety that would follow his identicfiation and refuse to tell of the affair. In several cases which have been brought to the notice of the Marshal and his deputies the women have declined to give any satisfactory information. The descriptions given by those who are willing to talk have been so vague and of such varietiiss that the officers have been unable to locate the man.

Marshal Richard Lloyd wiil not give the names of the huggers' victims.

1900

BERKELEY WOMAN VIOLATED GAME LAW AND IS FINED

Miss F. Louise Shepard of Berkeley has been fined $50 and Robert Poe and A. Jenks $25 each by Mendocino county judges for killing deer out of season. The lady conducted a camp and hired a man to violate the game laws to supply her table.

GATHER IN THE HOBOES

Eleven hoboes were arrested in West Berkeley Monday night by Deputy Constables George White and Joseph Taylor and taken to the County Jail.

The arrests were due to the fact that the Appellate Court has decided that the salary system for the payment of justices of the peace and constables is unconstitutional.

The decision of the Appellant Court is likely to be tested in the Supreme Court, which has once held the salary law to be constitutional, but the deputy constables are taking time by the forelock in making arrests, so that if the fee system is restored they will be entitled to compensation.

Under the fee custom the County Jail was always crowded with tramps and hoboes, while under the salary system very few vagrants were arrested. The fees of arresting officers are about $2 and justices of the peace $3 for each vagrant taken into custody and committed to the County Jail.

SERIOUS CHARGE MADE AGAINST WEST END MAN

August Wiesenhavern of 1328 Sixth street, West Berkeley was arrested yesterday by Policemen Lestrange and Farrar on a charge of indecent exposure. He was arrested February 4, 1902, on a similar charge but was acquited. Wiesenhavern had been placed in the County Jail.

Members of the Berkeley Fire Department on a hunting trip near Truckee, California. Courtesy of the Berkeley Firefighters Association.

OFFICERS PREVENT TRAGEDY

Detectives Parker and Jamison of the police department, who have a happy faculty of dropping in at the proper time, arrived at Third street and University avenue yesterday morning in time to prevent a tragedy. The behavior of a crowd of youngsters excited the suspicions of the detectives and they hurried to the scene of youthful gathering. In the center of the group was a large rock and on it lay a strange appearing object of tin. One small boy was in the act of striking the strange object, when his arm was caught by Jamison, while Parker captured the little tin object that lay on the rock.

An examination of the suspicious looking object disclosed the fact that it was nothing more nor less than a railway dynamite cap, used to place on the tracks after a wreck or washout as a warning to approaching trains. Had the youngster with the hammer succeeding in landing a square blow on the cap, Jamison says that at least three or four of the children gathered about the rock, would have suffered serious if not fatal injuries. The dynamite cap now occupies a place in Marshal Vollmer's desk. It is labeled "handle with care."

September 4, 1905

IS AFTER BREAKERS OF LAWS

That Marshal Vollmer is determined to enforce all the ordinances of the town and especially the one relating to the collecting of licenses was made evident this morning when R. E. Major was arrested at the corner of Grove and Allston way by Deputy Marshal Moran and booked at headquarters with violating a city ordinance. Major is a teamster and was carrying on his business, the quarterly license for which was due two weeks ago. The driver claimed that he had not been given notice to pay up. Major was released on bail.

Marshal Vollmer has issued a statement to the effect that all parties conducting businesses which require licenses must pay them immediately or take the chances of being arrested and fined or imprisoned. The last day which the law allows for the payment of license is July 15, at the beginning of the fiscal year, and all peddlers, expressmen, solicitors, etc., who have not as yet paid their assessment are guilty of violating a city ordinance.

Has Bicycle Stolen.

Arnold Barnett who is connected with the Berkeley Electric Light Company on Shattuck avenue reported to the police this morning that a bicycle belonging to him had been stolen last night. The wheel which is valued at thirty-five dollars was left standing at the door of the firm's offices while Barnett went inside with the intention of returning in a few moments. When he returned the bicycle was gone and the aid of the police was at once solicited. A number of wheels have been stolen in this city under similar conditions and the police are of the opinion that some one is systematically stealing the bicycles and pawning them in the city.

An Unruly Prisoner.

Berkeley Woman Creates a Disturbance in Alameda.

Jennie Hart, a woman 72 years of age, who claims Berkeley as her place of residence, was arrested Thursday evening in Alameda, on a charge of vagrancy. The act precipitating her arrest was her attempt to "lift" a box of fruit from a Park street grocery store.

Although Jennie Hart will be 73 years old on the day of her liberation, she is still full of youthful fire. On the night of her arrest she destroyed all the furniture in the woman's department of the City Prison, and let loose such a volume of oaths that the police found it necessary to lock her up in the steel tank. She made kindling wood of two chairs, a bed and a table, and twisted the gaspipe out of shape. Supper dishes were smashed into bits and thrown at the officers when they tried to subdue the women. The woman did not cease to swear roundly when finally reduced and forced into solitary confinement.

When brought before Justice of the Peace Morris, the prisoner exclaimed: "Look here, Judge, I don't want you to keep me in the jug any longer than you can help. My birthday comes on the 23d of August, and I've got to get out and enjoy myself."

The speech had its desired effect for instead of giving the woman a two months sentence as he had contemplated, Judge Morris ordered the woman to be confined in Sheriff Roger's hotel for forty days.

July 14, 1900

Plumbing and Laundry Crimes

ARREST WOMAN FOR VIOLATING TOWN ORDINANCE

Mrs. Harriet E. Guild of 1636 Virginia street, was arrested yesterday for violating ordinance No. 11, which provides for the connecting of dwellings with the sewer system. The house occupied by Mrs. Guild, it is claimed was built six years ago and never connected with the sewer. The woman was released on depositing $20 bail. Her case will come up in Justice Edgar's court to-morrow morning.

August 30, 1905

Case Continued.

The arraignment of Mrs. H. E. Guild, who was arrested for violating the town ordinance providing for connecting houses with sewers, was continued until next Tuesday afternoon at 2 o'clock. The continuation was granted upon the request of Mrs. Guild's attorney, George Perry.

Wanted to Go to Jail.

Mrs. Hanorah Bentley Tried Hard to Save Her Ten Dollars.

Mrs. Hanorah Bentley wanted to go to jail this morning. She tried to persuade Justice Edgar that a ten days' sojourn in the county resort would be first rate but he couldn't see it that way.

Mrs. Bentley was fined $10 for not connecting her house with a sewer. The amount of the fine had been deposited by Mrs. Bentley as bail some time before. Justice Edgar kept the money as a fine for breaking the law.

It was when Justice Edgar informed Mrs. Bently that she would not get her $10 back that she declared she wanted to go to jail. She was willing to spend ten days in jail if she could only get her money back.

Mrs. Bentley became quite indignant when Justice Edgar refused to send her to jail at the county's expense. She is a woman sixty-five years of age.

CHINESE IS UNDER ARREST

Last night Marshal Vollmer arrested Lo Yieng, a Chinese who recently opened a laundry on Blake street between Milvia street and Shattuck avenue, for violating Ordinance No. 112—A, which provides for the regulation conducting of laundries within the town limits. Yieng's offense consists of failure to make application to the Health Officer for a permit to conduct the laundry. Marshal Vollmer states that the Celestial will be arrested again to-day for violating the new ordinance, which prohibits the establishment of laundries within a prescribed district. As Yieng's laundry is in the district where such establishments are not allowed under the new ordinance, two charges will be made against him.

Some time ago residents in the vicinity of Dwight way station petitioned the Town Trustees to establish an ordinance prohibiting the conducting of laundries within the resident section. A territory was outlined, and an ordinance covering the question was presented and adopted by the board. The case of Lo Yieng will probably be the first instance where the new ordinance can be tested, provided the Chinese will fight the case.

The Marshal was informed some time ago that the Chinese had erected a building on Haste street, where they proposed opening a laundry. As soon as it was apparent that the Chinese proposed opening the laundry in direct violation of the ordinance, Marshal Vollmer placed the proprietor of the place under arrest. Lo Yieng secured his temporary release by depositing $40 bail. He will appear before Justice Edgar for arraignment to-morrow morning at 10 o'clock.

September 1905

Digging a sewer line trench in Sacramento Street in Berkeley in the early 1900s. This horse team was run by the Wileges family who lived nearby. Courtesy of the Berkeley Historical Society, catalog #1468.

Hoodlums

Annoyed by Hoodlums.

The residents of Peralta are complaining of the nightly disturbances of hoodlums who congregate at the corner of Ashby and Shattuck avenues. The youths perpetrate all manner of pranks much to the discomfort of the residents.

Will Be Put in School.

Marshal Vollmer was informed today by the parents of Eddie Johnson and Fred Gordon, the 11-year-old lad who recently ran away with a purse belonging to Johnson's aunt containing some $50, that the boys would be placed in private schools where they would be carefully watched.

Large Window Broken.

J. A. Christy of 2439 Shattuck avenue, has reported to Marshal Vollmer that a large steel washer was thrown through his window Saturday by a small boy. The boy, with another youngster, was throwing the washers at a Chinaman, but the missile failed to strike its mark, coming in contact with the window. The lad has not as yet been captured.

Hoodlums at Large.

A small band of ruffians prowling about the streets last Saturday night made a halt at the corner of Center street and Shattuck avenue, where one of them made an exhibition of the currish characteristics of his species. Stepping up to the front of the Berkeley Electric Lighting Company's office, he deliberately drove his fist through a large plate of glass in the front window, whereupon he and his associate scrubs took to their heels. The act was witnessed by a prominent young business man who chanced to be in the vicinity, and what he saw may lead to the apprehension of the miscreant and his gang. In which event a needed lesson will be given to evil-doers of his ilk.

March 5, 1900

Contractor Annoyed by Boys.

Contractor M. W. Davis reported to the Marshal that a number of boys had been taking lumber from a dwelling under course of construction of Francisco street, near California street, and also throwing rocks and other missiles at the building while the carpenters were working, endangering their lives. Marshal Vollmer detailed Detectives Jamieson and Parker on the case. After an investigation of the matter, they found that the disturbance was caused by a number of small boys residing in the immediate vicinity. The boys causing the trouble, according to their report, are the three Heaffey boys of Edith street, the Sherman boy of 1611 Delaware street and the Pizzano boy of Delaware and Magee streets.

Warrants will probably be sworn out by Contractor Davis for the boys' arrests this afternoon.

YOUTHFUL FOOTPADS USE GUN

Robert Bowles, the 9-year-old son of P. E. Bowles, president of the First National Bank of Oakland, was slightly wounded Tuesday afternoon while driving in the Claremont district, just south of the Berkeley town line, in an encounter with two youthful amateur highwaymen. That he was not killed is due only to the fact that he had succeeded in getting almost out of range of the weapon of one of the young knights of the road before the shot to enforce a command to halt was fired.

The banker's son and Eddie Leimert, a younger brother of Walter Leimert, the manager of the real estate department of the Realty Syndicate, were driving along Claremont avenue, in the vicinity of the Country Club, when they were suddenly ordered to halt by two boys, who stepped out of the brush at the side of the road. Seeing that the larger of the strangers was armed with a shotgun, Bowles ignored their order to stop and lashed the ponies he was driving into a run. After shouting to them once more to halt the boy with the gun threw his weapon to his shoulder and fired at the fleeing pair. One of the shots pierced the left ear of the banker's son and several struck the back of the cart.

At the time the shot was fired, however, the boys in the cart were almost out of range and the pellets that struck the vehicle simply marked the woodwork and fell to the ground. Bowles and his companion at once returned to their homes in Oakland and told their parents of what had occurred and yesterday morning the police were notified. The place where the two boys were fired upon is outside the city limits, but Detective George Kyte was detailed on the case and after a long search he found the youths who had essayed the role of highwaymen.

Robberies

CLAIMS TO HAVE BEEN HELD UP

Ex-Policeman James Campbell, now a teamster for Logan's Express, reported to the Town Marshal's office yesterday that he was held up Saturday night shortly after 10 o'clock by two men, who relieved him of $6 or $8 of his employer's money. The encounter with the thugs, he said, took place on Parker street, near Ellsworth, and was only a short distance from his home.

August 7, 1905

WOMEN SHOOT AT HOLD-UPS.

Highwaymen Stop Carriage on Lonely Road and Get Warm Reception.

Reno, Nev., Aug. 9.—Mrs. C. Brown and Mrs. A. Mathieson, wives of well-known residents of Gardnerville, south of here, had a thrilling experience with two highwaymen while out driving last evening. The women were on their way home, and when near the schoolhouse were ordered to stop. Instead of complying, they drew revolvers, and began firing at the would-be robbers, who started to retreat, at the same time emptying their guns at the two women. The women bravely stood their ground until help arrived. By this time, however, the bandits made their escape across the fields and have not been seen since.

August 9, 1905

Stage Held Up.

SAN FRANCISCO. August 17.—Word has been received here of the robbery of the Half Moon bay and San Mateo stage, which took place two miles from San Mateo at 11 o'clock this morning by a lone robber. The Wells, Fargo Express box and mail bay were taken.

August 1905

ROBBED BY HIS FRIEND

A warrant has been issued at the instigation of Nels J. Linstrom for the arrest of his erstwhile friend, Edward Daniels, on a charge of larceny. According to Linstrom, who got up from a sick bed to swear to the warrant, Daniels was visiting him in his room at 3130 King street, while he (Linstrom) lay ill in bed. After talking for an hour or so with his friend, Daniels went out to get Linsrom a cup of tea.

An hour passed and Daniels did not return with the beverage. Linstrom fearing that his friend had met with a mishap got out of bed and prepared to go in search of him. While dressing Linstrom made the discovery that his purse containing $32.25 was gone. He looked further and found that his watch was also missing. Then, instead of going in search of his friend, Linstrom went to the police station where he swore to a warrant for the arrest of Daniels.

Linstrom states that he left the purse containing $32.25 on a table near his bed, and lying near it was his watch. He is of the opinion that when Daniels got up he slipped the purse and watch into his pocket, stating at the time that he would get the invalid some tea, as an excuse to get out of the room with the money and watch. Linstrom says that he has known Daniels for some time and that he is a cement worker. He is not certain where the man resides.

Accused of Stealing Shoes.

Martin Slattery, from nowhere in particular, was arrested yesterday on a charge of petty larceny. Luke Dempsey, a plasterer claims that Slattery stole his shoes, and as Slattery was wearing the shoes in question at the time of his arrest, it appeared very much as if the Irish tourist would get his. Slattery, however, claims he is innocent of any wrong-doing. He says he found the shoes lying in the road, and as they were better than the pair he wore, he changed them then and there. Slattery's case comes up Monday.

September 11, 1905

YOSEMITE STAGE ROBBER VERY OBLIGING

Yosemite, Aug. 17.—Details of the daring hold-up which took place Tuesday afternoon by a lone highwayman who stopped and robbed a stage of the Yosemite Stage and Turnpike Company near the Cowan bridge, three and a half miles north of Ahwahnee, between Raymond and Wawona, have reached here. The robber was armed with a shot gun and six shooter. The shotgun was slung from his shoulder by a cord, so that he would still be armed while having the free use of both hands. His face was entirely covered with a cheesecloth mask. He stopped the stage with the gun and ordered the ten passengers, eight of whom were tourists and two stage company blacksmiths, to alight.

These were: G. H. Molson, A. G. Veith, Mrs. James Wilkinson and two daughters, the two Misses Fullerton and an Austrian lady.

Standing them up in a line beside the wagon, he stripped them of their valuables with one hand, keeping them covered with the revolver with the other. He secured in all about $100. He refused to take any money from the blacksmiths, saying that he didn't want a workingman's money. A tourist named Veith, of the Austrian consulate in Milwaukee, asked him to return his watch and a railroad ticket as being of no value to him, and the robber assented, throwing the watches into the crowd.

Veith, emboldened by his success, asked the favor of taking a snap shot of the bandit in the act of stopping the stage. The highwayman again consented and posed for the picture with his gun raised. He then ordered the passengers into the stage and made them drive on. He was quite gentlemanly throughout the affair, talked with an eastern accent and appeared to be inexperienced. He was about 40 years of age and had black eyes. The stage was driven by Walter Farnsworth of Mariposa. It carried neither mail nor express.

The scene of the hold-up was a lonely one, with no dwellings nearer than Ahwahnee. The robbery was reported at once to the sheriffs of Madera and Mariposa counties. The robber was tracked some distance, but has not yet been seen or heard of. The passengers continued their journey to Wawona and yesterday visited the Mariposa big tree grove, none the worse for their exciting experience of the day before.

August 1905

A MIDNIGHT DUEL

In Which Frank Sutton and Bur glars Participate.

Two Unsuccessful Attempts to Enter Upper Dwight Way Residence.

One of the most daring attemp at burglary that has ever been a tempted in this town was succes fully frustrated at an early hou this morning. The would-be ro bers were only beaten off after a exciting duel in which Frank Su ton and the marauders participate

At 2:10 o'clock this morning, tw burglars, who are given the usu description of "one short and on tall," tried to effect an entrance the residence of A. M. Sutton at th corner of Piedmont and Dwigl way. Frank Sutton, who is but 1 years of age, was awakened by crashing noise at the basement doo

THE DUEL.

As previous attempt had bee made, to burglarize the residenc Frank prepared himself for possib conflict. Arming himself with rifle he went to an upper back wi dow and called out "Who's there! The burglars did not respond bu beat a hasty retreat through th grounds at the back of the house.

Undaunted and with the air of a officer, young Sutton commande the fleeing men to throw up the hands. When they continued the course he fired a shot in their dire tion.

THE BURGLARS RESPOND.

The young man was astounded to see the thieves turn and fire two shots at him. By this time the whole household became aroused as well as many residents in the neigh borhood. An examination of the cellar door showed that they had tried to force it. On the screen were marks of one of the fellow's feet. Lying on the ground close by were their tools—a cold chisel, brace and bit, small hammer, a candle and a skeleton key.

A PREVIOUS ATTEMPT.

This morning's work of the bur glars does not constitute the only attempt to enter the residence. It develops that last Thursday a des perate attempt was made to bur glarize the premises. At that time a long ladder was used. This effort was also unsuccessssful, for the next morning a red handkerchief, which had evidently been used as a mask, and a box of matches were found under the dining-room window.

A peculiar part of the affair lies in the fact that no trace of the rob bers bullets can be found. The Sutton boys are exhibiting the flat tened missile which was fired from Frank's rifle.

Marshal Lloyd, to whom the case was reported, has been making in vestigations He is quite puzzled over the affair. Why the burglars should have fired shot when the way of escape was clear, he cannot comprehend.

"The tools which are supposed to have been left by the burglars," said Mr. Lloyd, "would be almost useless to a professional house breaker. The hammer was nothing but a toy. The only things that might have been used were the keys and cold chisel."

The affair assumes a more myster ious aspect as each phase of the case is brought to light.

August 28, 1900

BRAVE GIRL DEFEATS ATTEMPT OF TWO MEN TO ENTER RESIDENCE

While alone in her father's home at 2324 Fulton street late last night, Miss Genevieve Van Dyck, daughter of Henvy C. Van Dyck, frightened two burglars away from the house, who were attempting to enter by a rear window. The bravery and prompt action of the young women saved the possible loss of numerous valuables and what might have ended in a tragedy had the men succeeded in entering the house.

Shortly after 9 o'clock Miss Van Dyck was aroused by the ringing of the doorbell. Being alone and the house in darkness the young women instead of going to the door, peeked through a side window to see whom the visitor might be. The person at the door was a man, who, after waiting some time for a reply to the bell, left the place. In half an hour another man wearing a slouch hat rang the door-bell. He stood and listened for some time before leaving. By that time the young woman became nervous and fearing to retire she moved about the house looking cautiously through the half-drawn curtains.

About 11 o'clock while Miss Van Dyck was peeking through a rear window she saw two men climb over the back fence and creep toward the house. Although badly frightened the young woman knew that she would have to frighten the men away before they entered the house. She went quietly to the front part of the house and climbed the stairs to the second story. There she stationed herself in a room at the rear of the house where she could observe the progress of the supposed burglars. Upon looking out the window, however, Miss Van Dyck saw the men had got the start of her, as one was then half way through the lower hall window. Realizing that she must act quickly the young woman threw open a window and screamed to the burglars to "scoot." The strangers did not wait for a second invitation, but fled from the premises. After making sure the men were not coming back, Miss Van Dyck, fearing to remain in the house went out on the front porch, where she remained until her parents returned at 12:30 o'clock. Van Dyck reported the matter to the Marshal's office and Policemen Virgin and Lestrange made an investigation. They could find no trace of the men, however, as the case had not been reported until several hours after the strangers left the premises.

Brutal Bull Dog.

Yesterday afternoon a little girl was going down Center street with her dog, a peacable bird dog. When in front of Bowman's drug-store a big bull dog jumped on the bird dog and began to chew him. Half a dozen men came to the rescue and it was only after much kicking and pulling that they were able to get the brutal bull to loosen his hold. The little girl went crying down the street with her bleeding dog by her side. Detective Parker was present and saw the affair.

No one present know who owned the dog but Parker took the license number, which was 311. There is a town ordinance making it an offense to allow a vicious dog to run at large. This dog is a particularly vicious one and is the same one that a few months ago nearly killed a small dog at the corner of Center and Shattuck. The bystanders who saw the brutal attack were thoroughly aroused and demanded that the dog be shot. Today the police are looking for the owner of the dog. The tag was a last year's one and had evidently been taken from another dog as the 311 issue last year was for a collie dog. Marshal Vollmer has notified Poundmaster Coryell and if that official finds the dog loose without a 1905 tag he will go to the boneyard in short order. Detective Parker is anxious to swear to a complaint against the owner of the dog if he can apprehend him and the matter will not be dropped.

Kate Shot at the Thief.

It is owing to the dexterity with which Miss Byrne handles the revolver that the feathered flock of the Byrne homestead at 1313 Oxford street, remains intact this morning. About ten o'clock last evening the household was startled by a noise in the chicken house. Arming herself with a six-shooter, Miss Byrne proceeded to investigate. She discovered a thief red handed and coolly fired a shot in his direction.

The would-be robber beat a hasty retreat, dropping the poultry on the spot.

This is not the first time the Byrne premises have been raided. A few weeks ago nightly visits were made to their pantry. Thus far the marauders are not surely apprehended.

February 28, 1900

More "Funny Business."

The sleuths of the Berkeley secret service are trying to run to earth an amateur band of highwaymen who held up a delivery wagon last night and confiscated a lot of ice cream, which was on its way to the residence of Mrs. Phillips, 2511 Benvenue avenue. More than likely that the episode will result in an intelligent discrimination in the future, between "funny business" and robbery.

February 23, 1900

September 15, 1905

STUDENT ATTACKED BY THREE

While on his way home last night from the Berkeley station, Frank Abbott, a student in the University, was attacked by three men, and for ten minutes he held his own, keeping the men from reaching him using only his fists. The attack occurred on Addison street, near Shattuck avenue, the men being protected from observation in the shade of the Francis Shattuck building. Whether the men were merely drunk and quarrelsome, or whether they intended holding him up Abbott is unable to say. After escaping his assailants Abbott went to his room and securing a revolver he went out to look for the men with the intention of placing them under arrest. During his search Abbott met Deputy Marshal Moran who joined in the hunt. None of the men, however, were located, and it is believed that they must have left town immediately after their unsuccessful attempt to hold up the student.

According to the story told by Abbott he had returned from San Francisco, and upon leaving Berkeley station about 11 o'clock, he started down Addison street. About 100 feet from Shattuck avenue, he met three men who appeared to be intoxicated. As the student passed them he stepped off the sidewalk to avoid a collision, when one of the men struck at him. Abbott threw up his left arm and caught the blow on his shoulder and at the same time he gave the stranger a left arm jab in the chest. The other men then ran toward Abbott, while the student with his back against the Shattuck building held them off.

For a while the student feared he would be overcome by the strangers, until finally the three men turned and ran away. While the fight was on Abbott discovered that his assailants were not as intoxicated as they at first appeared. When the men had disappeared down Addison street Abbott immediately made his way home and returned with a revolver in hope of capturing the men whom he intended to march to the police station.

Million-Dollar Bank Robbery.

The Treasury of a Local Institution Completely Cleaned Out of Its Funds.

During the past few days the Atherton National Bank of Berkeley has been robbed twice, the aggregate loss being $1,350,000—too much for any Berkeley financial institution to spare without real inconvenience.

The bank in question is connected with Professor Atherton's business college, and it is sad to relate that suspicion clear and strong points to the male students of the college as the bold, bad cracksmen.

The first robbery was of $350,000 of the funds of the bank, and the burglary was committed in the early part of last week. While annoyed at the loss of the money, Professor Atherton did not see fit to make any great fuss over so inconsiderable a sum, but he "gave it out cold and flat" in the schoolroom that he wanted no more monkeying with the legal tender by the illegal toughs who had entered upon a career of crime while engaged in the pursuit of honorable and invaluable knowledge—and the resourceful professor straightway ordered a new issue of $1,000,000 of the college currency.

When banking hours commenced on Friday last it was found that the vaults of the bank had again been robbed. This time the burglars took $1,000,000 —all of the new issue.

President-Cashier Professor Atherton hastily summoned himself for a special meeting with himself and decided on vigorous action. He called all of his male students to book and tried to extort a confession. Not one of the class would confess to complicity in the daring burglaries, and never a mother's son of them would "squeal."

Firm in his resolve to get to the seat of the biggest robbery ever suffered in Alameda county and the only bank burglary in the history of Berkeley, all the boys of the school were suspended this morning, with the injunction to "think it over" and see if they could devise means for their reinstatement.

The boys are thinking it over.

Later: As the Gazette is going to press it receives intelligence to the effect that the bold boy burglars have made restitution of the money taken from the bank and compromised matters with the tender-hearted victim, Professor Atherton, who has received them back into good standing in the social and commercial circles of the business college. There is some talk in police circles, however, of indicting the professor for compounding a felony.

It is stated that the cause of the boys' quick surrender in this matter was the fact that they could not secure a lawyer to take the case with the retainer they offered—$850,000—the prominent legal light who was approached in the premises declining the tender with the cold announcement that he was 'no cheap man.'

March 12, 1900

Burglaries

BURGLAR WORKS IN DAY TIME

A daring daylight burglary was reported to the police this morning by T. Donovan of 812 Bristol street, who states that some one entered his residence yesterday morning between 9:45 and 10:30 o'clock, securing several articles of value. Entrance was gained during the temporary absence of members of the family, and it is presumed the burglary walked in at a rear door, which was found to be unlocked after the robbery.

Donovan did not report the matter to Marshal Vollmer until this morning. Detective Jamison was immediately set to work on the case.

Shots Fired at Night.

Shortly before 2 o'clock this morning residents in the vicinity of Dwight way and Bowditch street, were aroused by two pistol shots, which were fired in quick succession. L. C. Duff, who resides at 2435 Bowditch street reported the matter to the police station by telephone and Policeman Atcheson was sent to investigate. Although the policeman made a thorough canvass of the neighborhood, he could secure no trace of the person who did the shooting. He learned that many families had been awakened by the noise, but no one had seen anything of a suspicious nature.

Violates Ordinance.

Oscar Hanson, an Oakland boy employed by the Sunset Telephone Company, was arrested this morning by Deputy Marshal Moran, for riding on the sidewalk. He was released upon depositing $5 bail.

August 4, 1905

POLICE CAPTURE BURGLAR

Robert Linehan, a young man who has been rooming at 2114 Center street, was arrested yesterday morning by Detectives Jamison and Parker for burglarizing rooms in the building where he lived and the residence of M. P. W. Albee at 2415 Durant street. At first Linehan stoutly denied having entered the rooms, but under a severe sweating conducted by Marshal Vollmer, the prisoner finally confessed to the thefts and produced a number of the articles he had taken.

Saturday afternoon the room of E. Johnson at 2114 Center street, was entered during his absence and an overcoat, valued at $20 and two gold pins, were stolen. The same afternoon and in the same building, William Kidd's room was entered. An overcoat, gold pin, blue coat and vest, all valued at about $30, were taken.

On Friday evening some one entered the residence of M. P. W. Albee at 2415 Durant street and stole a ring, gold breast pin, Mystic Shriner pin, a razor and a pair of shoes, all valued at about $25. The police were immediately notified of the Friday night robbery and when informed of the thefts on Center street the following day, led them to direct their attention to that locality. Detectives Jamison and Parker were detailed on the case and yesterday morning secured their man. Vollmer has since investigated the case of Linehan and finds that he has been in similar difficulties before.

Linehan has been identified by John Gazanego as the man who entered the latter's barber shop Saturday and borrowed fifty cents on a ring, which has been turned over to the police. It is thought that Linehan is responsible for numerous small robberies recently, and a thorough investigation is being made of his case.

August 28, 1905

Wholesale Thievery.

Workmen Lose Valuables at the Berryman Reservoir.

The workmen's camp at the Berryman reservoir has recently been the scene of the operations of a marauder, who as yet has not been apprehended. Tents have been provided for the laborers by the contractors, Stone Brothers, and it is in these that the workmen keep their clothes and valuables.

Recently two ex-soldiers, Henry Holloway and George Grand were given employment at the reservoir. They had not been there many days before they were relieved of two suits of clothing, two hats, shoes, and a shotgun.

So incensed were the Stone Brothers when they heard of the theft that they offered a reward of $100 for the detection of the culprit.

October 1, 1905

Bundle of Rope Stolen.

Edward Rowland of Orinda Park reported to Marshal Vollmer this morning that a bundle of manila rope had been taken from his wagon while it was standing in front of Sather's blacksmith shop on Shattuck avenue near Dwight way yesterday afternoon. There is no clew to the thief, but the officers are looking for a man with a bundle of rope.

BUSY DAY
FOR THE
SLEUTHS

Detectives Jameson and Parker have been performing some very good work during the last two days. Yesterday the wily detectives located by a clever bit of deduction, the whereabouts of a ten-foot rope, stolen the day before from E. Rowland's wagon. Rowland is an Orinda park farmer. He came to Berkeley Monday and left his wagon and team standing in front of a store. During the few minutes he was in the store, a rope lying under the wagon seat was removed. Someone saw a small boy with a black bandage over his eye in the neighborhood of the wagon at the time of the theft.

The bandaged eye was the only clew in the possession of the detectives, but after working for half a day they found the lad with the injured optic, and located the rope. The boy was too young to be arrested. He acknowledged having taken the rope, stating that he needed it to construct a swing.

Locate Missing Pigeons.

Yesterday Detective Jamison discovered the whereabouts of ten pigeons belonging to the son of Thomas Rickard. The youth reported that his pigeons had been stolen several days before. Jamison found the pigeons in the possession of a small boy and returned them to their owner. No arrest was made.

August 2, 1905

Mobile Berkeley Police arrayed in front of old City Hall. Courtesy of the Berkeley Police Department Historical Preservation Society.

SHOP AND CONTENTS STOLEN

When the Spring Construction Company's gang of workmen broke camp at the corner of Magee avenue and Cedar street last Friday, it was found necessary to leave a small blacksmith shop, together with a number of wheelbarrows and heavy tools. When employes of the construction company returned to the camp site Monday morning, the blacksmith shop, wheelbarrows and tools had disappeared. Although the men searched the neighborhood for several hours they could find no trace of the missing articles; not even the lumber used in constructing the blacksmith shop could be found.

The case was immediately reported to Marshal Vollmer and for the past two days Vollmer and his policeman have been collecting the shop and its contents in sections. The shop had evidently been divided among certain persons residing in that end of the town, as sections of it were found in the possession of some twenty families. The entire neighborhood was searched by the police and almost every article has been located and ordered returned to the old camping ground of the construction company's workmen. Wherever Vollmer discovered any of the missing tools and even lumber from the little shop, he ordered the persons having them in their possession, to return them.

This afternoon the company sent several teams to the former camping ground and the stuff was removed. Only a few articles were not located by the police and Vollmer is confident that they will be found within a few days.

Berkeley Police Department lined up for inspection in front of City Hall, in the early 1910s. Courtesy of the Berkeley Police Department Historical Preservation Society.

BOYS AND COIN ARE MISSING

Eddie Johnson and Fred Gordon, 11-year-old youngsters who reside on Fairview street in the South End, are wanted by the local police. Simultaneously with their disappearance last night, Mrs. Jennie Sand, an aunt of young Johnson, missed a leather handbag containing $50 in gold and a silver dollar. The woman declares that her nephew took the money and in company with his youthful companion, has skipped the country. As Eddie has been in numerous escapades within the last few months, it is the belief of the police that he took the money and has gone to Sacramento.

Mrs. Sand has been stopping at the Johnson residence, 1600 Fairview avenue during the absence of Captain and Mrs. Johnson. Last night afer preparing for dinner Eddie went into his aunt's room, explaining afterwards that he was looking for a comb. After dinner he met young Gordon in front of the Johnson residence and the two went away together. About 9 o'clock Mrs. Sans missed her handbag containing the $51. A thorough search of the house failed to bring it to light and as Eddie failed to return home last night, the woman reported her loss to the police this morning.

The runaways are the same boys who were suspected of entering Hadley's store last May. During that month Eddie was taken into custody by the local police for stealing a bicycle, but was released on account of his age. Later he was again before the police, charged with stealing money from his mother. This time he was placed under probation and since then has reported regularly at the police station. During the past week, however, the boy became restless and talked of going to Sacramento, and it is believed that he has gone to that city. He is the son of Captain C. Johnson, a seafaring man. Young Gordon, who is about the same age as Johnson, resided with his parents at 1618 Fairview street.

September 8, 1905

Fairview and California Streets of South Berkeley, where Eddie Johnson and Fred Gordon lived and roamed. They were eleven years old in 1905. Courtesy of the Berkeley Historical Society.

Domestics

"In a place where your cook may be a Prince from Japan, your second girl, an American of good birth, an undergraduate Co-ed, your coachman also an undergraduate, snobbery is scarcely able to get a foothold. The motive that inspires the brave young men and woman to work their way through college raises labor above menial service, and gives the lie to false pride. Here Democracy is an actuality, not a political fiction."

—Katherine O. Easton, *Berkeley Reporter*, December 1906

Servant Left With Valuables.

W Mitchell, residing at 585 Thirty-third street, Oakland, reported to the police today the mysterious disappearance of the domestic employed at his home, together with a gold watch and some $15 or $20 in cash.

The servant is a short, thick-set woman of 40 summers, and had been employed at Mitchell's only a short while, her true name not being known to the family.

According to Mitchell's story she disappeared shortly after the evening meal Wednesday night, and has not been heard from or seen since. Later in the evening Mr. Mitchell missed his watch and coin.

Chief of Police Hodgkins immediately detailed several detectives on the case.

Charge Against Young Girl.

An information charging Luella Gardner, the young servant girl, with having burglarized the Gilbert residence on Telegraph avenue, Oakland, while employed at the residence of E. Barnet, next door, has been filed by the District Attorney's office and the girl will probably be arraigned on the charge before Judge Greene next Wednesday. She is at present confined at the county jail in default of bail.

November 24, 1900

Accuses His Former Housekeeper.

Captain Johnson Resorts to Search Warrants For Recovery of Property.

The story of the friendship of a sea captain for the woman who became his housekeeper, a tale of alienated affections, and subsequent charges of robbery are acts in the little drama which is now being enacted in the local justice court.

Captain Martin Johnson accuses Mrs. Barbara Hoffman of having robbed him. Search warrant proceedings were to have been heard by Justice Edgar to-daybut by consent of counsel for both sides the hearing was postponed until 2 o'clock next Wednesday.

The story leading up to the trouble which will be aired in the court is best told in the words of Attorney Button of Oakland who is representing the interests of Captain Johnson who commands a vessel which plys between here and British Columbia. "About a year ago Captain Johnson and his wife separated. Then his friends came to him and recommended Mrs. Hoffman as a housekeeper. She was engaged by him and all went very well for a while.

"But when he returned from one of his trips the Captain heard that Mrs. Hoffman was telling stories to the effect that she and Johnson were engaged. Then she said they were married and began running up bills on his credit.

"When Captain Johnson discharged her she took along a large quantity of his household goods. About two weeks ago Marshal Lloyd armed with a search warrant, went to where she was staying at the home of her sister, Mrs. Charles Wagner, Tenth street West Berkeley. There he disscovered a swing machine, glass and bedspread, which were the property of my client.

"We got out another search warrant, and yesterday afternoon Constable Williamson succeeded in getting some more household goods."

The whole affair will come come out in detail next Wednesday.

December 15, 1900

Scams and Confidence Crimes

COLLECTS, BUT KEEPS THE MONEY

A suave young man, representing himself to be C. C. McCann, a bill collecting agent, has been working the merchants of the West End for the past two weeks, according to H. W. De Leon of 1454 Sixth street. The method of procedure of the alleged spurious agent is an old one. He will call on a merchant, talk pleasantly with him for a while, present his card and ask the business man if he had any bad debts which he has been trying to collect for years. He declares that collecting of bad debts is his business and he is an expert at it. Generally the business man digs up some old bills and gives them to him to collect.

One of the heaviest sufferers by McCann's operations is DeLeon, who intrusted a bill of $8.85 to him for collection two weeks ago. McCann has never returned and today DeLeon learned the bill had been paid by the debtor. DeLeon makes known his loss in order that the other merchants of the town may be warned.

August 1905

POLICE ARE ON THE TRAIL OF CLARA SPIKES

From information secured last night Marshal Vollmer is of the opinion that he will soon be able to learn the whereabouts of Clara Spikes, the young colored woman who robbed Thomas Driscol of a wallet containing $220. Shortly after the theft Marshal Vollmer was informed and traced the woman to San Francisco. He learned that she had been visiting at the home of Miss Belle Clark at 2112 Fifth street, West Berkeley. Unfortunately the Clark woman did not assist the police, sending them off on wild goose chases, thus giving the Spikes woman time to get safely away.

ANNOYED BY FAKE GAS MAN

The local police are looking for a well-dressed young man who has been representing himself to be a gas inspector in the employ of the Oakland Gas, Light and Heat Company. Yesterday the young man visited three residences on Hilgard street and in each instance was ejected from the house on account of his objectionable manners. The matter was reported to Manager F. A. Leach of the gas company, who informed Marshal Vollmer.

Owing to the peculiar actions of the supposed inspector, who, so far as can be learned, did not steal anything from the houses he entered, Vollmer and the manager of the gas company are at a loss to understand the reason for his working the deception. According to the persons whose houses the fake inspector entered, he first looked into the basement window and discovering two meters presented himself at the front door. In each case the young man stated that he was a gas stove inspector for the company, and asked permission to inspect the stoves in the house. He was admitted but was asked to leave on account of his insulting manners. When asked to show his card from the company, the young man made excuses, which the people refused to believe.

August 30, 1905

Scene from the movie Officer 444, *filmed in Berkeley.* Courtesy of the Berkeley Police Department Historical Preservation Society.

A Clever Swindler

Victimizes a Landlady and a Prominent Drug Store.

The operations of a bold female swindler who visited this city last Wednesday have been reported to Marshal Lloyd. The woman, who succeeded in victimizing Mrs. M. C. Taber of 2220 Chapel street and a clerk in Pond's drug store, gave the name of Mrs. Moore.

She began her peculations last Wednesday. Going to the home of Mrs. Taber, who conducts a lodging house, she rented a room. Her actions were so clever and her manner and speech so guileless that she at once won the confidence of the lodging house proprietor. A room was engaged by the swindler who said that her trunk would arrive soon. She further stated that any delay would be occasioned by the fact that she might have misdirected the expressmen, telling them to go to Channing way instead of Chapel street. This mistake she explained was due to looking at so many rooms on different streets that she had became confused.

Nothing was thought of the trunk episode by Mrs. Taber, who comfortably ensconced the new guest in her lodgings. When Thursday morning had dawned upon Chapel street "Mrs. Moore" had fled, and with her an afghan settee covering, which was valued at $50. This was the first intimation that the landlady received that she had been victimized

Further swindling by the unknown woman is told in another chapter. Late that Wednesday afternoon "Mrs. Moore" complained of feeling unwell. Going to Pond's Drug Store she ordered $3.60 worth of patent preparations, giving the name of Mrs. Taber. It seems that the Channing way hallucination was still with her for she asked to have the drugs sent to 2222 Channing way. Half an hour later she came back and corrected the street to Chapel. The bold operator asked that a bill be sent with the goods.

When Druggist Pond's employe presented the bill he was asked to wait until the following day. As Mrs. Taber's credit was good the request was readily granted. It is unnecessary to state that Mrs. Moore has not put in an appearance

at either the drug store or lodging house again.

The petty larcenist is described as being plainly dressed having grey hair and being over 50 years of age.

September 8, 1900

Another Missing Man.

Captain Charles Hardy's Whereabouts a Matter of Grave Anxiety.

Captain Charles Hardy, first officer of the steamship Celia, has been missing since last Thursday evening, and his friends in Oakland, Berkeley and San Francisco are fearful that he has met with foul play.

On the night of his disappearance he was seen to enter the yards of the Humboldt Lumber Company shortly before midnight. He was on the way to his ship, which lies at Adams wharf, in Oakland, and it is known that he carried considerable money. The captain never reached his vessel, and the theory advanced is that he was struck down and robbed and then thrown into the bay.

Early Thursday evening Captain Hardy went into Thomas' saloon on the water front with a party of friends. He remained there until a late hour, and then left the place with Manuel White and "Bob" Belisco, two men who are also well known in shipping circles. They accompanied him as far as the lumber yards and then left him, as he insisted that he was able to make the ship without assistance.

Tuesday afternoon the crew of the Celia dragged the estuary about the boat, but could not find a trace of the missing captain. Yesterday the work was continued, with no better results, and it was then decided to notify the officers on both sides of the bay of his disappearance.

February 1, 1900

Marshal Vollmer's office around 1911. Courtesy of the Berkeley Police Department Historical Preservation Society.

POLICE PHONE SYSTEM

Acting upon the recommendation of the Police committee, the Trustees decided last night to establish a police alarm system, and a contract was entered into with the Signal Alarm Company of Milwaukee to immediately put in the system to consist of twenty alarm boxes for three years, provided the necessary right of way can be secured over telegraph and telephone poles. The contract with the company provides that the Milwaukee firm shall place the system at its own expense. For the first three years the city will pay a monthly rental of not less than $70 with the option to purchase the system outright within a period of three years for a sum in the neighborhood of $3500.

C. E. Wood, a representative of the Signal Alarm Company appeared before the board and explained the working of the police alarm box. A box was exhibited before the members of the board and the manner of its operation, its many advantages over similar contrivances and its great durability, were thoroughly explained by Wood. The system, he said, was capable of recording a call in three seconds, and was built to withstand rough treatment and practically indestructible as it contains no magnets and is almost entirely mechanical.

The Trustees inspected the alarm box with great interest and when the motion to adopt the report of the committee recommending the installation of the police alarm system, it was carried unanimously. Another motion was made by Trustee Hoff to the effect that the board enter into a contract with the alarm company to establish the system of twenty boxes for a monthly rental of not more than $70 with the option to purchase the system within three years for an amount in the neighborhood of $3500. The motion was carried unanimously.

Marshal Vollmer will immediately map out the town and settle upon the location of the alarm boxes, with a view to having the system installed as soon as possible.

The "Red Light Recall" board for responding to police calls was a technological leap. Circa 1914. Courtesy of the Berkeley Police Department Historical Preservation Society.

This Should Have Been a Crime

TO FERTILIZE WITH INDIAN BONES

SAN JOSE, April 9.—K. P. Ponce, an agriculturist of Mayfield, is arranging to market as a fertilizer a large Indian burial mound which he has discovered upon his land and which is rich in phosphates. Within a few months it is expected that the orchardists of this section will be growing produce with the bones of ancient Indians.

Ponce recently sent a sample of the earth to the University of California for examination and has received a report that it is full of phosphates and is one of the finest of fertilizers. He has promised to send a sample of the earth to the chamber of commerce in this city and will arrange to put it on the market as a fertilizer.

8. Children

Many children ran away from home at the turn of the century. A fifteen-year-old high-tailed it to Tilden Park and survived several days on squirrels his dog had caught. A father kidnapped his daughter from her mother's house on Allston Way. Youths were killed or injured in hunting accidents or while playing with guns. Though there were numerous articles on children being shot in 1900, there was little of the violence and hate that punctuates today's tragedies. Though gangs are noted in the *Gazette* articles, their crimes consisted primarily of petty theft, vandalism and loitering in schoolyards to smoke and drink.

Children often died of a disease shortly after it was contracted. Accidental childhood drownings were common as well.

Troubled and confused youths killed themselves. Others lashed out violently at strangers.

In 1900 Berkeley debated whether children had to attend school at all! Maybe five months of school a year would do. Many children worked to help meet their family's needs. Still, Berkeley set rules for child labor by requiring parents' signatures and school approval.

"It is not many years ago since most of our population, with the exception of the college people, a small number of wealthy residents and the tradesmen, derived their support through or from San Francisco.

"In those days, after the morning trains had borne the wage-workers, the clerks and the business men to the city, there were few signs of life in the little town; the children were at school; the boys and girls at the University were engaged in their studies; the house wives were busy with their domestic duties and the streets were so deserted that one might have fired a cannon down the main avenue without fear of hitting anything more important than a stray dog."

—H. A. Sully, *Berkeley Reporter*, December 1906

Classroom inside the Hillside School. Clara Germain Poturn was the first principal. Circa 1901. Courtesy of the Berkeley Historical Society, catalog #1484.

A Request to the Public.

In view of publications in the San Francisco morning papers with respect to alleged cruel treatment of pupils in the Lorin school I am constrained to respectfully request the public to suspend judgment until the committee of the Board of Education shall have conducted its investigation next Saturday evening and made its report.

March 25, 1900

A Berkeley girl. Courtesy of the Berkeley Firefighters Association.

Defended Their Men.

Berkeley High School Players Deny Charges of Rioting.

The leading students of the Berkeley High School are indignantly denying charges that have been made by Oakland High School students to the effect that the former started a riot after the baseball game between the two schools at Freeman's Park last Saturday. The Berkeleyans also disclaim feelings of jealously but state that they were discriminated against by umpire Kennedy, which they allege accounted for their losing to Oakland.

In speaking of the trouble this morning Manager Finley Eastman of the Berkeley team said: "After the game had been played, the Oaklandites felt so jubilant at winning that they went crazy. They jumped on our third baseman, Ray Jones, because last year he attended the Oakland High School. They claimed that he had held a runner at third base, and proceeded to punish him for it then and there. We were not going to see our man roughly used, so we protected him."

"We would not have lost the game," said Pitcher Plummer, "had it not been for the rank decisions of Umpire Kennedy. This morning we will attend the Oakland High School–Central High School game, but will not go there looking for trouble, as the Oakland contingent states."

Thus far the Berkeley and Stockton High School teams are tie in the race for the championship pennant. The winner of today's game will complete the trio of contestants.

April 14, 1900

Berkeley High School. This picture was taken in the 1896–97 term. Courtesy of the Berkeley Architectural Heritage Association, photo #114.

Class at McKinley Junior High School. Courtesy of the Berkeley Architectural Heritage Association, from the Muriel Durgin Backman album.

A Rush Aftermath.

President Wheeler Warns High School Students.

If the students of the Berkeley High School rush on the University campus again they will be denied the use of it for athletic purposes. Such is the edict as set forth by President Benjamin Ide Wheeler, in a letter which was read at a meeting of the Associated Students of the Berkeley High School this morning.

A few weeks ago a good-natured mix-up was indulged in by the pupils of the Oakland and Berkeley High Schools after a baseball game on the campus. But in the future it seems that the boys will be compelled to curb their partisanship while on the University grounds.

Principal M. C. James announced the program for the Senior class graduation. Class Day, upon which the class play is presented, is set for June 6th. Graduation will be held on the 7th and the dance on the 8th of June. It is probable that all these affairs will be held in Shattuck Hall.

Notice was given that the election of the associated students would probably be held next Friday.

April 25, 1900

Lillian Dell'Ergo at about four years old by her family home at 3035 Ellis Street, Berkeley. This was an often repeated scene as photographers would travel around neighborhoods with their goat cart and, for some small amount of change, take pictures of neighborhood children sitting in the cart. Courtesy of the Berkeley Public Library, South Branch, Vincent Dell'Ergo Collection, photo #sb000-559.

<table>
<tr><td>Schools</td></tr>
</table>

Urgent Need for New Buildings.

S. D. Waterman, Superintendant of City Schools, Writes of the Present Crowded Condition of Our Schools and the Necessity for Building New Ones.

The demand for additional school rooms for the Public School Department of Berkeley was never more imperative than at the present time. Only twice during the last ten years have the school accommodations for the primary and grammar grades been sufficient. In 1891-92 children in the 9th grade were forced to travel from what was the extreme southern boundary of the town to the Rose street school for a room. During this time eleven rooms were rented in various parts of the town for school purposes. In 1892, after the annexation of the Peralta or Ashby avenue district the pressure was relieved for a year by the erection of the Le Conte, the Whittier and the Columbus school building. It was only for a year, however, for almost immediately the Board of Education was forced to supply additional room Two additional rooms were erected on the LeConte school lot an addition of two rooms was made to the Lorin school building, and one additional room was fitted up in the basement of the Rose street school. The Maloney building at the corner of Shattuck avenue and Channing way and, later, the Old Berkeley Gymnasium building on Atherton street were rented and fitted for school purposes. It should be remembered that these rented rooms only served as shelter. They were in no way suited to the demands of the school room. None but those connected closely with the School Department understand fully the difficulty of managing schools under such discouraging conditions.

With the completion of the Dwight way and Bancroft way school buildings there was a temporary relief, but the rapid increase in population has been such during the last two years that we are again cramped for room. During the present school year children have had to wait for weeks for seats in their proper grades.

It is not necessary to state here how school work has been handicapped during all these years by this lack of suitable room.

Owing to the removal of the ninth grade classes to the Allston way school and to the opening of the Business Department, the High school has had better accommodations during the last two years, but during the present year the principal's office has been used during the entire forenoon for a class room and one class has used the Superintendent's office for recitation purposes.

The question is often asked, "What additional rooms will be gained for the Primary and Grammar Grades if the proposed bonds are issued and the plans of the Board of Education are carried into effect?" The answer is briefly,

Four additional rooms on the Dwight way lot.

Four rooms in the Scenic Tract, which is at present without a single school room.

Children living in the Scenic tract north of the University grounds have had to attend the Dwight way school. Pupils who really belong in the Dwight way school district have thus been compelled to attend the LeConte school producing in that school a crowded condition in some of the grades. This will be remedied fully by the erection of the proposed new building in the Scenic tract.

A new building on the San Pablo avenue lot to take the place of the old, out-of-date and tumble-down building which at present occupies the site.

With the completion of the new High School building, the twelve room now occupied by the High School can be utilized wherever needed the most, as the building can be easily moved. This gives a total of 20 additional rooms which will be available for the use of the Primary and Grammar grades.

The proposed new High School building includes the following: 16 large class rooms, 2 small recitation rooms, a principal's office and reception room, a library room and an assembly hall on the second floor large enough for all lectures and school exercises, thus doing away with the expense of renting a hall whenever any school exercise is to be held.

In addition to the main building, a separate one-story building of 3 rooms is to be erected for a chemical laboratory, a physical laboratory and a room for the recitations in chemistry and physics. These laboratories for obvious reasons should never be under the same roof as the other class rooms.

These accommodations will be sufficient for a school of from 600 to 700 students.

In 1891 we had an enrollment of 72, in 1900, 300.

With the prospective influx of people when the new University buildings, under the Hearst plans, are begun and the new High School is completed, we may reasonably expect at least 500 students in the High School within five years.

The Berkeley High School will be essentially a preparatory school. It must be so by reason of its location and with suitable facilities and accommodations for doing the work it should be the model secondary school of California.

As to the new location. While the present location has some advantages, the new one, taking everything into consideration, is infinitely better. The noise of trains, the continued passing on the street to and from the University, the fact that almost every street demonstration of the U. C. student body includes Center street in its line of march, the nearness to the business center of the town—all these interfere seriously with school discipline and work.

The proposed new site is admirably located, fronting Grove street. It has streets on three sides and thus good air and ventilation can be secured.

In view of the pressing needs of the School Department it is hoped that every voter will at least express his will at the polls. If a majority of the voters of the town are satisfied with the present condition of things the vote will show it; but if on the other hand the majority of the voters desire the improvements indicated to be made—the only effective way to secure them is to so indicate by the ballot.

This is written for the information of those residents of Berkeley who are not familiar with the past conditions of the Department, as well as to remind old residents that the town is growing and that the educational interests must suffer materially if financial aid is not forth coming. S. D. WATERMAN,
Supt. of City Schools,
Berkeley, Cal.

McKinley School, from the book Berkeley, A City of Homes. *Courtesy of the Berkeley Architectural Heritage Association.*

FOR OUR SCHOOLS.

Proposition to Raise Money for Extension and Improvement.

Meeting of Joint Committee to Consider Plans for the Issue of Bonds Which Shall Yield the Necessary Funds.

The committees of the whole of the Board of Trustees and the Board of Education met at the office of Mason & McLenathen last night for a joint conference on the school bond proposition.

The especial purpose of the meeting was to inform the town trustees fully as to what the members of the board of education had accomplished in the investigation of the subject and to furnish the official representatives of the town government with estimates of the amount necessary for school purposes.

The committee representing the Board of Education requested the town trustees to call an election and to issue bonds, if the people approved of the contemplated issue, on the municipal plan, in the sum of $100.000. Of this amount $70,000 is recommended for the purchase of a lot and the erection of a building for the High School, and the balance for the uses of the grammar and lower grades.

The Board of Trustees was requested to take up the matter immediately and forward it as vigorously as possible. It is understood that the subject will be considered at the next meeting of the board, and that definite action will then be taken in the matter.

The meeting last night was entirely harmonious, the only difference of opinion being as to the comparative merits of the municipal and the district plans for the issuance of the bonds. The former is somewhat more expensive in its legal requirements, but it is decidedly preferable for the reason that bonds under that plan are more readily sold and bring a better price than those under the district plan. It was finally agreed, therefore, to favor the municipal plan.

The consensus of opinion among Berkeley's best citizens seems to be enthusiastically in favor of this proposed bond issue for the badly-needed improvement of our school facilities, all progressive people believing that the money spent in advancing the interests of our excellent and overcrowded schools will be money very well used.

February 24, 1900

Rose Street School on Berryman Street. Courtesy of the Berkeley Architectural Heritage Association, photo #5.

Franklin School at the corner of Delaware Street and San Pablo Avenue. Courtesy of the Berkeley Historical Society.

Wulburn child with both her grandmothers at 1609 Fifth Street in 1901. Courtesy of the Berkeley Architectural Heritage Association.

TEACHER MAKES A CORRECTION

Editor Gazette—Will you kindly correct a statement made in to-day's Gazette, to the effect that I had some boys arrested for frequenting the Hillside School premises. The Marshall came into our neighborhood looking for boys who had been reported as having been troublesome, but for what offense, or by whom reported, I did not know. Later in the day when we found our telephone wires had been cut, I notified the Marshall to that effect.

C. GERMAIN POTWIN,
Principal Hillside School.
August 31, 1905.

[Ed.—We are glad to make the publication. We don't see where any correction is needed but still we are pleased to give the hearing. We said, "Acting upon the complaint of the principal of the Hillside school, Marshal Vollmer has been keeping a close watch on the behavior of a gang of small boys." The principal says: "When we found our telephone wires had been cut I notified the Marshall to that effect." There may be a wide divergence between these two statements that needs correction but we fail to see it. Still we gladly give the space for the alleged correction.]

Emi and Fumi Manabe as children in front of their home at 1725 Stuart Street, Berkeley. Courtesy of the Berkeley Public Library, South Branch, Fumi M. Hayashi Collection, photo #sb000-212.

A Berkeley class. Courtesy of the Berkeley Firefighters Association.

Would Have Compulsory Attendance.

Berkeley Educators Favor Such Legislation.

The State Educational Commission, composed of prominent men and women from all parts of California, convened yesterday in the assembly-room of the Board of Education in San Francisco, and laid the foundation for much important legislation in behalf of the public schools of California.

The meeting was presided over by the chairman, Henry Weinstock, and the following other members were present: Edward F. Adams, Wrights; F. W. Anderson, Alden Anderson, Suisun; James A. Barr, Stockton; H. M. Bland, San Jose; Professor Elmer E. Brown, University of California; Mayor James D. Phelan, Frederick Burk, C. W. Mark, Charles A. Murdock, W. D. Kingsbury, San Farncisco; President David Starr Jordan and Professor E. P. Cubberley Stanford University. The proposed law to enforce the attendance at public schools of all children between the ages of 8 and 14, during at least five months of the year, unless physical disability, unusual conditions or other instruction should excuse non-attendance, providing for the creation of truant schools, and prohibiting the employment of children to the detriment of their education, led to a prolonged discussion upon minor proivsions of the clauses of the law as it is now framed.

December 10, 1900

GRAMMAR TEACHERS ARE SCARCE

Owing to several causes, the supply of available teachers from the University of California is smaller this year than in former years, while the demand has been greater than ever before. The appointment secretary asks for volunteers, especially for the grammar schools. There are a number of positions to be filled this week, many of them in country schools, but with salaries ranging from $65 to $75 per month. There are always calls for teachers for this class of schools, late in the summer, and each year the number of grammar schools for which University teachers are wanted grows larger. It would be well for undergraduates to bear this in mind, especially the men who wish to become superintendents of schools or to teach for a few years before preparing for some other profession. Grammar school principals are in demand, and salaries are being increased for the purpose of attracting men teachers to them. More men should fit themselves to fill these positions, as it is being found that they are more competent than women for work of this kind, and very good inducements are accordingly being made

August 1905

Berkeley teachers at the turn of the century. Courtesy of the Berkeley Firefighters Association.

ANTI-VACCINATION LEAGUE DECIDES TO OPEN A NEW SCHOOL

With reorganization last night of the Berkeley branch of the Anti-Compulsory Vaccination League at a meeting held in Golden Sheaf hall, it was definitely decided to proceed with the establishment of the new free public school for children who are not vaccinated. The meeting, which was well attended, was presided over by Dr. S. H. Frazier.

Dr. Frazier opened the meeting with remarks relative to the league. He asked to be informed whether the organization had ever been actually established, and if so, he wished to see the constituion and by-laws. His remarks brought out the fact that he minutes of the league contained no information bearing on the permanent organization of the league, whereupon the chairman stated that before the school directors appointed at a recent meeting, could proceed intelligently with their plans for the new school, it would be necessary to establish a permanent organization and elect new officers for the ensuing year. A meeting of the school directors had been held last week, Dr. Frazier stated, at which time a committee was appointed to draw up a constitution and by-laws for the league. These, he said, would be presented by the committee, with the recommendation of the school directors that they be adopted.

Before hearing the report of the committee, however, Mrs. Dr. E. Campbell reported that some fifty children had signified their intention to join the school. She also reported that more than $100 a month had been subscribed toward the maintenance of the school, the money being subscribed by parents whose children will attend and many who merely wish to assist the movement.

Dr. Frazier stated that the school directors of the league had decided to _____ the use of Golden Sheaf hall, _____ ced at their dispo-_____ G. Wright, to be _____ l. Besides Mrs. _____y T. Wilson, who has been selected principal of the school, Dr. Frazier stated that two other teachers had offered their services free for several hours each day. Beginning to-morrow morning, between 10 and 11 o'clock Mrs. Wilson will be in the school room for the purpose of enrolling pupils and assigning them to their classes.

During the evening Dr. Frazier expressed the desire that some definite date be set for the opening of the new school, but as the committee appointed to secure seats and desks for the school room could only report progress, it was decided to leave that question to be settled by the school directors, which body will meet to-night. Should desks and seats be secured this week, the school will open next Monday morning, that date having met with the approval of last night's meeting.

S. Taylor reported that he had visited a firm in San Francisco with regard to purchasing desks for the school, and had found forty that could be purchased at a reasonable figure. In Berkeley he found about twenty. He believed that little difficulty would be experienced in securing the desks.

Chairman Frazier then addressed the meeting on the question of effecting a permanent organization of the league in order that he school directors might proceed with their work. The chairman of the committee from the board of school directors, Mrs. A. V. Holloway, was requested to read the report of the commitee relative to this matter.

The report recommended the adoption of a constitution and by-laws, accompanying the report. These were read and with but one minor change were adopted. The constituion provides that the organization be known as the Anti-Compulsory Vaccination League, Berkelely Branch, that the secretary act as secretary of the board of school directors, consisting of seven persons. It provides that regular meetings be held on the first Tuesday of each month and that fifteen members constitue a quorum. Otherwise the organization differs but little from the former organization. The by-laws were adopted as read.

A recess of fifteen minutes was then taken in order to permit those present who wished to join the league, to sign the constitution. Thirty persons signed, and as the constitution provided that an initiation fee of $1 be paid upon signing the roll, the treasury was enriched by $25, the other members promising to pay at the next meeting.

The election of officers resulted as follows: President, Dr. S. H. Frazier; vice-president, George H. Wright; secretary, Mrs. A. V. Hollowar; treasurer, J. G. Wright; auditors—S. A. Hulin and John A. Wilson; school directors— J. T. Wright, Dr. S. H. Frazier, Samuel Taylor, Mrs. A. H. MacDonald, Mrs. Alice V. Holloway, Mrs. L. Moller and Mrs. E. Campbell. For the office of secretary, two candidates were voted upon—Mrs. Holloway and Mrs. Campbell, the former securing the office by a majority of four votes. The school directors elected last night are the same as were elected at a previous meeting.

August 2, 1905

APPOINT VACCINE DOCTORS

Acting upon the recently rendered opinion of Town Attorney Harry H. Johnson, who advised that a physician be appointed for vaccinating children unable to pay as well as to furnish vaccine virus, under the State law, the Board of Education appointed three doctors for this purpose at a special meeting of the board last Saturday evening in the town hall. Upon the recommendation of Health Officer G. F. Reinhardt, Dr. M. M. Rowley, Dr. J. J. Benton and Dr. David Hadden were appointed. One dollar out of the town school fund is to be paid for each vaccination when the child brings a statement from the parents saying they cannot pay the bill.

In taking this action the Board of Education is acting contrary to an opinion given by John Allen, District Attorney, who stated that the school funds cannot be used in paying for the expense of vaccination. Town Attorney Johnson advised the board that in his opinion they were legally justified to make the move, and despite these contradictory opinions, the board concluded to let the expense for vaccinating the poor children fall upon the school funds.

Upon motion of Director A. T. Sutherland, and seconded by Director E. P. Lewis, Health Officer Reinhardt's report was adopted and Clerk Merrill instructed to place vaccination posters in various sections of town in accordance with the State law.

Additional Cost at Lincoln.

Director A. T. Sutherland called the attention of the board to the plans of the Lincoln addition, drawn by Dickey & Reed. "As progress in the work is made," said Sutherland, "we find that several errors were made in drawing the plans. As the plans stand, the arrangements for the doors to the lavatory are neglected. In the new plans which I have here, this defect, as well as the one of only one entrance for the boys and four for the girls, is remedied. The cost will be $663 ad——"

Upon the suggestion of President Weir, the plans for the correction in the Lincoln school were submitted to A. H. Broad, the supervising architect of the board, for his approval, a report on them to be made at an adjourned meeting to be held to-night. Owing to the amount involved, the clerk was instructed to advertise for bids on the work.

Ruth Witherspoon, longtime Berkeley resident, at one month with her mother Naomi Oliver. Courtesy of the Berkeley Public Library, South Branch, Ruth Witherspoon Collection, photo #sb000-308b.

Dale children in 1902. Courtesy of the Berkeley Architectural Heritage Association.

"*It is an excellent thing, that here, and there, on the tumultuous ocean of this industrial world, an island springs up, islands of peace and knowledge, where a few quiet, wise men are segregated and free from hurry, free from self-interest, piously honor the arts and sciences under the soft murmuring trees, at the foot of the thoughtful hills. The painters, musicians and sculptures of California ought to swarm here, as to their natural headquarters.*"

—Robert Duponey, *Berkeley Reporter*, December 1906

SCIENTIFIC RAISING OF CHILDREN

ST. LOUIS, July 31.—Luther Burbank, the famous California horticulturist, declares that the great object and aim of his life is to apply to the training of children those scientific ideas which he has so successfully employed in working miraculous transformations in plant life.

This phase of the great naturalist's character, hitherto kept secret from the world at large, was revealed in a recent interview with Rev. Dr. James W. Lee, pastor of St. John's Southern Methodist Church, who returned yesterday from a trip to Santa Rosa, Cal., whither he went for an interview with Burbank.

The clergyman told Burbank that he had referred to the latter's work in an address at Portland and had expressed the wish that he might introduce into the method of rearing children some of the scientific ideas that Burbank was applying every day to the improvement of plants. Dr. Lee says that Burbank's eyes immediately flashed and he replied: "That is the great object and aim of my life."

Dr. Lee was astounded at the unexpected reply of Burbank's, as he had presumed that the latter was completely wrapped up in his studies of plants. Continuing, however, Burbank declared that plants, weeds and trees were responsive to a few influences in their environment, but that children were infinitely more responsive, and the failure to recognize the fact of the spiritual elements in the environing conditions of children had been the fatal lack in dealing with them.

Dr. Lee asked Burbank if he was familiar with the works of Thomas J. Barnardo of London, who had educated some 60,000 waif children in the ninety-three homes which he has founded in various parts of England, with the result that only 2 per cent of them have turned out bad. Burbank replied that he had studies Barnardo's methods of rearing children, and that the latter was doing in the realm of human life what he (Burbank) was doing in the real of plant life.

"Barnardo," he continued, "has demonstrated that infinitely more can be done with children than with weeds and plants. Whenever human beings recognize these realities in the realms of human life and begin to apply scientific principles to the training of children, then humanity will enter upon a new stage o. existence.

Burbank said that, in his opinion, every person should be physically, morally and spiritually perfect, and could be if the same attention were paid to his or her training that he was giving to weeds. He declared that, just as he had wrought miracles with plants by bringing them into contact with those elements of their environment to which they rapidly responded, should with the care of children seek to do for them and to train them by bringing their natures into relation with all the elements in their environment to which they are potentially responsive.

Children playing in front of Lincoln School (now Malcolm X School). Left child is Robert Kinney, boy holding brother on shoulders is Robert Dell'Ergo with Vincent Dell'Ergo standing on his shoulders. The other two children are unidentified. Vincent says the forked tree still stands on the school grounds. Vincent grew up to become Vice Principal at Willard Junior High and district liaison to the School Board and was in the school system for 30 years. Courtesy of the Berkeley Public Library, South Branch, Vincent Dell'Ergo Collection, photo #sb000-573.

SMALL BOY INJURED BY PLAYMATE

A warrant was issued to-day for the arrest of Alton Brown, a 14-year-old boy, who resides in South Berkeley. Brown is accused of having thrown a stone which struck Ben Parker, a playmate, over the eye, causing a painful wound. The complaint was made by Mrs. Pearson, mother of the injured lad, who resides at 2206 Woolsey street. The Browns reside at California and Felton streets.

PONY FALLS INJURING SMALL BOY

Charlie Bennett, a boy of fourteen, living with his parents on Canyon road barely escaped serious injury by a fall from his Shetland pony last Sunday afternoon. The pony became frightened at the tooting of an approaching automobile and reared on his haunches, finally falling over backwards and rolling on the prostrate youth.

It was mere fortune that the boy was not injured worse than he was. The horse fell squarely over his body, the saddle horn just striking to the side of him. As it was Charlie's leg and side was severely bruised and it will be some days before he will be able to ride his pony again.

Shootings

Accidentally Shot.

William Norris, While Hunting in West Berkeley, Painfully Wounded.

William Norris, a young man residing on Fifth street, near Bancroft way, West Berkeley, accidentally shot himself in the right arm while hunting yesterday evening. He was taken to the County Receiving Hospital and the wound dressed.

The gunshot wound is a severe one and amputation may be necessary. At present, however, the physicians still have hopes of saving the arm.

Norris was hunting on the water front when the accident occurred. The gun was discharged and the shot passed up through the right arm just above the elbow. The injured hunter is still at the hospital.

January 9, 1900

A Boy Shot at Mrs. Engebretzen.

While out riding on San Pablo avenue Sunday afternoon, Mrs. Christian Engebretzen, wife of the Assistant Superintendent of Streets, was the victim of an unpleasant experience. She was returning from her drive when she noticed several small boys on the road handling air rifles in a promiscuous manner.

Driving on a little further Mrs. Engebretzen turned and saw one of the youths take deliberate aim and fired a shot at her. The bullet struck her on the back of the head. Mrs. Engebretzen became thoroughly frightened. Had the rifle been of any other than the air pattern serious consequences might have resulted.

March 20, 1900

GIRL IS SHOT IN THE EYE

The story of a frolic that may result in a tragedy, of a girl's playfulness that will certainly result in the loss of one of her eyes and may end her life, became public last night. On Wednesday evening Carrie Terry, a young woman whose home is at Woodland, but who was visiting the family of William Hind at 1918 Channing way, was playing the hose in the garden in front of her friend's home. At the time Harry Hind, son of of proprietor of the home, and the lad's chum, young Windham, were comfortably ensconced in the branches of a tree directly in front of the house.

In the spirit of sport Miss Terry sprinkled the eight-year-olds with water from the hose, and they made frantic efforts to get out of her reach. Young Winham had a light air rifle, loaded with BB shot, in his hands, and as he moved the rifle was discharged. Whether he discharged the rifle purposely or whether it was discharged by contact with a branch of the tree may never be known, as the little fellow is too excited and terrified to be coherent; but, whatever the cause, the shot entered the young girl's right eye and she sank to the ground in pain.

A physician was quickly summoned, but his efforts to secure the shot through probing proved unsuccessful, and last night the young woman was reported to be in a precarious condition. The eye will never, in any event, be of use again, and it is feared that the presence of the leaden pellet will produce blood poisoning and that it may be impossible to save the girl's life.

August 19, 1905

BULLET WHISTLES BY EAR

A small boy recklessly shooting off a 22-caliber rifle within the town limits almost caused the death of Mrs. E. A. Norton of 2404 Ellsworth street this morning. As it was the bullet whistled by barely an inch from her head and imbedded itself in the wall behind her. Mrs. Norton immediately notified the Marshal's office and the police are now hunting for the culprit.

Mrs. Norton wah standing near the telephone on the second floor of her dwelling when the shot was fired. She had just bent down to pick something up when the bullet passed by the spot where her head had been a few seconds before. The police believe that some small boy was shooting birds in the tall trees that surround the Norton home.

July 8, 1909

ANOTHER BOY SHOT IN HILLS

Frank Clement, a cash boy in the employ of Collins, the Oakland druggist, was taken to the Receiving Hospital, yesterday morning, suffering from gunshot wounds incurred accidentally while hunting in the North Berkeley hills. He was treated by Steward Borchert, who, after dressing his wounds, had the boy removed to his home, 715B Castro street.

Young Clement, accompanied by a boy named White, who lives at the corner of Eighth and Jefferson streets, Oakland and another youth, whose name they refuse to reveal, started out early yesterday morning on a hunting trip. Young Clement is hard of hearing, and as the third boy was about to fire a shot he cried out to warn Clement that he was in range. His warning was not heard, and about twenty of the bird shot with which the gun was loaded penetrated Clement's left side and lower limbs, causing painful wounds. Clement's companions tried their best to stanch the flow of blood, and failing in this, hurried him to the receiving hospital.

When seen at his home this afternoon the boy was suffering severe pain, but is emphatic in his statement that the shooting was accidental. "I was slightly in advance of my companions," he said, "when suddenly I heard a shot, and at the same time felt a stinging sensation in my left side and legs. I did not fall, but I thought for a while that I was going to die . I guess, though, I am all right."

Both of the boys refuse to give the name of their companions, but state that the best of good feeling prevailed at all times, and that the shooting was simply an accident.

BULLET
IS NOT IN
HER EYE

It is no longer feared that fatal consequences will result from the remarkable accident which befell Miss Rose Terry of Woodland, who on last Wednesday evening was shot in the eye by Rudolph Windham, nephew of William G. Hind of 2228 Channing way, with whom she was making a visit. At first it was supposed that the little BB shot from the lad's air rifle had penetrated the eye and great apprehension was felt for blood poisoning by her physician, Dr. J. E. Shafer. As no serious complications have appeared, the young woman's friends now believe that the eye socket must have been struck a glancing shot and the led pellet is not in the eye at all. Dr. Shafer is not so positive and is waiting until the swelling in the eye has subsided in order to make a careful X-ray examination. He still entertains serious doubts as to the possibility of saving the organ, as the eyeball itself was badly torn by the bullet.

Young Windham, who is the son of Harry G. Windham of 2220 Haste street, has declared repeatedly that the shooting was accidental. Miss Terry had been sprinkling the garden with the hose and had teased the Windham boy and his cousin, Harry Hind, son of W. G. Hind. Having caught them both up a tree, she frightened them with threats of a ducking, and in the excitement of getting out of reach of the stream from the hose, the lads scrambled awkwardly out of the branches. In the tumble the air-gun went off with disastrous results to the young miss playing the hose.

Young people of Berkeley with a rifle, a common scene in 1900. Courtesy of the Berkeley Firefighters Association.

SHOT OFF TOP OF HIS HEAD

Seventeen-Year-Old Boy Commits Suicide through Fear of Operation.

Marysville, August 19 —John His son committed suicide last night a the home of his father, E. W. Hixson in Sutter county, ten miles west of Marysville. He was 17 years old and apparently in good spirits. He knelt on the grass beneath an orange tree and blew the top of his head off with a shotgun. The fear of an operation for appendicitis is believed to ha been the cause of his rash act.

July 19, 1905

VICTIM OF
LOADED
REVOLVER

Believing that the pistol was already discharged, George Amasa, the son of G. Amasa of 2634 Grove street, carelessly placed the middle finger of his left hand over the end of the barrel and pulled the trigger, laughingly shouting that he would shoot himself. But it was the millionth and one rehearsal of the old story—there was a loud report and the lad's finger, torn and bleeding, was another offering at the altar of "I didn't know it was loaded."

Fortunately it was a 22-blank revolver, so that young Amasa only lost the flesh off his finger, instead of losing the entire member. His whole hand was badly burnt by the powder, and it was necessary to take several stitches in the finger. Dr. Gray was called to dress the wound.

July 6, 1905

REPORT CHILD IS MISSING

With the disappearance of little Esther Van Velsor is involved what the police believe to be a successful attempt on the part of a father to kidnap a daughter he has long been separated from. The Van Velsor child has been missing since Thursday last and unless she is being forcibly detained she is apparently in league with the interests her mother has long sougth to prevent her becoming intimate with. No one has thus far come forward with any evidence to support a theory of foul play.

The missing girl is 15 years of age, and the daughter of Mrs. Joel Agee, 1240 Allston way. Mrs. Agee's first matrimonial venture with Jesse Van Velsor was a failure on account of alleged intemperance.

After the separation, some years ago, Mrs .Ellen Steele, a relation of the Agee family, took a fancy to the daughter by the first marriage, and Mrs. Agee permitted her daughter to take up her residence at the Steele home.

The girl has lived with her foster-mother for the last four and a half years, and of late it is known that she has been in the habit of visiting her father, who resides in Temescal. The intimacy was clandestine in order that the mother might not be disturbed. Recently Mrs. Agee was informed that her daughter was not being as kindly treated by Mrs. Steele as she wished, and after consultation with her husband, it was decided that Esther should come to the Agee home for the future. With this object in view Mrs. Agee waited upon Mrs. Steele last Friday afternoon to learn that the girl had disappeared the preceding day. The mother was greatly surprised when she learned from Mrs. Steele that the daughter and father had become friends within the past few weeks and all the circumstances indicate that the girl was either kidnaped by him or else voluntarily fled the Steele home for his shelter.

What would strengthen this theory is that Van Velsor has quit his former abode in Temescal within the past week and has not been seen or heard from.

Mrs. Agee blames Mrs. Steele for allowing the girl to become intimate with her father despite her express promise to the contrary when she was allowed to take Esther to her home. The police of the cities about the bay have been informed of the disappearance of the little girl.

July 28, 1905

BERKELEY BOY ARRESTED
IN SANTA CLARA COUNTY

Marshal Vollmer received a dispatch to-day from Chief of Police Carroll of San Jose, stating that George Malcolm of West Berkeley had been arrested in that city. Malcolm ran away from home last week and his father has informed Vollmer that he will try to have the boy sent to the reform school.

August 21, 1905

LEAVES HOME OF MOTHER

Claiming that she had been driven to desperation and almost to the verge of suicide by the harsh conduct of her mother, Miss Anne Jorgenson of 2223 Byron street in West Berkeley left the roof of her parent on the first day of this year and went to live with friends on Fifth street. Mrs. Jorgenson, the mother, appeared at that time to be no whit disturbed by the departure, but last night she went to the house where her daughter has been staying for the last seven months, and demanded that the girl be restored to her immediately. The friends of Miss Jorgenson refused to comply with her request and the girl herself shrunk from the idea of returning to the home where she says she was treated with great cruelty. Mrs. Jorgenson was insistent, however, and the protectors of Miss Jorgenson fearing that a disturbance was imminent summoned Policemar Acheson.

Mrs. Jorgenson immediately demanded thatt the officer take the girl from her new friends and compel her to stay at the home of her mother. This Acheson refused to do unless a complaint was sworn out and the irate parent was forced to depart unaccompanied by her daughter.

Miss Jorgenson, who is only seventeen years of age, was formerly employed at the Ramona Candy Factory. When she left home she also abandoned her position at the factory and went to work in an Oakland candy store. Miss Jorgenson says she will, under no circumstances return to the home of her parent. According to the story she tells the treatment accorded her at home borders on extreme cruelty. At times she says her mother behavior became such that she often threatened to kill herself. The people with whom she is staying corroborate her story and intend to keep the girl at their house unless the police intervene.

July 28, 1905

RUNAWAY BOY CAPTURED BY DETECTIVE

Upon information furnished the local police department by the San Francisco police, Detective Parker took a trip up Wild Cat Canyon late yesterday afternoon and captured James Kearney, a 15-year-old boy who had run away from his home in the metropolis. The boy had been camping for several days with companions in the Berkeley hills, and his capture was effected only after a hard trip on the part of the detective. Parker took the lad to San Francisco and turned him over to the police of that city.

Young Kearney and his companions claim to have been without food for several days, eating only rabbits and squirrels caught by their dog.

September 1, 1905

Small Boy Is Found.

A small boy of five years, wearing a white sweater and green trousers, with light hair, was found wandering aimlessly around the streets this morning by S. H. Speigelmyer of 3198 Adeline street. The lad was brought to the Marshal's office, but was unable to tell Marshal Vollmer his name. All he could say was that he came from Santa Clara and was visiting "Uncle Allen and Aunt Nellie." Detectives Jamison and Parker were detailed on the case.

September 4, 1905

GIRL IS REPORTED MISSING

Pretty Josie McGregor, 23 years of age, has been missing since July 22, and the police have been asked to aid in the search for her. Her disappearance was reported to Chief Hodgkins of Oakland yesterday morning by Frank Snook of 2035 Hearst avenue. She was working at the Snook home up to the time of her sudden flight. Snook says she was a modest girl and he is at a loss to account for her absence.

The missing girl is slight of stature. She weighs 120 pounds and is 5 feet 3 inches in height. What makes Snook believe she has met with violence of some kind is the fact that she left her trunk and all her clothing behind her. These are now at the Snook home, and have never been demanded, either personally or by letter; nor have any of Miss McGregor's acquaintances seen her since the day she disappeared.

August 5, 1905

EXPLAIN THE DISAPPEARANCE OF LITTLE GIRL

Mr. and Mrs. F. M. Steele of West Berkeley, who up to last week, had charge of little Esther Van Velson whose mother believes has been kidnaped by her father, have explained the mystery of the child's disappearance. Steele stated to-day that the child, who had gone to her father from their home, had been placed by her parent with a good family in San Francisco. The little girl, Steele said, had lived at his home for the last three years. He declares emphatically that she had never been abused while residing with them.

August 1905

MISSING GIRL IS LOCATED IN OAKLAND

Several days ago the Oakland police were requested to search for Miss Josie McGregor, a domestic, aged 23 years, who has been missing from the home of Dr. Frank Snook, 2035 Hearst avenue in this city since July 22d. She was located Saturday afternoon at the corner of Seventh and Clay streets, Oakland, where she has been living for some time under the name of Mrs. Frank Hopkins. The young woman refuses to be interviewed, nor will her friends advance any explanation as to why she disappeared mysteriously from Berkeley, leaving behind all of her personal property.

August 7, 1905

Captures Runaway Boy.

Marshal Vollmer received word from Chief of Police Carrol of San Jose yesterday morning telling him of the capture of Eugene Desimo, the 10-year-old son of E. Desimo of 1617 Prince street who ran away from home yesterday morning and left no trace of his whereabouts for his anxious parents. The distracted father failed to notify the Berkeley police, but went to work individually to find his runaway boy. He made an ineffectual hunt through Oakland, and was still engaged in the chase when Carroll's telegram came this morning. It is supposed that the lad gave himself up.

August 1905

A Berkeley class outing. Courtesy of the Berkeley Firefighters Association.

ENFORCING CHILD LABOR REGULATION

Enforcement of the child labor law has caused the discharge from canneries of many young persons, who do not hold certificates from the School Department as to their age and condition. Superintendent of Schools Mc-Clymonds has been flooded with requests for certificates. Boys and girls between the ages of 14 and 16 years must show written consent of their parents to work during the vacation period. Children between the ages of 12 and 14 years must show a certificate that they have attended school during the last term, as well as a certificate of consent from their parents or guardians.

A SUSPICIOUS DEATH.

A most mysterious death was reported to Deputy Coroner Streight-iff from South Berkeley this afternoon.

It was reported to him that a 3-months-old child named Delwyn Trimble, had died while in the care of Mrs. Fathour of Felton street, Lorin, or Mrs. Hoover of Ward street.

Mrs. Hoover, who it is alleged is grandmother of the child, gave it into the care of Mrs. Fathour last Monday. This morning the latter reported that the child was ill. The Hoovers removed it to their home. While it was enroute it was found, it is said, that the child was dead.

Mrs. Fathour claims the child did not die while with her, while the Hoovers say its body was rigid when they took it.

October 3, 1900

CHILDREN DIE FROM DIPTHERIA

The sad news comes from Santa Cruz that Mr. and Mrs. W. T. Mushet of 1831 Derby street have lost two of their little children, Muriel and Douglas from diphtheria at the former town where they went to spend the summer.

Mr. and Mrs. Mushet left Berkeley two weeks ago with their four children for a trip to Santa Cruz. On the way down on the train, there was a child aboard suffering from diphtheria and, by the time the family arrived at Santa Cruz, the four children were taken ill. Two of theme have recovered but two of them passed away. Muriel was six years old and Douglas five.

Mushet is the assistant manager of the Risdon Iron Works at San Francisco. Mr. and Mrs. Mushet's many friends sympathize with them in their great bereavement.

August 21, 1905

Seventh Street. Circa 1900. Courtesy of Berkeley Firefighters Association.

CRUELTY TO BABIES.

"That Saturday Post is a nuisance," said a prominent Berkeleyan (all Berkeleyans are prominent, you know), the other day as he boarded a Key Route train after having fought his way through a crowd of seventeen urchins, who were clamoring to sell him a copy of the Saturday Post six days old.

We quite agree with the citizen. The Post is a nuisance or least its method of having infants in arms...

Y. M. C. A. BOYS ARE TO CAMP AT CAZADERO

Preparations are now completed for the Y. M. C. A. boys' camp at Elen Grove near Cazadero, Sonoma County. The director of the camp has just returned to Berkeley and reports that everything is in shape for receiving the campers. Wm. H. Popert and six of the boys of the local organization leave early tomorrow morning, some for two weeks and some for a month.

MEET TO PROTEST AGAINST ENFORCING THE TUITION RULE

For the purpose of taking action on the strict enforcement of the State tuition law, requiring the children of all fathers, who are not registered here and are therefore non-residents, to pay a yearly tuition of $50 in the high school, the Berkeley Real Estate Exchange is holding a meeting this afternoon in the office of Juster & Baird. The enforcement of the strict letter of the law by the Berkeley Board of Education has aroused a general protest, especially among the realty dealers of the town.

Many Families Affected.

Over a hundred children, representing about 75 families, will be affected by this law in the high school. It is reported that several families are already preparing to move to San Francisco or Oakland, if this law is carried out. A Sonoma county woman, intending to live here, says she will go somewhere else. Not only does the law work an injury to the town in the driving away of families with high high school pupils, but it also affects families having children in the grammar schools where they intend to send them right up through the high school.

State Law Is Optional.

The particular section covering this matter is the last provision of section 9, chapter 65, and reads: "Provided further, that after July 1, 1905, a non-resident pupil shall, in the discretion of the high school board of the high school district where he attends school, be required to pay a tuition fee to such school equal to the difference between the cost of pupil for maintenance of said high school and the amount per pupil received during the school year by said school from the State." In all other sections of the chapter, "pupils" are spoken of, but here the singular is used, evidently inferring that the high school board are to consider tuition cases individually. The only city in which the law is enforced strictly is want to make him pay tuition for his child in high school, because he can't register here, being a banker in another town.

High School Has Good Name.

"Our educational advantage is all we possess. Take away our schools and what would there be left? Now the Berkeley high school is becoming known throughout California as one of the best high schools in the State and more and more people are attracted to Berkeley by its fame. Now, if we enforce this most unreasonable rule, we will simply drive these prospective citizens to Oakland, or San Francisco or some other town, where they are not shortsighted enough to cut off their own heads. What if we do have to cramp ourselves for a while to pay for our schools. They are our all and we should be glad people come here to enjoy their advantages."

Should Not Enforce Law.

"It is an outrageous rule," declared F. H. Lawton this morning, "and will drive people away from Berkeley. There is no reason at all for enforcing it to the letter, for it is an optional law and in Berkeley it is wisdom not to enforce it strictly. We want to get as many desirable residents here as possible, but if we are going to deny them the right of free schools, we won't get any. Take the case of Mr. Nichols, whose family has lived here for five years and who intends to build a handsome home here. He spends at least $2000 a year here and yet the Board of Education would throw this away for a miserly $50. What matters it if a man is not yet registered here or own extensive properties?

GANG OF SMALL BOYS IN HILLSIDE DISTRICT DISBANDED BY POLICE

Acting upon the complaint of the principal of the Hillside school, Marshal Vollmer has been keeping a close watch on the behavior of a gang of small boys who have been meeting after dark on the school grounds. The investigation resulted in disclosing the existence of an organized gang of youngsters who met on the school grounds to smoke and drink. The finding of an empty whiskey flask on the school grounds several days ago created almost as much excitement as would have been caused by the presence of a rattlesnake, and as a result the gang has been broken up by the police.

The investigation, which was conducted by Policeman Farrar, brought out the existence of the gang, which had its headquarters in an oak tree on Bonte avenue. On the trunk of the tree the members had inscribed their names, together with the signs of the order and it was by this means that Farrar located them.

It was also discovered that two members of the youthful gang were responsible for a number of recent thefts reported by Contractor F. E. Armstrong. The boys had removed a quantity of lumber and building material from houses in process of construction and were using it to construct pigeon lofts. Owing to the youthfulness of the offenders and the fact that most of the material was returned, Contractor Armstrong will not take action against the boys. Neither will the police proceed further in the matter as the boys have been severely reprimanded and told to keep away from the school house after dark on danger of arrest.

August 31, 1905

Fell Into a Well.

Little Gladys Hart Has a Narrow Escape.

Had it not been for the fact that she possesses a lusty pair of lungs, 8-year old Gladys Hart of Claremont might have been drowned in a peculiar manner this morning.

Little Gladys was playing alone in a field which faces on Claremont road when she fell into an abandoned well. The child was running at the time of her mishap and fell feet foremost into the hole.

The soft mud at the bottom of the well allowed her to sink until it would only have been a short time when the small amount of water in the well would have covered her head.

But Gladys yelled so loudly that some teamsters who were passing were attracted by her cries. The little girl was taken to her home, where she rapidly recovered from her fright.

July 31, 1900

Ruth Witherspoon, Berkeley resident, as a young girl. Courtesy of the Berkeley Public Library, South Branch, Ruth Witherspoon Collection, photo #sb000-310.

WHISKEY HELPS TO BREAK UP GANG OF SMALL BOY ROBBERS

Too much indulgence in whiskey last night proved to be the undoing of oneof the most successful juvenile robber bands that has infested Berkeley for some time. As a result the gang is broken up and five small boys—Willie Small, aged 8; James Small, aged 9; Fred McNamara, aged 10; John McNamara, aged 13, and Gustav Palache, aged 13, have been made to feel the stern rebuke of the law.

This morning at 9 o'clock, Fred Wagner, who resides at the rear of the house at Dwight way and Spaulding street, complained at police headquarters that during the night his house had been broken into and several articles stolen. Among the things that were taken were a bottle of whiskey, a demijohn of the same fluid, a box of cigars and a pair of trousers, having five cents in one of the pockets. Wagner stated that this was the second time during the week that his house had been entered. It was his opinion that a number of small boys in his neighborhood were the perpetrators of the deed. Wagner did not want to have the lads arrested but thought that it would be sufficient if they were admonished by the police to refrain from pilfering in the future.

Accompanied by Wagner acting Marshal Moran took a trip to the neighborhood of Dwight way and Spaulding street to locate the young robbers. His discovery of the identify of the lads came about in a peculiar way. Some of Wagner's neighbors had, on the night of the robbery, seen five small boys, acting as though int a complete state of inebriation. Three of the elder boys were helping two of their younger comrades and making the night hideous with their shouts. Two of the lads were recognized and through them Moran located the remainder of the juvenile gang.

The gang of small boys in that neighborhood have been operating for some time. Several people have been missing things from their yards and stores and the police are of the opinion that the lads accused by Wagner are in a great measure responsible for most of the depredations committed.

McNamara denied that both his boys were there. He states that only the younger was involved.

July 15, 1905

Arrested for Jumping Trains.

H. W. Lair Hill and Fletcher Monson, two small boys, were arrested by Marshal Lloyd yesterday afternoon for jumping on the trains at Berkeley station. They were taken to the Town Hall.

Justice Edgar released the boys upon their own recognizance and set their arraignment for four o'clock this afternoon.

The arrested children are from well known families.

On the Santa Fe tracks near Addison Street. Courtesy of the Berkeley Historical Society.

San Pablo School. Miss Poller is the teacher. Courtesy of the Berkeley Firefighters Association.

Dale kids at 1805 Fifth Street. Courtesy of the Berkeley Architectural Heritage Association.

Child's Narrow Escape.

Saved by an Oakland Woman From the Wheels of a Train.

Margaretta Rastor, the 2½ year-old daughter of Mr. and Mrs. C. Rastor, was rescued from a horrible death by the quick action of Mrs. R. H. Hammond, wife of the vice-president of the M. J. Keller Company, Oakland, yesterday evening, at Seventh and Grove streets, Oakland. The little one was playing across the track from the house, where the mother was visiting, and upon the approach of the down train started towards her mother, who at the same time ran to the rescue of her child. Both crossed just ahead of the engine, and then the little one again attempted to cross to her mother when Mrs. Hammond dashed forward and caught her by the dress and pulled her to safety. The mother one side of the locomotive, thought her child was surely killed, while those on the other side supposed the mother was mangled beneath the wheels.

"It was Providence that saved the child's life,' said Mrs. Hammond, who had saved the little one from death. I thought the mother was dead, but was surprised to see her alive. I shall never forget my experience."

The engineer did good work in bringing the train to a stop by applying the brakes. The many people who gathered about the scene could not explain the escape of both mother and child from a horrible death.

September 27, 1900

9. Injuries and Fatalities

The Fourth of July was a joyous holiday, celebrated with great enthusiasm and bravado in Berkeley at the turn of the century. A number of residents owned cannons, and during the festivities many people were injured or maimed.

One learns in reading the *Berkeley Gazette* that horses were involved in the greatest number of injuries and deaths. It was commonplace for horses to kick people or throw riders from their backs, or for horse-drawn carriages to career and topple. New noises and sights associated with the burgeoning town frightened the horses and in panic they ran off, often while still harnessed to carriages or carts.

Trains were another major cause of injury and death in 1900. Trains collided with horses, cows, carriages, a milk wagon, a fire engine, people or, in some instances, other trains. Many passengers were injured as they boarded or debarked from the trains. Pedestrians found it difficult to gauge the speed of the massive steam trains and electric streetcars, though they traveled only fifteen miles per hour. Lawsuits were filed against companies involved in these accidents.

Suicides and attempted suicides were reported in the *Gazette*. Many people ended their suffering after long illnesses. The names of their emergency contacts were found in their pockets.

Steam train on Shattuck Avenue. Courtesy of the Berkeley Firefighters Association.

A view of the Lorin District, the business district of South Berkeley. Courtesy of the Berkeley Firefighters Association; photo from *Berkelely Reporter*, December 1906.

UNKNOWN MAN IS KILLED

An unknown man stepped in front of a West Berkeley north-bound train at 10:20 last night directly opposite the stockyards and was ground to pieces under he swiftly moving train.

The remains were re noved to the Oakland Morgue by Deputy Coroner Van Vrankin, and an effort will be made to establish the man's identity. The engine, No. 1016, was in charge of Engineer Farley, while Conductor Maus was in charge of the train.

January 3, 1900

Broke Her Arm.

An unknown woman fell from the local train at Lorin last evening at 10 o'clock while attempting to alight before the cars had stopped. In falling she put out her right arm to protect herself and that limb received the full force of the contact. The woman at once screamed out that her arm was broken. She was immediately taken charge of by a female companion. The two women refused to divulge their names or give their addresses.

March 22, 1900

Berkeley Local.

Receives Injuries Last Evenings Which Caused His Death—His Father in Wyoming.

Otis J. Adams, the 18-year-old son of G. R. Adams, was run over by the Berkeley local last evening and received injuries which caused his death. He sank rapidly under the shock and died this morning at 11 o'clock.

The accident occurred just after the 6:45 o'clock train left Dwight way station. It was the custom of young Adams, who works in San Francisco and resides with his parents on Haste and Grove streets, to jump off the train each evening at Haste street, one block from Dwight way. The road-bed is being cleaned along this part of the track and piles of dirt and weeds were left beside it. It is supposed that Adams, in jumping, fell over a pile of dirt and was thrown under the rapidly moving train

H. C. Ingram, the switchman at Haste street, was the first to see the accident. Other persons, walking along the street, came to his aid and the injured young man was removed to the Dwight Way Pharmacy. From there he was taken to Dr. H. N. Miner's, 2227 Dwight way.

Besides being badly bruised about the head and body young Adams' left arm was crushed to a pulp and had to be amputated at the shoulder. There was also a compound fracture of the right forearm, and his right ankle was injured.

The mother of the injured boy was immediately informed of the accident, and arrived at the drug store soon after her son had been taken there. The scene was heart-rending.

Adams' father left yesterday for Wyoming where he is engaged in mining. A message was sent to him this morning telling him of the accident.

January 3, 1900

Dwight Way Station at the southeast corner of Dwight Way and Shattuck Avenue. Courtesy of the Berkeley Historical Society, catalog #1506.

Hurt at Dwight Way.

James Davis commenced suit yesterday afternoon against the Realty Syndicate and the Oakland Consolidated Railway Company to recover $15,500 damages for permanent personal injuries alleged to have been sustained September 28, 1898, by reason of the negligence of defendants' servants in running an electric car at the rate of eighteen miles an hour at the crossing of Grove street and Dwight way.

The complaint, prepared by Attorneys Chapman and Clift, and Read and Nusbaumer, recites that plaintiff had been engaged as roadmaster of the Piedmont district at a compensation of $3 per day; that by reason of the speed of the car in question a horse, attached to a cart in which he was seated, was frightened, and, running away, caused him to be thrown from the seat, and that as a result he sustained a contusion and concussion of the spine, besides bruises on the head.

He claims that his injuries will prove permanent and asks for $15,000 damages on that account, besides $500 expended for medical treatment, medicine and a nurse.

Louis Erickson returns from hauling Byron Jackson pumps to San Francisco. Photo taken on Addison Street near the Santa Fe tracks. Courtesy of the Berkeley Firefighters Association.

WAGON HIT BY LOCAL

The 10:25 o'clock Southern Pacific train down from North Berkeley this morning struck a large four-horse wagon belonging to the Spring Construction Company of this city, at the corner of Shattuck avenue and Cedar street, completely demolishing the rear end of the vehicle and hurling the driver, T. Miers, from his seat. Miers clung to the reins after he was thrown out of his seat and was dragged several yards over the rough pavement, receiving many severe bruises, but no serious injury. The horses were unhurt. The few witnesses to the accident state that the engineer failed to blow his whistle or slow up when he saw the wagon on the track.

Miers had just come from the company's quarries and his wagon was loaded with four tons of crushed rock. He came down Cedar street and started to cross the railroad tracks. Owing to some repair work on the track the planks for the crossing were removed, making it difficult and slow work to cross the high rails with a heavily loaded team.

According to stories told by witnesses, the engineer of the train, evidently thinking that the wagon would clear the tracks in time, neglected to blow his whistle or ring the bell, but pulled out quickly. Miers tried desperately to force the horses across, but the high rails proved too much for the wagon. The locomotive struck the rear end, breaking the wheels and axle and smashing the woodwork.

Miers was hurled to the ground by the shock of the compact and dragged several yards by the frightened horses. That he escaped being thrown in front of the engine and instantly killed was considered a wonder. Beyond a severe fright, the four-horse team was uninjured.

July 20, 1905

Injuries and Horses

WOMAN'S NARROW ESCAPE

Mrs. C. Christensen of North Berkeley and her 18-months' old child, had a narrow escape from death yesterday afternoon in an exciting runaway. That both mother and child were not killed or seriously injured was due to the bravery of George Meyers of the South End who seized the child from its mother's arms as the buggy dashed past him, and the fact that the horse broke from the buggy a moment later without overturning the vehicle.

The horse started its mad race on Shattuck avenue near Center street shortly after 4 o'clock and ran to the corner of Harmon street and Adeline street before breaking from the buggy. At the time the horse started to run Christensen was not in the buggy, he having climbed out to examine the harness that had become unfastened. Christensen's feet had hardly touched the ground before the horse started to run. The father's frightened cries brought hundreds of people into the street, but no one was able to stop the horse as it ran frantically down Shattuck avenue. The screams of the woman, who could only hold the reins with one hand and her child in the other, could be heard for blocks. Men dashed in front of the horse, but were unable to stop the animal or change its course.

2811 Benvenue Avenue. Circa 1895. Courtesy of the Berkeley Firefighters Association.

DRIVER'S NARROW ESCAPE

R. Emerson, driver of the delivery wagon of the American Biscuit Company on this side of the bay, displayed unusual courage this afternoon when he clung desperately to the reins of his runaway horse, whose flying hoofs threatened every moment to dash out his brains, until the animal literally kicked himself loose from the wagon. The runaway was one of the most exciting witnessed for some time and that several persons were not injured or killed is considered a wonder, as Shattuck avenue, down which the animal dashed, was crowded with pedestrians and wagons.

Emerson was just about to alight from his wagon to enter Morehouse's grocery store on the corner of Shattuck avenue and Berkeley way to get an order, when the 1:05 local train came tearing down the grade from North Berkeley. His horse, a huge but nervous mare, took fright at the engine and started wildly down Shattuck avenue.

Though Emerson, who is scarcely more than a boy, had an excellent chance to jump, he stuck bravely by his post and sought to hold in the flying animal. He succeeded to slowing the horse down in front of Berkeley station, but at the critical moment the brake gave way. All the while the horse was dashing down the street, he was kicking wildly with her hind legs, pieces of the front end of the wagon flying through the air. Finally in front of the Town Hall, she broke away and ran up Allston way, going for many blocks before she was finally captured.

The front of the wagon was badly smashed, but strange to say, only one of the boxes of crackers was lost during the flight. Had it not been for the fact that the mare was hitched so close to the wagon that she was unable to kick over the dashboard, Emerson would have been severely injured or killed.

July 19, 1905

RUNAWAY ON MAIN STREET

A runaway horse that dashed madly across the pavements on Center street in the busiest part of the town at 2 o'clock this afternoon caused great commotion and several persons barely escaped injury from his flying hoofs. The sidewalks were crowded at the time and it is almost a miracle that no one was hurt. The infuriated beast was finally stopped in front of Joe Ruben's barber shop, by the colored porter, Dan Jones.

The horse, which was attached to a delivery wagon belonging to Hatch & Gibson, a grocery firm at the corner of Dwight way and Telegraph avenue, started on its wild race from Hearst and Milvia streets. The Driver E. B. Gond had unfastened the bridle from the horse's head preparatory to feeding it when the animal taking sudden fright started off down the street knocking its driver into the dust. The horse, dragging the wagon after it dashed along Milvia street into Berkeley way and down Shattuck avenue. Just in front of where the Southern Pacific freight sheds used to be is a telegraph pole. The vehicle was dashed into the pole and remained fast while the horse freeing itself from the shafts continued its mad course down Shattuck avenue and into Center street where it was finally stopped.

Golden Sheaf Bakery wagon. The Golden Sheaf was located on Shattuck Avenue between University Avenue and Addison Street. Courtesy of the Berkeley Historical Society, catalog #1469.

WAGON IS STRUCK BY KEY ROUTE

Owing to the fact that the train was slowing down, a serious accident was averted this morning at Berkeley station. A large meat wagon from Richertown, crossing the tracks, was struck by the 10 o'clock Key route train, but was fortunately turned sidewise by the blow. No damage other than tearing a gate off the train and breaking a piece of the brake off was done. The driver was uninjured.

August 1, 1905

SAN FRANCISCO BOY IS HIT BY LOCAL TRAIN

Arthur Kahdeman, 16 years of age, was struck by the Berkeley local at the pier near tower No. 1 last evening, thrown into the air nearly to the height of the smokestack and fell to the side of the track suffering a broken shoulder and possibly internal injuries.

The boy had just alighted from the Fresno train and was walking along the track. He failed to see the other train approaching. Kahdeman lives at 37 Bruce place, San Francisco. He was removed to the Oakland Receiving Hospital. The engine was in charge of Engineer Louzzadder.

August 22, 1905

DEMURRER FILED IN AUTO CASE

A determined effort is being made to protect and keep from public gossip the two young women who accompanied Morris White on his $299 automobile ride which resulted in the suit brought by G. A. McPherson, the owner of the machine. Yesterdy morning a demurrer was filed by H. H. Johnson, attorney for the young defendant. In the event the demurrer is overruled the two girl friends of White will be compelled to come into court and testify. To prevent this every effort is being made by the attorney and his defendant client.

White, who conducts a livery stable, had the McPherson machine. The owner had left it for safekeeping. White had just finished his work when his two young lady friends came along. Immediately a "chug" wagon ride was in order and the party of three embarked. At that moment McPherson hove in sight just in time to see his car buzz down the road. Before White returned the car had been ditched, the ladies had to return to their homes on the street railway, and the damages amounted to about $99. Then McPherson sued. He asks rental to the amount of $200 and the $99 for damages.

So far, White has succeeded in keeping the names of his mysterious lady companions from the Marshal's office, but unless Johnson has something better than a demurrer they will be forced to come into court and tell what they know of the disastrous pleasure trip in the unlucky automobile.

September 18, 1905

OAKLAND MAN DIES AS RESULT OF FALL FROM HODGE BLOCK

Lester Snodgrass, a carpenter who resides at 1025 East Sixteenth street, Oakland, died at 1 o'clock this afternoon at the Roosevelt Hospital, from injuries sustained in a fall from the second story of the Hodge block at the corner of Fairview and Adeline streets. The man's injuries consisted of a terrible fracture which extended half way across the top of his skull, and although Drs. Rowley and Reinhardt performed an operation to relieve the pressure on the brain, the injured man never regained consciousness, passing away an hour and a half after the accident. He leaves a wife and several children.

Snodgrass was working on a scaffold about half-past eleven, when the staging began to slide to one side. Realizing his danger, the carpenter attempted to grasp a windowsill, but failed and fell to the ground a distance of some forty feet. The man struck squarely on the top of his head and was rendered unconscious.

The police department was informed of the accident by persons who had witnessed the carpenter's fall, and Marshal Vollmer had the man removed at once to the Roosevelt Hospital on Dwight way. Drs. Reinhardt and Rowley were soon in attendance, and although trephining was resorted to in an effort to relieve the pressure on the brain, too much blood had gathered in the brain and the carpenter died without regaining his senses.

Marshal Vollmer sent word to the family of the injured man as soon as the address was learned, but the wife was unable to reach Berkeley until after the death of her husband. Snodgrass was 38 years old.

September 8, 1905

ENGINEER LORING OF WEST BERKELEY LOCAL HAS NARROW ESCAPE IN COLLISION TODAY

A collision between the 7:30 East and West Berkeley, Southern Pacific locals this morning at Sixteenth street station in Oakland, came near resulting in the death of C. A. Loring, engineer of the West Berkeley train, who was dragged from the debris of the wrecked engine cab by his fireman Archie Carlton. But for Carlton's bravery and presence of mind, Engineer Loring would have been scalded to death in a few minutes. As it was he escaped with numerous bruises about the body and a severe cut on the head. Engineer Loring was the only person injured in the collision, although his engine was badly wrecked together with considerable damage to the passenger coaches on the East Berkeley train.

As far as can be learned the accident was caused by the giving of a wrong signal. Loring's train was lying on the sidetrack at the Sixteenth street station waiting for the 7:20 East Side train to pass it. Finally Loring claims he got a signal to go ahead, the train that was to have passed him being late. Loring then started ahead and just as his engine reached the main track and in a moment would have been on it, the East Berkeley train dashed past. The cylinder head on the East Berkeley train struck Loring's engin and was almost torn off. Before the engines would be stopped the through train has dragged past the West Side train, ripping the sides and gates from three coaches.

The force of the collision jammed Loring's engine back onto the train telescoping it with the tender and throwing the engineer to the floor of cab, where he was pinned beneath the window seat. A steam cock was broken off and in an instant the cab was filled with steam. Fireman Carlton jumped and saved himself from injury. As soon as the engines came to a standstill, however, Carlton was back in the wrecked cab.

In the burning steam Carlton searched until he found Loring pinned beneath some heavy timber and the cab-seat. Seizing him by the arms Carlton dragged Loring from his dangerous position. The engineer was bleeding from a gash on the head and complained of his legs. He was immediately removed to the receiving hospital and later to his home 1019 Channing way in this city.

The injured man is the father of Dr. E. L. Loring, member of the Board of Education. Engineer Loring has been in the employ of the Southern Pacific Company for the last thirty years, and for the last eight years he has been an engineer on the West Berkeley line. He has always been considered one of the best and most careful engineers in the service. Although he is suffering from numerous bruises, it is not feared he will be permanently injured or confined to his bed for any great length of time.

As a result of the accident the Southern Pacific service to Berkeley was tied up until 10 o'clock this morning. Both trains were so badly wrecked as a result of the collision that it required several hours to clear the tracks. Samuel Bones, conductor of the train that collided with Loring's engine, reports that although he had a large number of persons aboard his train, no one was injured. Six gates were torn from Bones' train, and the passengers were thrown from their seats, but not even a bruise was reported. Passengers on the West Berkeley train experienced a shaking up, but no one was injured.

August 30, 1905

INJURED
BY FALL
FROM RIG

Louis Stein in front of bakery at 2116 Vine Street. Mr. Stein's butcher market was on the same block. Courtesy of the Berkeley Firefighters Association.

Andrew Bell, a negro who resides at 1614 Todd street, was thrown from a buggy at the corner of Grant and Delaware streets this morning, sustaining injuries that necessitated his removal to the receiving hospital in Oakland. Bell was intoxicated at the time of the accident, and was driving rapidly. Upon turning the corner at Grant and Delaware streets, the man was thrown out. He struck squarely on his head and shoulders, which resulted in his scalp being laid open for several inches.

Bell was rendered unconscious by his fall, but upon regaining his senses he walked a block from where he fell and was found sitting by the roadside. Policeman Atchison and Detective Jamison found the man and supporting him between them, they took him to the police station. Still dazed and complaining of a severe pain at the base of the skull, Bell could not give an intelligent account of how he had been injured. E. L. Coryell, the real estate man, however, supplied that information, he having witnessed the accident. It was learned that the rig used by Bell the property of E. Powers, who resides on Seventh street in West Oakland. Late this afternoon it was reported that Bell was in a critical condition his spine being injured. It is also feared he may be suffering from a slight concussion of the brain.

September 1, 1905

Kicked by a Horse!

L. L. Stein's four-year-old son, Jack, was kicked in the head by a horse while playing in the yard back of the house at 1448 Shattuck. He had a deep gash cut in his skull just over the left eye, but was not otherwise injured. He was taken to Squire's drugstore, and Dr. Kelsey was summoned and found there was a cut of one and a half inches which was laid open to the skull, besides a light skin incision running up into be hair. He took three stitches.

He said he was playing in the yard and for fun began throwing at he horse. which kicked him.

Equine Amphibian.

Quite an excitement ensued on the West Berkeley water front yesterday afternoon when a loose horse gave a free Wild West show for the benefit of the populace. The animal had got on the railroad track at Fleming station, ahead of a freight train. Frightened by the approaching engine, the horse scampered along the track at a wild pace for fully half a mile until he reached Camellia street, fully half a mile from the station at which he took passage on the railway, and then he broke away from the railway and made for the wharf at Judson & Shepherd's chemical works. Arrived at the water's edge, he took a sudden notion to water travel and jumped into the bay and turned his prow toward Sheep Island. Half a dozen workmen at the acid works, who had seen the wild antics of the equine tramp, followed him in boats and headed him toward the shore after he had got about two miles out. The horse was finally got back onto dry land, and captured after he had been in the water two hours. He is a fine young, sound animal, and he will be well cared for and held for his owner.

November 7, 1900

RUNAWAY COLLIDES WITH RIG

While driving south on Shattuck avenue about 8 o'clock this morning in a light road buggy, F. C. Cunningham, who is connected with the Lindgren-Hicks Company, met with a narrow escape from serious injury through the unusual performance of a runaway colt. Just as Cunningham's rig reached a point opposite Dwight way he observed a horse racing toward him. Thinking the horse would either stop or turn to one side Cunningham paid no further attention to the animal until it was almost upon him.

It was then too late to avoid a collision and the runaway struck Cunningham's rig squarely between the front and rear wheels, and then occurred one of the most remarkable exhibitions ever witnessed outside a circus ring. The runaway colt, going as it was at a high rate of speed, turned completely over the rig in which Cunningham was riding. The animal immediately gained its feet, started to run, having apparently not been injured.

The buggy was wrecked and Cunningham sustained numerous cuts and bruises as a result of the smashup. The runaway is a colt owned by Charles A. Cain. The animal had only recently been brought into town and this morning it became frightened and broke away from the man who was leading it.

September 1, 1905

Expressman Erikson. Courtesy of Berkeley Firefighters Association.

Photograph of woman on horse who had won an award at the Berkeley Flower Show for the best riding. The photo was signed to "Mr. A Vollmer," likely the police marshal's wife or a family member. Courtesy of the Berkeley Firefighters Association.

KICKED ON THE HEAD.

A Woman Physician of Petaluma Receives a Fracture of the Skull.

Petaluma, Aug. 3.—Dr. Ruth French, a prominent physician of this city, was kicked on the head last evening by a horse and suffered a fractured skull. It is feared that the accident may prove fatal. Dr. French was driving along the streets, when suddenly, without warning, her horse reared up on its foreleeet and kicked clear over the dashboard. Both hoofs struck her in the forehead and she received the full force of the blow. Her head was badly fractured, and, despite all medical attention, she does not appear to be improving.

Died From Injuries.

Mrs. Delon While Cycling Was Struck by a Buggy.

Mrs. Julia Delon of 831 Harrison street, Oakland, died last night at the receiving hospital of the injuries which she received yesterday morning in a collision with a horse and buggy while riding a bicycle on Clay street. During the entire day she did not regain consciousness. She was attended by Drs. Milton and Porter and her aged mother was at her bedside when she passed away. The immediate cause of her death was was internal hemorrhage. Mrs. Delon, while riding her bicycle down Clay street, came into collision with a horse and buggy driven by R. F. Fleming, manager of the telephone compay. She was knocked unconscious by a blow on the back of the head, presumably given by one of the horse's feet. The animal itself fell over the wheel, which struck directly between its fore feet and it was by a narrow margin that the woman escaped being crushed beneath the horse's body.

The accident happened between Ninth and Tenth streets. Mrs. Delon, with a handbag on her arm, was riding towards Ninth street, while Mr. Fleming was driving in the opposite direction. Each started to turn to the right in order to pass, when Mrs. Delon, apparently becoming confused, lost control of her wheel, which veered to the left, striking the approaching horse in the forelegs.

Mr. Fleming, who was very much concerned over the accident, was seen at the hospital, where he had called to ascertain the patient's condition. He stated that he was driving slowly up Clay street when the accident occurred; that he had seen the woman approaching and had started to turn out to the right when suddenly she seemed to lose control of her wheel and swerving to the left, ran directly into the horse, which fell down over the wheel.

1900

INQUEST TONIGHT

The inquest on the body of W. H. Berger, district organizer of the Order of Americans, who was killed at Lorin Saturday morning by the Berkeley local, has been set for this evening at 7 o'clock at the local branch Morgue.

A later search of the dead man's pockets brought forth a brief note wherein Berger requested that if anything happened to him Estelle Stevenson of 821 East Twenty-eighth street, Los Angeles, should be notified at once. This Deputy Coroner Streightif attended to.

Berger was riding a bicycle at the time he was struck by the local. His skull was fractured. He was 40 years old.

Died of Indigestion

George Harding, known to the sporting world as "Liverpool George," glass-eater and sideshow freak, who died in a hospital yesterday afternoon, was well known in Marin county. Three months ago in San Rafael he ate three whisky glasses, and it is believed that his death resulted from complications caused by that feat.

January 8, 1900

EYES RUINED IN SPRAYING OAK TREES

Believing that Paris green spraying has caused the ruining of his eyesight, J. Monson, one of the workmen on the University of California grounds, is preparing to submit his bill for damages and medical treatment to the Board of Regents, with the request that he be reimbursed on account of the carelessness of those under whose directions he worked.

Monson claims that the mixture of Paris green and whale oil, used in spraying the campus oak trees for predatory insects, was too strong in the former ingredient and that, when he was engaged in the act of applying the spray, the powerful poison in the air so affected the organs of sight that their value has been hopelessly impaired.

September 11, 1905

Farm Laborer Almost Drowned In Wildcat Canyon.

News was brought over the hills this afternoon to the effect that Hirman Coles, a farm laborer was almost drowned at Wildcat creek this morning by falling into an abandoned well. It was only by the merest accident that he escaped death.

Coles had been herding cows when he stepped into the well which had been overgrown with brush. He fell clear to the bottom, the water covering his head. It was impossible for him to climb up the sides, and his struggles were of no avail.

A friend who was with Coles, happening to miss him, followed in his tracks. The unfortunate man's struggles attracted his companion's attention, and led to a rescue.

In a few hours Coles was none the worse for his submersion and close call to death.

OLD MAN KILLED BY CANNON

San Francisco, July 5.—John Barry, an aged longshoreman sacrificed his life to the ardor of Louis Lettis a boy, who was celebrating the Fourth of July.

Lettis was firing a toy cannon and it is said the gun was loaded. The cannon exploded and Barry, who was passing by, was shot through the head and instantly killed.

At 12 o'clock, Barry, who was a longshoreman and worked at the Pacific Mail dock, went to a restaurant on Brannan street for his lunch. He remained there until 12:45 o'clock, and then started back in the direction of the dock.

Young Lettis, together with a number of other youths, was firing the toy cannon. The chamber of the gun was heavily loaded with powder, and it is declared by a number of those who witnessed the affair that there was a ball in the barrel.

Just as Barry passed the boy touched off the gun. The charge of powder was too heavy and the weapon exploded, flying in pieces. Barry was seen to stagger and fall. It was found that a bullet or a piece of the cannon had passed through his face and he died within a few minutes.

A police officer was notified and young Lettis was placed under arrest, charged with murder.

ON THE FOURTH OF JULY

In another day we shall reach another Fourth of July and parents might give a little forethought to the present method of celebrating the day, says the Ladies' Home Journal. Why must we go on, year after year, and make the day practically a day of terror, and, what is infinitely worse, a day of deaths and casualties Each year a longer list of killing, maining and burning confronts us. Take such a list as this, summing up one year's deaths and injuries:

Died of lockjaw, caused by injuries 406
Died from other injuries. 60
Totally blinded 10
Number who lost one eye........ 75
Arms and legs lost 54
Number who lost fingers 174

Oakland Accidents.

The attendants and surgeons at the Receiving Hospital in Oakland had a very busy time yesterday. Among those who celebrated too much were William Cordray of 610 Woolsey street, who was shooting a cannon, which prematurely exploded and blew away a large part of the dorsal portion of the right hand; George Cavagnara of 660 ...

One of the first trucks owned by the City of Berkeley in a parade on Telegraph Avenue. At one time, volunteer firemen identified the driver as Jim Nealon and the dog on the hood as Ding-a-ling. Courtesy of the Berkeley Firefighters Association.

WANTED TO GO TO ASYLUM

While Marshal Vollmer sat at his roller-top this morning perusing a list of "those wanted," a small man with a pale face and a wild eye, slipped quietly into the office. For a moment the visitor stood in the center of the room surveying the Marshal then burst forth:

"I'm a raving maniac, and unless i'm locked up soon I'm apt to do something desperate."

For a moment the startled officer of the peace stiffened in his chair. But only for a moment, when, with his usual sang-froid Vollmer replied: "Well, I guess we can accommodate you, won't you sit down?"

Yes, the maniac would sit down, but he insisted that he be taken to an asylum without delay, else there might be something unpleasant happen. He wasn't quite certain as to the nature of the impending catastrophe, but he was certain it would happen unless something was done at once.

"We like to accommodate every one in here," explained Vollmer, "and I suppose we can help you out. What charge do you wish to have placed against you?"

"Insanity," shouted the visitor. "Don't I look insane?"

"Sure you do," replied the Marshal, "but just wait till I summon the judge."

Justice Edgar was called and the stranger again asked to be arrested. He stated that he came here from Nevada and that his name was Matthew C. Bailey. Further than to say he was single, the man refused to discuss himself. He insisted that he was a raving maniac, asking the Justice and Marshal repeatedly if they did not think he appeared insane.

After hearing the man's story Justice Edgar informed him that he would be pleased to do all he could and issued a warrant for Bailey's arrest on a charge of insanity. "We do all we can here for strangers," explained Justice Edgar when the warrant was ready.

I'm very grateful, replied the stranger and thus closed one of the most startling events in the history of the local police department.

August 19, 1905

Bullets Wouldn't Go Into His Head.

San Francisco, Aug. 25.—William G. Munzenmayer, formerly a porter employed at Haas Bros.' candy store, attempted suicide yesterday morning by shooting himself twice in the head. Munzenmayer used an old-fashioned navy revolver of 44 caliber, which had been loaded and undischarged for years. The rusty barrel retarded the speed of the bullets and when both balls flattened on the would-be suicide's head he gave up in disgust. He was treated at the central emergency hospital for two scalp wounds. Munzenmayer had been out of work for nearly a year, and despondency is attributed as his motive of attempted suicide.

August 25, 1905

NEUBER NAME OF SUICIDE

Frank Neuber, 38 years old, for several years employed at the wine cellars of C. Schilling, 230 Brannan street, San Francisco, is believed to be the man whose body was found June 10 hanging to a tree in La Loma Park, Berkeley. Schilling made inquiry at the Morgue Monday concerning the case.

The body corresponded to Schilling's description of Neuber, who had written to a brother in Germany that he intended to end his life at Berkeley because of ill health. Neuber left Schilling's employ May 13, saying he intended to return to Koenigsberg, Germany, where relatives resided. The name of Edward Musack was found in a note left by the suicide. In his letter to his brother Neuber said he would commit suicide under an assumed name.

July 12, 1905

10. The Italian Immigrant and the Fountain

Wanted: A Fountain at Berkeley.

Editor GAZETTE: Day after day as I am seated in my office (tail-board of my wagon,) the question is asked by strangers, Where can I get a drink of water? Echo answers, "Where?" but don't supply the aqua. Only yesterday a lady, accompanied by three children inquired of me where she could get water for herself and children Of course no one would refuse a stranger a drink of water, but no person not acquainted likes to intrude and ask for it.

Some men would sooner go and pay for a glass of beer, but they can't do this in the temperance town of Berkeley. Now what's to hinder our temperance people from erecting a fountain in the neighborhood of Berkeley station? A pretty and attractive fountain would be an ornament, and it might be placed conveniently near the station at a moderate cost. Kindly give this matter your attention, Mr. Editor, bring it before the people; let the temperance societies take hold and urge the erection of this much needed fountain and our children shall call you blessed, even unto the third and fourth generation.

TAX PAYER, alias JOHN E. BOYD

March 30, 1900

Many comments and heated debates one might hear about recently immigrated populations today were also heard at the turn of the twentieth century.

Some believed that recent immigrant groups would populate too fast and overwhelm the general population and its resources. It was thought by some that particular immigrants were incapable of being educated. Italian immigrants were consistently belittled, mistrusted and ostracized.

Italian or Greek immigrants might find themselves confronted with some resident's ire if they sold food on the street or washed their hands in a public fountain. Though not everyone participated in this discrimination, the *Gazette* articles illustrate the condescension immigrants endured from some established Berkeley residents.

Berkeley Station at University Avenue and Shattuck Square. Note the fountain at the lower left; a young girl is ready to drink from it. Courtesy of the Berkeley Historical Society.

NEEDS ARE MULTIPLYING.

A correspondent has today called attention to a matter that has been frequently discussed, that of a fountain, or drinking accommodations at or near Berkeley station. A thirsty visitor to Berkeley has just cause for calling it a "dry town." It is well known by business men about the station that there is constant need of some means of supplying the public, and especially strangers, with water. Children brought with parents on the trains have to go without until they go home or get into the next county. There is no water supplied by the railroad for its patrons in either trains or depot, and never will be. It is no less than a shame to treat the thousands of visitors coming to Berkeley in this manner. They are entitled to respectful treatment and the ordinary accommodations. But in this, as in other improvements, we are met with, "Well what are you going to do about it?" With a town all feet and no head the answer closes the question. There are clubs, societies, boards of trustees and education Missionary workers, and the W. C. T. U. which wants visitors to drink water only, and yet there is no body of citizens organized for general utility, to look after the common interests of the whole body. It is unfortunate, and this condition should not long be continued.

March 30, 1900

PEANUT VENDERS.

At the meeting of the Board of Town Trustees last night President Rickar offered the suggestion that the time had come in the history of Berkele when peanut and popcorn vender should not be allowed upon the streets

We most heartily agree with ou Mayor. These peanut men obstruc the street with their wagons and pre sent an unsightly appearance.

On Center street in front of th Wright block there is a peanut stan which is not only an obstruction to th street but a nuisance. It is run by great, big, husky foreigner, who shoul be handling a pick and shovel. Whe interviewed this fellow says that h does not like hard work and prefer the easier vocation of vending peanuts At least one of the venders on Stan ford place, near the Southern Pacifi depot is entitled to some consideratio —as he is unable to earn a living at man ual labor. Still the venders at th depot are allowed to stand too fa south and thus obstruct travel.

While on the subject of streets ou attention has been called to the fact by a lady subscriber, that the express men, and particular the noted poetica baggage-buster, obstruct the street op pose the depot to a degree to be a men ace to life. This is a matter which J E. should take up in a communication

The peanut vender of Center stree should be made to move at once an it is the duty of the Marshal and hi force to remove him. This fellow o Center street has no pull and he doe not write poetry and hence there ca be no possible reason for his continu ing to violate the law.

July 11, 1905

LAVES HIS HANDS IN FOUNTAIN

The large husky Italian who vends peanuts and popcorn down by the station was washing his hands and face in the bowl of the Hearst fountain yesterday afternoon when John E. Boyd meandered along. Now, John has always taken a peculiar interest in this municipal ornament and mighty was his wrath at the actions of the dark-skinned foreigner. In no unmeasured terms Evergreen ordered Luigi to discontinue his ablutions but the native of Italy, with his native sang-froid and nonchalance merely favored Boyd with a withering smile.

John's rage was terrible to behold. His fists clinched and he started forward as if to fell the grinning Latin to the macadam, but suddenly realizing where he was at, Boyd stopped short and started for the Marshal's office to invoke the aid of the law. Deputy Marshal Moran, who is in charge of the office during Vollmer's absence, summoned the Italian vender to his office and administered some advice to him on the subject of putting things to their proper use.

July 13, 1905

FROM THE PEANUT ARTISTE

Mr. Paper Mana—Corpi de Blanco! What for you say in you paper I musta taka da pick, da shovel instead sell da peanuta, da popa corno? What for you no go to do Presidente of the U. C. and speake him, "You big husky mana, Mr. Presidente, you go geta da pick de shovel, you too much strong to be da Grand Duke of da U. C. You go worka da sewer. Digga da foundation for da new casa.' You understatnd Mr. Paper mana, I da artiste in da peanutta and da pop-corna. Cambretti! Suppose you try to cooka do pop-corna and da peanutte, you no savee and you spoila da cuisine. You say I no pulla. I pulla da peanutta wagon every night. S'pose you letta me lone, you come every night, getta da peanutta, getea da popcorna, no pay da nick. We good friends and you pitch into da Boyd, say him da tenita garcon, all same big nuisance.

VENEDO DE GRAMPHINO,
Peanutta Artista.

July 13, 1905

LAW IS WORKING HARDSHIPS

Editor GAZETTE: The peanut butchers around Berkeley station are in trouble. There was a law passed some years ago, saying, "No vehicle shall stand on Stanford place within sixty feet of Center street," and Marshal Vollmer greatly to his credit is going to see this and every ordinance enforced. Still my object in writing this, Mr. Editor, is to call the attention of the town officials to the hardship this law is working on two elderly men who trouble no one, and who are trying to make an honest living, one of whom has a wife who has kept a sick bed for the lasts fourteen years.

Now, it does seem hard that these men should not be allowed to sell their wares in a place where people congregate. It puts one in mind of Robbie Burns' lines, where,

"He begs a brother of the earth,
To give him leave to toil."

If these men, Mr. Editor, were fit for manual labor, I should "keep my eating apparatus closed and sing low," but when a poor fellow explains to me that he has expended his last dollar fitting up his peanut cart and to move means the loss of a chance to make a living, then I feel called upon to say to our town officials, "Be merciful, even as you hope for mercy."

JOHN E. BOYD.

July 24, 1905

AFTER PEANUT VENDER

After Peanut Vender.

In hope of driving a peanut vender from one of the fashionable resident sections of town where his stand has become an eyesore to the community, the 20-year-old son of Dr. John Snook of 2301 Bancroft way, turned the hose on Guiz Paponis, who conducts a stand at the corner of Bancroft way and Telegraph avenue. Dr. Snook declares the watering down of the peanut vender and his ungainly stand, was an accident, but the Greek says the water was played over his place of business for ten or fifteen minutes, destroying a portion of his stock and driving him into the street.

For several months Paponis has conducted his stand on the corner it now occupies, causing much annoyance to the residents in that vicinity. Paponis the neighborhood of his presence. Paponis declares he will not leave the corner and will have Dr. Snook's son arrested on a charge of malicious mischief. No warrant has as yet been applied for, however.

In speaking of the peanut vender, Dr. Snook said: "The peanut stand has been an eyesore in the neighborhood for a long time, and it is a disgrace to Berkeley. We have appealed to the Town Trustees, but have received no satisfaction. I spoke to Mayor Rickard about the matter a few days ago, and he said he would attend to the case. So far, however, nothing has been done to relieve the neighborhood of the nuisance. The water that was thrown at the vender was not directed against him, but wet him accidentally."

The presence in Berkeley of a large number of unsightly peanut stands, have been the source of considerable complaint of late, and an effort will be made to rid the town of these objectionable street venders.

II. African American Focus

The Colored Aristocracy Co.

At the Opera House Tonight---A Rag Time Carnival.

This is the best traveling minstrel troup on the Coast, and among the members of the company will be found Madah A. Hyer (of Hyer Sisters fame) who will sing "The Holy City," Miss Kate Carter, America's best Buck and Wing dancer, the "Komical Kusses" Brown and Howard, Tom Logan, Comedian, Kid Alston and Miss Mable Hearde, Sketch Team, Fred Kerrisy, Tenor.

The Colored Aristocracy Co. have been playing to the largest houses of any organization of its kind in all parts of the States.

This company again has visited Australia and the Hawaiian Islands scoring tremendous hits in those parts of the foreign world.

At 12 o'clock sharp today a big parade was formed in front of the Berkeley Opera House consisting of a large band of fifteen pieces and the balance of the artists numbering twenty-five people who will appear in gorgeous costumes as only colored people can show to advantage,

At 7:30 in the evening an open air concert will take place in front of the Opera House.

Popular price for the performance will prevail—25 cts and 50 cts. No extra charge for reserved seats.

November 8, 1900

When I read about African Americans in the *Berkelely Gazette* articles of 1900, I expected to find both subtle and blatant racism. I found those articles, but more common was the reporting on the organizational efforts of African Americans in 1900. These modern-sounding organizations, businesses, social and community endeavors among African Americans in Berkeley and throughout the nation have faded from the voice of history but are well-recorded in the *Gazette*.

Booker T. Washington, the African American educator, philosopher and orator, is quoted in the *Gazette*. In support of admitting the Chinese, he stated, "It will pay from every point of view to give the Chinese people a fair chance." On the state of race in America, Washington said, "The white man of this country has tremendous opportunity. To him every door is open. Such strength should never be used to crush, but to uplift." There are notices of the Afro American State League of California selling stock to open a general merchandising company. What became of them? An advertisement placed by an African American barber thanked the people of Berkeley for making his business successful and for their kindness.

The *Gazette* covered national news as well, including the work of the Colored Women's Club in Alabama and the separate election held for a black governor by blacks in Connecticut.

The Old Virginia Minstrels were scheduled to perform at the Berkeley Theater on Shattuck

Fred Tillman, Berkeley resident, at twenty-one years old. Fred was born in 1901 and lived until 1996; he was very active in the Berkeley community, especially with senior care. Courtesy of the Berkeley Public Library, South Branch, Fred and Ethel Tillman Collection, photo #sb000-660.

Avenue. Two of the performers got into an argument with the theater manager over advance pay, ending in the performers' arrest and fine for disturbing the peace.

A *Gazette* article reports on efforts by Southern agriculturalists to bring Chinese into the region for farm work, in effect pushing out African American farm workers.

In perhaps the oddest article found in this collection, an anonymous author writes an editorial with the chilling title "The Negro Question." The fact that the *Gazette* printed this editorial would seem to indicate that these views fell within the norms of their readership. The writer puts forth his belief that the single barrier to the local African American community's ability to achieve its true potential is the lack of government-provided school facilities and compulsory education. He further states that until African Americans receive such education they will not have access to the fruits of citizenship. Though this is a worthy view, the racially offensive language continually assaults our ability to trust the writer's intent.

Gazette writers often identified the race or ethnicity of people in their articles, but never identified any subject as white.

NEGRO FAVORS CHINESE.

Booker T. Washington Thinks Gates Should be Opened to All.

New York. July 6.—In an address at Montclair, N. J., Booker T. Washington spoke of the progress of the negro since the days of slavery and the service the negro has rendered to the commercial and professional world since then. He endeavored to show that progress and freedom are inseparable. He added:

"Russia just now is drinking to the drevs the cup of sorrow because of her failure to learn that her people could better serve it in a state of freedom. In this connection I believe our own country has a lesson to learn and to put into practice regarding the Chinese who wish to come into the United States. I believe that we will soon learn that it will pay from every point of view to give these people a fair chance. I am glad to see some such impression is gaining ground, but I wish it had happened before that Chinese boycott had been spoken of or before our conscience had felt the value of the Chinese dollars.

"The white man of this country has tremendous responsibility and a tremendous opportunity. To him every door is open. Such strength should never be used to crush, but to uplift.

"There is no slavery more hurtful than hatred, whether it be one section for another or one of race for another, for as is shown in history, in the end the oppressed become free and their oppressors are lost."

July 1905

Afro-American Council at Indianapolis.

Indianapolis, Aug. 11.—Some of the most distinguished colored citizens of the country are present at the annual meeting of the Afro American Council, which is being held here today. This meeting is of great importance and one of the largest ever held. Booker T. Washington and T. Thomas Fortune are both expected to deliver addresses. Bishop Walters, the president of the council, is presiding. Mrs. Ruffin, at the head of the Federation of Colored Women's Clubs, who refused to affiliate with other women's organizations, because they would not recognize the rights of the colored women, is also present.

August 11, 1900

MINSTREL SHOW AT THE BERKELEY THEATRE TONIGHT

Manager Lerner of the Berkeley Theater has secured a new attraction for his local playhouse in the shape of the Old Virginia Minstrels, which will open a week's engagement beginning to-night. The troupe carries its own orchestra and brass band, and has its own private car, which has been sidetracked at the Berkeley station. Manager Lerner is confident the minstrels will meet with success, as the show comes here well recommended.

MINSTREL MEN MIX IN A ROW

In place of ministrel jollity and darkey song there was weeping and cursing Saturday night at the performance of Wm. Mitchell's "Old Virginia Minstrels" in the Berkeley Theater on Shattuck avenue. Tom Massey and John Rishel, two actors and musicians, created a disturbance by demanding their pay before the show started, and, on being put off by Frank T. Homer, the advance representative of the troupe, they lost no time in expressing themselves forcibly over their troubles, creating such a row that the local police were called in and the two belligerent negroes were arrested and booked on charges of disturbing the peace. In lieu of bail they were taken to the County Jail in Oakland.

Massey and Rishel complain bitterly of the hardships that have fallen to their share since they essayed the life of the footlights. They insist that they are the victims of a plot to keep wages from them while they are kept busy singing and dancing in false merriment night after night. Homer says that the two negroes had only a few dollars coming to them and that the trouble started because they were temporarily "stood off."

August 8, 1905

HEAVY FINE FOR COLORED MINSTREL MEN

Thomas Massie and John Risher, the two members of the Georgia Minstrel troupe arrested last week on a charge of disturbing the peace, appeared before Justice Edgar this morning and were fined $10 each. The disturbance leading up to the arrest of the minstrel men was the outcome of their demand for the payment of their salaries.

Two Good Colored Barbers.

The O. K. barber shop is prepared to give you the best possible service to be had in barbering. Cigars and tobacco; soft drinks in connection. Roy Nemeyer, proprietor, 2004 Shattuck avenue.

A Card of Thanks.

I have just completed a year of very successful barbering in your midst, and take this means to accord to you the many thanks for the support given me and realizing as I do that not a people, elsewhere can excel the hospitality or the generosity of the people of Berkeley and vicinity, I am indeed grateful to all that have been patrons of the O. K. Barbershop. Wishing you all a merry Christmas and a full and rounded up measure of the pleasures of the ensuing year I remain,   Respectfully yours,
ROY NEMEYER,
The colored. barber, 2004 Shattuck avenue, Berkeley.   d18-3t

Mr. Hickerson. Courtesy of the Berkeley Public Library, South Branch, photo #sb000-138.

NEGRO CAUSES ALARM

Alarm has been occasioned in the West End through the actions of a young negro who has been lurking in empty freight cars and trying to lure little girls into his hiding place. So strong has been the feeling against the negro that he has disappeared within the last few days and no trace can be found of him.

The negro took his warning none too soon, for a number of men, heads of families, had banded together to deal with him in a vigorous manner without an appeal to the officers of the law. The high feeling against the negro was fanned by rumors that the fellow had actually assaulted a couple of girls. The police have been unable to corroborate this report, the families named refusing to verify the stories. Little Josephine Boiard of 2216 Fourth street had a narrow escape from falling into the clutches of the man last week. Her home is only a block from the railroad track, which, at Allston way, runs close to the bay shore. The child left the house alone intending to take a stroll on the beach. She passed the Standard Soap Works, where a number of freight cars were standing. Suddenly the head of the negro lad appeared from the door of one of the box cars and then she was hailed.

The girl was surprised to hear the summons and stood still, undecided what to do. Taking advantage of her hesitation, the negro climbed out of the car and made for her. Then the frightened child took to her heels and ran across lots to her home. Here she told her father, Joseph Boiard, a gardener, who made a prompt investigation of the case. He made inquiries to see if the negro was, by any chance, an officious watchman for the soap works or a train hand, and found that he had no connection with either railroad or factory.

Boiard, on inquiry, has found that his little nine-year-old girl is not the only child to have been approached by the negro. A number of neighbors have met with similar experiences, and it was the comparing of these stories that made the angry fathers unite to drive the fellow out of town. Arthur Hoffer's twelve-year-old daughter, Agnes, had an experience almost identical to that of Josephine Boiard over a week ago. Henry Wiener of Sixth and Bancroft way also reports a case where the young negro gave chase to two little girls that were playing along the street near the railroad track. The children screamed and Wiener drove the fellow away, supposing that he was merely trying to frighten the children in a spirit of mischievousness.

July 3, 1905

THE NEGRO QUESTION.

Uncle Sam has a difficult question to answer in regard to what will be done with the negro. Since the Emancipation Proclamation which set all slaves free, there has been felt the necessity of bringing the negro into the condition of full citizenship, able to vote wisely and to act in a manner destined to do most good for our country. It was not expected that the old slave could be changed in a few short years into the educated citizen, capable of governing and being governed. But it was expected that the children as they grew up would receive an education and that they would be taught to realize the full responsibilities of the duties of citizenship. However, as the years have passed the negro has been allowed to remain in the same condition as he was at the time of the Civil war.

Education has not been made compulsory. In fact the government and the states have not made provision for the education of the negro in a way that all could be accomodated. Thus it is that while a few have received the common school training, the vast majority have been allowed to live in ignorance, being wholly unacquainted with the laws of the county and the duties of citizenship owed to the government. It is not so much the fault of the negro as it is of the government and the states that he is not a better citizen. Of course, it must be understood that after their years of darkness, it is impossible to bring this race, in a single generation, to the same high standard as the white people are to-day. It takes time to educate a people; it takes years to raise a people from darkness and superstition to the condition of intellectual enlightenment. But because of the present inactivity of the government, the time has been lengthened and the negro has been prohibited from becoming an educated citizen. Through the school house the negro can be changed into the educated citizen, without it he will remain in his present condition. So that the future of the negro race depends almost entirely upon the providing of educational facilities, and the making of attendance in the schools compulsory. Until this is done the negro will remain in his present condition, and instead of making advancement he will not be able to absorb enough education and moral strength to overcome the supremacy of his savage nature.

April 10, 1900

Afro-Americans Organize.

The Afro-American State League of California filed articles of incorporation Saturday with a capital stock of $10,000. The sum of $14 has been subscribed toward the capital stock by the following directors: George Ingerman, J. F. Summers, William Tipton, E. H. Barrett, George R. Cashen, J. K. Dickenson, George Sequie, J. A. Hackett, Dr. G. R. H. Rutherford, S. A. Derick, J. C. Rivers, I. Beal, F. F. White and C. P. Duncan. The purpose of the incorporation is stated to be to fraternally unite all persons of the negro race, to carry on and conduct a general merchandise business for the benefit of the members and their material aid, to educate the members socially, morally and intellectually, and to advance their interests politically.

November 12, 1900

Ruth Witherspoon with her brother and sister, Henry and Mary, and her mother, Naomi Oliver. Ruth is a longtime Berkeley resident. Courtesy of the Berkeley Public Library, South Branch, Ruth Witherspoon Collection, photo #sb000-309.

Negro Women Discuss Negro Culture.

Birmingham, Alabama, September 7—The general discussion at today's session of the State Federation of Colored Women's Clubs being held here, was on the subject "Shall We Have a Reformatory, and Where?" Among the speakers who advanced views were Mrs. Booker T. Washington, of Tuskeegee, and Mrs. A. A. Bowie, of Selma. Other papers were read bearing on this subject, the general trend being that the establishment of a reformatory for young and wayward negroes would have good moral effect. The closing paper was read by Miss M. Gibbs, of Mobile, on the "Evolution of the Colored Woman."

September 7, 1900

Margaret Williams (bottom) and her sister. Courtesy of the Berkeley Public Library, South Branch, photo #sb000-590.

Chinese vs. Negro.

By the way, a Southerner whom I met at one of the hotels the other day tells me that if the South succeeds in breaking down the barriers against Asiatic immigration that it will import coolies to work in the South, thus practically freezing out the negro, and that many Southerner planters consider that the solution of the race problem in that section. The Chinese will not desire to mix socially or in other ways with the whites and will keep to themselves, and since the south wants cheap labor and wants to get rid of the negro without losing the labor he supplies for a trifling cost, the idea of substituting coolies for negroes and thus forcing the latter out of the country has originated. Thus new race complications would appear to be in sight, not only on this Coast but in other parts of the country as well.

Immigration Officer Sargent tells me that he is busy getting his plans ready for the new detention and immigration shed on Angel Island. The War Department has agreed to let the Department of Commerce and Labor have ten acres of the island on the eastern side, which will be fitted up with buildings to accommodate a large number of immigrants. They will be given rooms and food, and when their period of detention is over will be carried to San Francisco by the government on one of its own boats. Congress had already appropriated $200,-000 for the purpose and as Secretary Metcalf is now home he is helping Sargent in making the necessary arrangements. The present detention pens will be abandoned as soon as the Angel Island buildings are erected.

PROPHET.

July 24, 1905

Connecticut's Negro Governor.

The negroes of Connecticut were formerly accustomed to elect a governor for themselves. "Negro election," as it was called, generally took place on the Saturday following the election day of the whites. Just what the negro governor's duties and privileges were does not appear. At all events, he was respected as "gubernor" by the negroes throughout the state. The custom was established before the Revolutionary war and was continued as late as 1820.

NEGRO SUFFRAGE IN NORTH CAROLINA.

Indication That the Amendment Will Be Carried.

Every Man in the State Armed and Only Slight Disturbance Needed to Cause General Riot

Oakleigh, N. C., Aug. 2.—Today decides the fate of Negro suffrage in North Carolina. Practically every man in the state went to the polls armed and only a slight disturbance is necessary to lead to a riot all over the state. Three men shot, one fatally cut, another badly beaten, was Wednesday's record. The indications are the amendment and the state Democratic ticket will win by forty thousand.

August 2, 1900

Lena E. Pickett Holland, Berkeley resident and founder of the New Light Senior Citizens Center. She was also a seamstress, award-winning quilter and producer of plays. Courtesy of the Berkeley Public Library, South Branch, Joy Holland Collection, photo #sb000-614.

12. Asian American Focus

LIST OF ASIATIC WORKERS

Men and women both are engaged in the work of collecting statistics which has been undertaken by the Chinese, Japanese and Korean Exclusion League. The first reports, although they are not yet in shape for publication, show that some interesting and perhaps startling facts will soon be proved. By next Friday night the League expects to start in upon the work of classifying the returns as by that time it is expected that a large number will be able to make their reports, partially at least if not in full.

From the partial reports it appears that a large number of Asiatics in Oakland are doing housework, most of them as cooks, some as waiters, some even in chamberwork. In other walks of life are the Japanese tailors, shoemakers, window cleaners and hotel employes. There are the Chinese laundry and vegetable men, saloon employes and in the country districts both Japanese and Chinese employed in picking fruit and other agricultural pursuits. There are also the Celestials at the canneries and at the manufactories. The statistical collection includes the work of getting all sorts of facts about these people. A number reported that the difficulty of understanding the foreigners and making them understand, and their natural reticence toward giving out facts that may ultimately work to their disadvantage made the work very difficult. The canvassers have, however, been persistent in their duties and believe that, although some time will be needed in its completion, the canvass will be an ultimate success.

August 25, 1905

Chinese were called "Celestials" because it was said they believed they would be pulled to heaven by their queues or long pigtails. An Exclusion League had been established in 1900 to keep Japanese, Chinese and Koreans out of California and to boycott businesses established by Asians. League members surveyed the county to ascertain which jobs Asians held and the wages they were paid.

The League found Japanese tailors, shoemakers, window cleaners and hotel workers. The 1890 U.S. census reported nineteen Japanese living in Berkeley; in 1900 there were just seventeen persons of Japanese descent. They were young bachelors, students, laborers, a cobbler, teamsters and domestic help. These men averaged seventeen years of age and had come to California temporarily to earn money and return to Japan. They were generally not well-received. They mainly socialized among themselves.

In 1900 Japanese immigrants founded the Sake Brewing Company in Berkeley. After five years the viable company closed mysteriously. Did these men return to Japan or pursue other interests in Berkeley?

Chinese men were listed as laundry workers, vegetable vendors and saloon employees. Chinese and Japanese men worked in the fruit orchards and canneries. Koreans were present in Berkeley in 1900 but not emphasized in the *Gazette* articles.

Asian woman who worked in Berkeley for Professor Sengers's family as a housekeeper. Courtesy of the Berkeley Architectural Heritage Association, photo #609.

California had for the first time as an American state begun to participate in international markets. The state was particularly competitive in the agricultural arena and the pressure to remain competitive was great. As improvements to machinery were maximized, some business people argued that the only remaining way to maintain competitive prices was to reduce workers' wages.

Some people were afraid of losing their jobs since newly arrived immigrants commanded lesser wages. Others were concerned that their standard of living would decline. These people were poised for membership in the Exclusion League.

An editorial in the *Berkeley Gazette* supported importing cheap Russian workers during beet harvests and Japanese workers for other crops. Some agriculturists and businessmen believed that the Russians and Japanese laborers were superior to the white American laborer since the American laborer was better adapted to skilled work and was a little afraid of common hard work.

The fighting between Chinese associations in Berkeley fueled sentiment against the Chinese. As Lew Wah Get, officer of Suey Sin Tong, was quoted in *Walking San Francisco on the Barbary Coast Trail*, "If anyone threatened you or interfered with your business, the Tong would help you out. If you couldn't find a job, the Tong would introduce you to someone who could give you work. This was why so many people wanted to join them. Most Tong wars started from turf battles over criminal enterprises."

Some non-Chinese used battles between Tong associations and cultural differences to try to deny the Chinese freedoms enjoyed by other residents. One *Gazette* writer proposed, "The Chinese can be kept under subjection if they are properly handled. In the first place they are given too much freedom. Transported from a country where they are accustomed to obey the Emperor and the officials in every thing that they say, they have freedom suddenly thrust upon them and they are completely lost."

Several articles in the *Gazette* supported the rights of Chinese and other immigrants to decent livelihoods and denounced the Exclusion League's activities and intentions.

A COMING LABOR PROBLEM.

California must in the near future decide what will be done with the labor question. With the cheapening of the food products, the increased competition and the higher development of the farm comes the necessity of fixing the wage of the farm laborer. During the past few years this State has undergone a wonderful change. Its products are shipped all over the world. They are entering into competition with the products of other countries and the question now confronts the State. How can California successfully maintain her position in commercial life? From year to year, through improved machinery, the cost of production has been lessened, and now the only way to further reduce the cost is to sacrifice the man. Every State, every country has had to face this question. California has yet to learn the lesson of economy. It is only a question of time when this will be brought more directly before the people. At the present time there are propositions on foot to import several thousand Russians to work in the California beet sugar fields, and also many thousand Japanese for other labor purposes. The question is will this importation of of cheap labor have any effect on the price of labor in general in this state. For the purposes for which these people are to be brought to this state they are far superior to the California laborer. The producer of the sugar beet is at present unable, with the high price of labor, to raise the sugar beet with profit. Besides the American laborer is undesirable for the simple reason that he is better adapted to skilled work and he is a little afraid of common hard work. By the importation of these Russians the sugar beet industry in this State will grow, and quantities large enough to supply at least the home markets will be produced. The question is whether we will sacrifice all that has been done along this line in this state and refuse to allow these laborers to come, or to further develop this industry by allowing cheap labor to enter the state. We must decide either one way or the other. It is impossible to continue to cultivate the beet under the present conditions for new capital will not be invested and new factories built. One great objection to the American laborer is that he cannot be relied on. On the other hand these Russians will be always available. And the Japanese laborers will be found to be good in these lines of work which are tedious and require the closest attention. It is in this work that the American laborer fails.

March 30, 1900

TO HOLD ANTI-JAP MEETING

The first big rally of the Alameda county campaign against the Japanese invasion will be held in Maple Hall in Oakland to-night and from present indications the meeting will be largely attended and will be enthusiastic. The meeting will be opened at 8 o'clock sharp and in addition to President Marshall, who will preside, there will be five speakers of known ability to present and discuss the subject.

E. J. Livernash, State Senator Edward Wolfe, Assemblyman Philip Walsh of this county; O. A. Tveitmoe, president of the San Francisco Exclusion League, and Walter Graham, also of the San Francisco organization, will address the meeting giving an exposition of the plans of the Alameda County League and setting forth the great and imperative need of the work that is planned.

It is the intention of the Alameda County Chinese, Japanese and Corean Exclusion League to compile a census of the Japanese population of this county, showing the occupation and place of business and the amount of wages, wherever possible, in each individual case. Efforts will then be made to arouse public opinion to such a pitch as to amount in effect to a practical boycott of all Japanese in the county.

The statistics and proofs secured by the local league will be properly compiled and will be placed in the hands of the representatives of the State of California in the national legislative bodies, to be used by such representatives during the coming session of Congress in support of their fight for the exclusion of Mongolians from the United States. At to-night's meeting every detail of the anticipated campaign will be made plain and the support of mercantile bodies and individual merchants and workers will be sought. The league has enough money on hand to pay the rental of Maple Hall during the present month, and public meetings will be held there regularly.

August 14, 1905

A Japanese Dinner.

He who does not like the way the Japanese cook fish must be hard to please. They are better fish cooks than the French. The Japanese waters are very prolific, and the natives seem to have learned in cooking to preserve the inherent flavor of the fish, while their sauces are very simple. And as for eels, as they are cooked at the kandagawa, a teahouse in Tokyo, he who has tasted them has established a standard in his mind by which to judge other eels.

Seaweed we had, too, thin as paper, and crisp. It is the weed of the sea that is left on the rocks and scraped from them by the fisher women with shells and then dried in the sun. It is eaten as a relish and has a delicate flavor, suggesting cinnamon.

Rice we had in abundance. It was served from a bucket (not unlike ours, but not quite so deep) of unpainted white pine, with a little wooden shovel somewhat like those our children use in playing at the seashore. Our rice bowls were filled again and yet again, and when we covered our bowls it meant we had finished dinner. I have seen the Japanese look with indifference at a fish cooked in a way that made my mouth fairly-water with desire, but when they are served with rice it receives their immediate attention.—Harper's Magazine.

January 20, 1900

Japanese Social.

The young ladies of the Christian Endeavor Society of the North Berkeley Congregational Church gave a social to the same society last evening at the residence of James Lee on Hilgard avenue. It was a Japanese social. The young ladies were in Japanese costume and the parlors were decorated in Japanese style. Tea was served.

About sixty members of the society were present. An informal musical program was rendered, and all sorts of games played. The affair was a very pleasant one.

February 24, 1900

TO BEGIN ANTI-JAP CAMPAIGN

Now that the preliminary meetings of the movement to exclude, or at least restrict, the threatened influx of Japanese labor have been held, and the movement has made manifest its strength and popularity, the men behind the guns are preparing to establish the movement in this county on a sound, working basis, and to this end will hold a meeting to discuss ways and means to-morrow evening.

At this time the work done by the San Francisco organization will be reviewed, and it is probable that the work here will be modeled largely on similar lines. The one great desire, of course, is to interest and secure the co-operation of other than union-labor bodies, and it is designed to make a strong effort to bring into line as many of the secret societies of the country as possible.

The argument that will have to be overcome by the men interested in the anti-Japanese movement, is that their movement is "political." The workers admit frankly that the movement is both political and economic, for it is political in that it is intended to influence the policy of government and economic in that it is intended to affect existent conditions as they affect the condition of the Caucasian worker. But, and this is the nub of the argument in favor of the movement, it is not political in the sense of being the policy of a party or of a distinctive class or type, and it is a movement in which all American citizens, despite creed or political belief, may unite.

Where it is found impossible to persuade the influential organizations whose support is desired as organizations, the effort will be made to secure the support of their members as individuals, and it is hoped in this way to gain all the support that will be found necessary.

Japanese bachelors enjoying an outing. Circa 1900. Courtesy of T. Robert Yamada from his book The Japanese American Experience: The Berkeley Legacy 1895-1995.

At Friday night's meeting two well-informed workers will be present to outline the methods that experience has proved best, and much of the time of the meeting will be given up to listening to the advice of these men. Further than this, however, important working committees will be selected, and because of the desire to make all such committees in every way representative, it is urged that every delegate be present and that those organizations that have not previously been represented at these meetings send properly accredited delegates.

August 6, 1905

The lawlessness of the Chinese in this State should be dealt with in such a manner that there would be no possibility of its growing as time passes. The Chinese can be kept under subjection if they are properly handled. In the first place they are given too much freedom. Transported from a country where they are accustomed to obey the Emperor and the officials in every thing that they say, they have freedom suddenly thrust upon them and they are completely lost. The ordinary Chinaman that comes to California is only half-civilized, and it is the height of injustice to treat him as a civilized being. The ordinary method of dealing with such a people is to keep them under restraint until they become civilized and capable of knowing the difference between right and wrong. Then again the authorities have allowed the Chinese to become collected together in a small space of ground where they can carry on their lawlessness without the possibility of being caught. They should be kept from congregating in such closely settled colonies, and especially be kept from gaining a foothold in the heart of a civilized community. Then again the Chinese should be disarmed. The idea that in a State of the size and population of California the authorities should permit them to carry arms, a constant menace to the people. A Chinaman would just as soon kill a man as be friendly with him and his religion bears him out in this. The Chinaman should be kept under strict and rigid laws and not allowed the freedom he at present enjoys.

March 3, 1900

WARNING AGAINST JAPANESE

Walter MacArthur of San Francisco, in a stirring address, informed the members of the Chinese, Japanese and Corean League of Alameda County last night of the dangers of unlimited immigration of Asiatics. The speakers gave the members of the league much good advice and urged them on in their campaign to secure more stringent exclusion laws.

"It is a question," said MacArthur, "whether or not all the territory of the United States west of the Rocky mountains shall be saved to the American people, or whether it shall be abandoned to the people of Asia." Continuing, he said that when the people of the United States had been told the condition as they exist they "will arise and demand that this country remain, and absolutely so, in the possession of the American people."

MacArthur then outlined the inroads the Oriental laborers are making in the labor market, and said they were gradually crowding more and more into the industrial and business world, and that their encroachment was being felt, and seriously so, by the people of the West. He concluded his address with an eloquent period, in which he said: "I feel that the people of the West will be worthy of their noble heritage, and that they will settle this grave problem, peaceably or otherwise, as necessity command, but it will be settled right."

President T. F. Marshall in opening the meeting created considerable enthusiasm with a brief address in which he said the league had been gaining members rapidly; that the membership now numbered over 400, and that within a short time there would be at least 1000 members enrolled. Efforts, he said, had been made to secure money with which to pay the expenses of the league, and controbutions had been coming in rapidly, and he believed no trouble would be encountered in securing sufficient funds to carry on the work.

President Marshall appointed J. R. Kelley, G. T. Stone, H. C. Matthews, E. E. Travis and J. O'Byrne, members of the organization committee. A. E. Maliden was elected financial secretary.

December 8, 1900

JAPANESE NOT FARM LABORERS

The change from Japanese labor to white labor in the apricot orchards of California was affected through the failure of the Japanese contractor to "make good" in the matter of supplying help to pick the fruit, says the Watsonville Register. That work is now being done by white men and women, boys and girls, and it is being done in a most satisfactory manner. This is not at all surprising to those who are familiar with the Japanese methods of labor.

The little brown man, taking him in a lump, is not and never will be a success as a farm laborer in this country. The contract system under which he works frees him from all sense of responsibility to the employer who has hired his labor from a third party—the Japanese contractor. If the Jap laborer does not do his work well, which is the rule instead of the exception, the employer's only recourse is the contractor, and that wily individual is never around when he is wanted. And when it does happen that the contractor is at hand and can be reached with a complaint, he is very apt to shrug his shoulders and mutter something in his native tongue that may be interpreted into the familiar interrogation, "What are you going to do about it?"

The experience of the apricot-growers of the Pajaro valley with the Japanese laborer does not differ materially from the experience of othr mployers of the same class of labor. Such labor, no matter how cheap it may be is a failure, so far as practical results are able to determine it.

It is a good thing for the apricot-grower of the Pajaro valley that circumstances have directed his attention to white laborers and that the latter have been given a chance to show their mettle.

The Sam Wakeham home at the northeast corner of Berkeley Way and Shattuck Avenue. Picture shows Mrs. Wakeham investigating the products brought to her door. Courtesy of the Berkeley Firefighters Association.

It is even a better thing for the town that white labor is supplanting Japanese labor, and the Register hopes that the time is not far distant when every fruit that grows in the Pajaro valley will be cultivated, picked, packed and sold by white men.

To bring about this much desired state of affairs, however, the white laborer must play his part. He must, by faithful service, prove his superiority over the Jap and convince the fruit-grower that he not only can, but will, do better work than his coolie competitor.

August 17, 1905

GOOD WORK OF CHINESE STUDENTS

Among the Chinese students who are at present in the University of Californai there are some who have already distinguished themselves in the literature of their own country before coming to America. Several of theme have obtained the bashelor's or "Hiu-tsia" degree at the regular Government examinations; while some have the master's or "Chu-jen" degree. The amount of study of the Chinese classics and of exercises in the highest styles of prose and poetical composition, which are involved in these degrees, is almost incredible. It is to this severe mental discipline that the ability to learn English and to carry on further studies in our universities, side by side with the best of our American students, is to be attributed.

One of these literary characters is Chang-tsung-yuen, a gentleman of 29 years of age, who came to the University of California from the Nan-yang government college at Shanghai three years ago and expects to graduate from the college of commerce·in 1907. He has already published ̗four important treatises in the Chinese language which are everywhere well received and appreciated among the thinking part of the nation. As Mr. Chang is presenting copies of these four works to the University library, a few works about them may not be out of place.

1. The Constitution of the United States of America.
2. A short American Colonial history.
3. An outline of American commonwealth.
4. A compendium of American history.

Asian fraternity brothers around 1900. Courtesy of the Berkeley Public Library, South Branch, Michiko Uchida Collection, photo #sb000-011.

It may be mentioned that these four works, which are translations or compilations from our best American authors, show a remarkably intelligent appreciation of the constitution, government and history of the United States, expressed in the most clear and elegant literary style. Four such work coming from any university in the world would suffice to raise the writer to a high place in the estimation of the thinking and reading public. The University of California may well feel proud of having such a distinguished student in its ranks. It is needless to point out the vast benefit of such publications to the governing classes of China, who are seeking now to remodel the constitution and government of that ancient nation, as far as it practicable, on the models of the different countries of America and Europe.

Chinese House Burned.

Leong Joe's Property Destroyed By Fire at Two O'clock.

Another event in the epidemic of fires occurred shortly before two o'clock this afternoon, when the house of Leong Joe, a Chinese vegetable gardener, who resides on Bancroft way and Magee street, was totally destroyed by fire. All that was saved by the celestials consisted of a farm wagon, some household goods and agricultural impliments.

How the fire originated the bewildered Chinese who work for Leong Joe, could not tell. All that Leong Joe could disclose was the fact that he had lost $1000.

Leong Joe has been troubled considerably of late by theives, who have raided his melon patch. Whether the fire was of incendiary origin or not is a matter of corjecture.

Although several fire companies responded they were unable to render their services on account of the lack of a nearby hydrant.

SHOULD ADMIT CHINESE

Professor Bernard Moses of the chair of history in the University of California at the Taft banquet held in San Francisco a few nights ago was reported to have said in talking with a fellow banqueter, that if America is to compete for trade of the world the wages of American laborers must come down.

Asked if he made such a statement and if so, to go into further details on the subject, Professor Moses expressed surprise that what he is supposed to have said in private conversation should have been reported. He was more than surprised, he said, that if quoted at all he had not been quoted correctly and continued:

"The statement purported to have been made by me in private conversation with Senator Patterson at the Taft banquet is evidently a misquotation. Anybody knows that there may be high wages and yet such efficiency on the part of laborers that they may successfully compete with a system of production when the wages are much lower. The reason of this, of course, is that the highly paid labor may be relative to the wages paid, more efficient than the labor with low wages. This has, however, nothing to do with the other question as to whether wages and standard of living in this country must tend to become equalized with those of other countries.

"Hitherto the abundant resources of this country and certain legislative restrictions have made it possible for us to have conditions different from those of our neighbors. But recent developments in the means of communication have made it possible for large numbers of foreigners to come into the United States, where they constitute an addition to the supply of labor. As our natural resources become more and more fully appropriated and the number of laborers increases, it is to be expected that the wages will ultimately tend to decline, particularly when the additions to the laboring population are inferior in strength and skill to those who have been hitherto employed. Many of the recent immigrants from Southeastern Europe are clearly of this latter class. But as yet the immigration has not even in the Eastern States been sufficient to produce what may be expected to be ultimately result. At present the facilities for distributing immigrants to places when this labor is needed are very much better than formerly, so that the vast immigration is, at present, being, in a large measure, absorbed without overstocking any particular labor market. But this, of course, is only a temporary result. Ultimately all civilized nations will tend toward common geonomic standards of wages and living. Drawing away the laboring population from any country will naturally tend to improve the opportunities of those remaining. The people of Ireland are unquestionably better off because of immigration to the United States. And the large number of Italians who have in recent years left Italy for the United States and the Argentine Republic have made a beginning of relief in some parts of Italy. It would thus appear that the equalizing process does not mean merely a reduction of wages and standards of living in this country, but an improvement in the wages and conditions of other countries as well."

Professor Moses holds with Secretary of War Taft concerning the way in which Chinese coming to this country should be treated. He does not believe in throwing open our ports absolutely to the Chinese; and yet he thinks it would not be wise by any discourtesy towards the Chinese in the enforcement of the regulations at the ports of entry to take the risk of closing the markets of China to the products of American labor. That policy which treats every Chinese seeking admission as a coolie until he can prove himself otherwise is in accord with neither the spirit nor the letter of the treaty between China and this country.

July 12, 1905

Mummy Frightened Him.

President Wheeler's Celestial has a Terrifying Experience.

An expressman drove up to the residence of President Benjamin Ide Wheeler of the University of California yesterday in Berkeley and deposited a large but not very heavy box upon the steps. President Wheeler was not at home, and his Chinese servant received the box and at once removed it to the kitchen.

Not having taken all of the higher courses in the university over which his employer presides, the Chinaman grasped only the fact that the box was for Mr. Wheeler. As the president is in frequent receipt of presents, particularly at this time of the year, and as many of thses presents are of an edible nature, the Chinaman followed precedent and arranged to prepare the contents of the box for dinner.

The box was long and narrow and tightly built. It required ardent application of hammer and chisel to remove the top, and then the Chinaman found generous quantities of excelsior, underneath which was some felt packing.

Layer after layer of all kinds of packing was removed, until suddenly the Chinaman emitted a yell that would have done credit to a Berkeley rooter when the ball was almost over the Stanford goal line. His pigtail stood up straight in the air and he ran shrieking through the house.

"Heap dead man in box!" shouted the excited Celestial.

At last Mrs. Wheeler was induced to make an investigation of the Chinaman' excitement, and she found that the box that the cook had supposed contained materials for a feast contained an Egyptian mummy that had been sent by Mrs. Hearst to President Wheeler for the university.

The Chinaman was so much disturbed over the discovery of the body in the box that he declined to allow it even to be stored next to his room, and President Wheeler had to keep it in his library over night.

August 12, 1900

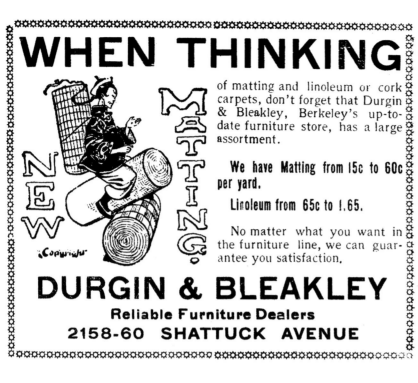
NO CHINESE RESTAURANTS IN PALO ALTO

PALO ALTO, July 6.—The fact that wo Chinese restaurants are about to be opened here is arousing much public indignation. The citizens have never permitted a Chinese business place of any sort to become established in alo Alto. This has ordinarily been revented by peaceful means, but on ne occasion both the Chinaman and the landlord were given twenty-four hours to leave town—and they went. Threats are being made that if the Chinamen persist in their purpose the contents of the places they are fitting up will be thrown into the street and the Mongols forced to decamp.

July 6, 1905

SITUATIONS WANTED.

Wanted—Situation by first-class cook. W. J. Richardson, 2238 Telegraph.
8-3-1m

Wanted—A Japanese boy wants a situation as plain cook or waiter. Address George P. O. Box 247, Berkeley.
8-22-1w

Wanted—Woman wants to go out cooking by day or part of day, or assist in light work. 1847 Russell st.
8-26-1w

Wanted—Good Japanese girl wants sitnation as plain cook or house worker. Phone Stuart 1051, or call 2551 Telegraph.
8-28-1w

Wanted—Position by Japanese school-boy, or cooking in private family. Address Y. Hama, 2130 Dwight way; ng an phone Berkeley 991.
8-23-1w

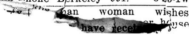
han woman wishes
have rece...

SITUATIONS WANTED.

Wanted—An honest Japanese school boy wants position. Address T. Naka, 2130 Dwight way.
7-25-3t

Japanese House Cleaning Co.—Cook, waiter, washing, contract, keep garden, cleaning new house. 1514 Louisa st., North Berkeley. Tel. Mason 905.
2-13-6m

Aetna Employment Agency—Mrs. M. Dean and Mrs. E. Kadderly, 411 11th st., Oakland; first-class help furnished. Office phone Clay 702; res. phone, Alameda 1477.
7-13-r

Wanted—A young lady, experienced, wishes work to do at the homes in manicuring, facial and scalp treatment; also general massage. Telephone Berkeley 1043.
7-19-1w

Wanted—Japanese Union Club; reliable employment office; all kinds help and any kind of day work. 2130 Dwight way, phone Berkeley 991.
6-14-3m

Wanted—Japanese Employment Office and House Cleaning Co.—General agency of trade; all kinds of skilled help furnished. N. Oba, prop., 319 Seventh street, Oakland. Red. 8452.
7-19-6m

13. Focus on Women

In 1900 a twelve-foot-high board fence had to surround campus women before they could play basketball outdoors. Philanthropist Phoebe Hearst donated the thousand dollars for the court. Women were given editorial responsibility for a campus publication, the *Occident*, but only for a day!

"Surely Berkeley's maids and matrons can compare most favorably with those of any time and any land."

—Miss Lucile Wollenberg, *Berkeley Reporter*, December 1906

Women at the turn of the century were sometimes depicted as courageous in the *Gazette* stories. One woman rescued a drowning football star; another climbed to a burning roof and extinguished a fire. Women passengers returned gunfire as bandits attempted to rob their stagecoach. Another woman dove in the path of a moving train, saving a child from a sure death.

Suffragettes convened in Alameda County. Susan B. Anthony delivered a speech in San Francisco in 1905. At eighty-five, her eyes were still clear and she was, as reported by the *Gazette*, in full possession of her faculties and had the intellectual resistance of the trained debater. Meanwhile abundant advertisements for patent medicines littered the *Gazette,* proclaiming women nervous, fragile and prone to the blues.

Lottie Shelly Bartlow, Berkeley resident at about age 50. Courtesy of the Berkeley Public Library, South Branch, Bartlow Family Collection, photo #sb000-075.

Unidentified Berkeley woman. Courtesy of the Berkeley Firefighters Association.

Women as Editors.

The issue of the Occident for October 31st will be entirely in the hands of the women students. A board of editors has just been appointed by Miss Frisius, president of the A. W. S. U. C. They are as follows: Miss Eleanor Gates, editor in-chief; Miss Elise Wenzelberger, society editor; Miss Celeste Granice, athletic editor, and Miss K Courtenay Johnson, news editor.

October 26, 1900

"For the Berkeley women are discriminating, and only the worth whiles gain admittance. The aristocracy of wealth does not overrule the aristocracy of brains and breeding. The mere jingle of money is not an open sesame. Many a social climber, richly upholstered with this world's goods, but only sawdust filling, has given up in despair and gone to fields where money talks, and throws its golden glamor over every deficiency.

"In dress as in everything else the Berkeley women display the best of taste, always wearing the proper gown for the occasion, and never indulging in the bad form of overdressing. There are society ladies who can ply the needle quite as cleverly as a high priced modiste. To their credit they do not hang the secret of these home productions in the closet with the family skeleton. They are justly proud of their versatility."

—Miss Lucile Wollenberg, *Berkeley Reporter*, December 1906

U.C. women, probably seniors at graduation, on the U.C. Berkeley campus. Courtesy of the Berkeley Historical Society, catalog #1498.

Negro Women Discuss Negro Culture.

Birmingham, Alabama, September 7—The general discussion at today's session of the State Federation of Colored Women's Clubs being held here, was on the subject "Shall We Have a Reformatory, and Where?" Among the speakers who advanced views were Mrs. Booker T. Washington, of Tuskeegee, and Mrs. A. A. Bowie, of Selma. Other papers were read bearing on this subject, the general trend being that the establishment of a reformatory for young and wayward negroes would have good moral effect. The closing paper was read by Miss M. Gibbs, of Mobile, on the "Evolution of the Colored Woman."

September 7, 1900

The daughters of George and Leontine Braux. George was a Civil War veteran. Courtesy of the Berkeley Public Library, South Branch, Betty Reid Collection, photo #sb000-252.

Basket Ball Team.

Miss Emma Stoer of Oakland has been elected captain and Miss Ethel Cotton manager of the University of California basket ball team. Practice will commence in an open court after January 1st. This will be the first time the young ladies of the State University have ever played outside of a building. The court will, however, be enclosed by a 12-foot board fence.

Mrs. Phebe A. Hearst, who has taken such an active interest in the athletic sports of the women students, has set aside $1000 with which to construct the court. It will be the best that can be built. The grounds will be 150 feet long by about 100 feet wide. Seats will be arranged on the side. Work of preparing the court will commence soon, and it will be ready for occupancy by the first of the year.

November 14, 1900

Sybil Marston as a U.C. student. She was a daughter of Mayor Marston of Berkeley. Courtesy of the Berkeley Firefighters Association.

WOMAN RESCUES P. GRAY

Prentiss Gray, football player and president of the Associated Students of the University of California for next term, was saved from drowning recently by a frail young woman.

The heroine of the hour is Miss Genevieve Dowsett of Honolulu, the beautiful sister of Mrs. Frederick Knight, whose guest she is in San Francisco. Miss Dowsett has won for herself a reputation for bravery and presence of mind such as might be envied by any one, but she bears her honors with becoming modesty and is disposed to make light of her own courage in the matter. She was last week the guest of the George Grays of Oakland at their country place at Noyo, Mendocino county, and one morning went rowing on the Noyo river with young Prentiss.

Miss Dowsett was in the bow of the boat and some slight jar resulted in her falling overboard. Gray leaped at once to her rescue, although, as was proved by subsequent events, Miss Dowsett is a remarkably strong and confident swimmer. As he jumped overboard, Gray, in some manner, became unconscious; whether he struck his head on a submerged pile or on the oar, or what was the reason is not known, but as he rose Miss Dowsett saw his condition. She manifested a remarkable presence of mind, for, as soon as she grasped the situation, she swam to the young man, seized him firmly and kept him above water until she could receive aid. Gray's sisters and Al Coogan, a fraternity brother, were on the shore, and were greatly alarmed by the occurrence—so much so, in fact that Miss Gray fainted. Coogan started to jump into the water also to relieve Miss Dowsett of her unconscious burden, but she, with the calmness which characterized her actions throughout, called to him to get a boat, as he would otherwise be unable to do any good. Coogan, in his haste, jumped into a boat which

was tied firmly to the landing, but soon discovered his mistake, and rowed to where Miss Dowsett and Gray had drifted some distance down the stream. Gray was a heavy burden to attempt to lift into the boat, and in their efforts they nearly caused the boat to capsize. They finally got him to the shore, but he was unconscious for some hours, and the greatest alarm was felt as to his condition. He has since entirely recovered and is now feeling no ill effects from his accident.

Gray is the football player who went through the great game last November with two broken ribs and a foot in which he had had blood poisoning for two daps; but so great was his desire to fill his place on the team that he played during the first half in spite of the excruciating agony he suffered. The result was so serious that it was feared for some time that amputation of the foot would be necessary. Miss Dowsett is a Honolulu girl and has been visiting California for some months past, during which time she has made many friends and has been extensively entertained.

July 3, 1905

WOMAN RESCUES INFANT

Mrs. S. Hulin from her window at 1803 Shattuck avenue saw a child standing on the Southern Pacific tracks, his pudgy fists pushed into his eyes, and sobbing aloud. The train was approaching from Dwight way, but the boy did not seem to notice it. He stood facing the approaching local but the tears blinded him so he could not see the train and he was too much involved in his great grief to pay any attention to the rumble or the whistle. Mrs. Hulin watched the child awhile and since it made no move to save itself, she hastened from the house and lead the child to the sidewalk.

The child who appeared to be only two or three years of age gave but one answer to Mrs. Hulin's question. "I want papa," he kept sobbing and the tears rolled down his cheek making streaks of clean through his grimy countenance. He did not know his name, nor where he lived—simply "I want papa."

Mrs. Hulin was in a quandry. She telephoned to the Marshal's office and Policeman J. T. Farrar went over to see about the matter. He no sooner saw the child than he recognized him as "Teddy" Allen, the two-year-old son of C. R. Allen of Vine and Shattuck streets. Farrar started to North Berkeley with the child, but half way to his destination he encountered the distracted father who had been hunting all over the town for his lost child.

The boy had left his home early in the morning and had wandered about all the forenoon. He was a half a mile from Vine street when he was found. It was shortly before noon and the child was probably hungry when he stopped in the middle of the tracks and started crying for papa. "Teddy" was well dressed when he left home but when he was returned to his "papa," his hair was tousled, his face dirty, his clothes torn in different places and scratches on his legs where his stockings had rolled down over his shoes.

July 1, 1905

MEET TO DISCUSS SUFFRAGE

The woman suffragists of Alameda county meet in annual convention to-morrow in two sessions to be held in Maple Hall, corner of Webster and Thirteenth streets, Oakland. The morning session will be devoted to the business of the association and the election of officers.

The afternoon session, which will open promptly at 2 o'clock, will be an attractive one to persons of a variety of interests, as well as those specially concerned in the suffrage work. Miss Mary Fairboother, who has been so successful with her classes in parliamentary law in the cities about the bay, will speak on parliamentary usage. Mr. Austin Lewis will make one of the principal addresses of the afternoon and will take for his subject, "Woman Economically Considered, and Socialism."

Among the other speakers on the program will be W. C. Petray of the Labor Council, "Why We Organize," Mrs. Austin Sperry, State president, "Status of Work in California;" Mrs. Nellie Holbrook Blinn, "Equal Suffrage;" N. M. Burnside, "Object of Wm. Morris' Club;" Mrs. John F. Swift, "What the National Council of Women has Accomplished;" Albert Elliott, "The Laws of California Pertaining to Women;" Mrs. Horace Coffin of San Francisco, president of the Equal Suffrage League, "Object of the League;" Mrs. Lawrence Groulund of Seattle, "Prominent Figures in the Humane Movement."

The public is cordially invited to attend the sessions.

September 15, 1905

RECEPTION FOR SUSAN B. ANTHONY

Miss Susan B. Anthony, for more than fifty years an advocate of equal suffrage, will stop in San Francisco on hear way East after presiding at the recent equal suffrage convention in Portland, and the visit will be accorded due honor by those among local clugwomen who are in sympathy with the cause. Two notable affairs will mark the brief sojourn here of Miss Anthony. The first will be a reception given her at the Sequoia Hotel, on Geary and Hyde streets, next Friday afternoon from 4 to 6, at which the Rev. Anna H. Shaw, president of the Women's National Suffrage Association, will share the honors, and the second a lecture at the Alhambra Theater on Monday evening, the 24th, when both Miss Anthony and Dr. Shaw will speak.

Among the notable women who will be present on these occasions will be Miss Sue Lombard, president of the State Federation of Women's Clubs of Washington, one of the delegates sent to Portland, and a member of the committee appointed to entertain Miss Anthony and Dr. Shaw while in San Francisco. Others on this committee are Mrs. John F. Swift, Mrs. Austin Sperry, Mrs. C. H. Blinn, Dr. M. E. Kibbee, Mrs. Ellen C. Sargent, Dr. Avery, Mrs. Campbell, Mrs. J. G. Scoville, Mrs. Lloyd Baldwin, Mrs. Gertrude Andrews, Mrs. Hester Harland, Mrs. Laura Bride-Powers and Miss Gertrude Yates.

WOMEN! REMEMBER THIS.

In addressing Mrs. Pinkham you are communicating with a woman — a woman whose experience in treating woman's ills is greater than that of any living person.

A woman can talk freely to a woman when it is revolting to relate her private troubles to a man.

Many women suffer in silence and drift along from bad to worse, knowing full well that they should have immediate assistance, but a natural modesty impels them to shrink from exposing themselves to the questions and probable examination of even their family physician. It is unnecessary. Without money or price you can consult a woman, whose knowledge from 20 years' actual experience is unequalled.

Women suffering from any form of female weakness are invited to freely communicate with Mrs. Pinkham at Lynn, Mass.

All letters are received, opened, read, and answered by women only.

This is a positive fact — not a mere statement — easily verified — thus has been established the eternal confidence between Mrs. Pinkham and the women of America, which has never been broken, and has induced more than 100,000 sufferers to write her for advice during the last few months.

Out of the vast volume of experience which she has to draw from, it is more than possible that she has gained the very knowledge that will help your case. She asks nothing in return except your good-will, and her advice has relieved thousands. Here are some of the cases we refer to:

A Woman who Doctored Eight Years and got No Relief Cured by Lydia E. Pinkham's Vegetable Compound.

"Before taking the Vegetable Compound I was troubled with irregular menstruation, and suffered great agony. My physician gave me morphine, and I remained in bed. I doctored eight years and got no relief, and the doctors told me there was no relief for my trouble. Finally I tried Lydia E. Pinkham's Vegetable Compound. While taking the first bottle I felt that I was improving. I have taken seven or eight bottles, and never had anything to do me so much good. Every month my troubles have grown less and less, and now at this time I am cured." Ella Quinney, No. 22 Stage Street, Haverhill, Mass.

Another Woman Who Acknowledges the Help she has Received from Mrs. Pinkham.

"DEAR MRS. PINKHAM — The doctor says I have congestion of the womb, and cannot help me. There is aching in the right side of abdomen, hip, leg, and back. If you can do me any good, please write." Mrs. Nina Chase, Fulton, N. Y., December 20, 1897.

"DEAR MRS. PINKHAM — I followed your instructions, and now I want every woman suffering from female trouble to know how good your advice and medicine is. The doctor advised an operation. I could not bear to think of that, so followed your advice. I got better right off. I took six bottles of Lydia E. Pinkham's Vegetable Compound, and used three packages of Sanative Wash; also took your Liver Pills, and am cured." Mrs. Nina Chase, Fulton, N. Y. December 12, 1898.

Mrs. Voss cured of Periodical Pains and Perpetual Headaches by Following Mrs. Pinkham's Counsel.

"DEAR MRS. PINKHAM — I have been suffering for over a year and had three doctors. At time of menstruation I suffer terrible pains in back and ovaries. I have headache nearly every day, and feel tired all the time. The doctor said my womb was out of place. Would be so glad if you could help me." Mrs. Carl Voss, Sac City, Iowa, August 1, 1898.

"Please accept my sincere thanks for the good your advice and Lydia E. Pinkham's Vegetable Compound has done me. I did everything you told me to do, and used only three bottles, and feel better in every respect."— Mrs. Carl Voss, Sac City, Iowa, March 23, 1899.

Mrs. Pinkham has Fifty Thousand Such Letters as Above on File at Her Office -- She Makes No Statements She Cannot Prove.

Nervous Women

Their Suffering Are Usually Due to Uterine Disorders Perhaps Unsuspected

A MEDICINE THAT CURES

Mrs. M. E. Shotwell

Can we dispute the well-known fact that American women *are* nervous?

How often do we hear the expression, "I am so nervous, it seems as if I should fly;" or, "Don't speak to me." Little things annoy you and make you irritable; you can't sleep, you are unable to quietly and calmly perform your daily tasks or care for your children.

The relation of the nerves and generative organs in women is so close that nine-tenths of the nervous prostration, nervous debility, the blues, sleeplessness and nervous irritability arise from some derangement of the organism which makes her a woman. Fits of depression or restlessness and irritability. Spirits easily affected, so that one minute she laughs, the next minute weeps. Pain in the ovaries and between the shoulders. Loss of voice; nervous dyspepsia. A tendency to cry at the least provocation. All this points to nervous prostration.

Nothing will relieve this distressing condition and prevent months of prostration and suffering so surely as Lydia E. Pinkham's Vegetable Compound.

Mrs. M. E. Shotwell, of 103 Flatbush Avenue, Brooklyn, N. Y., writes:

"I cannot express the wonderful relief I have experienced by taking Lydia E. Pinkham's Vegetable Compound. I suffered for a long time with nervous prostration, backache, headache, loss of appetite. I could not sleep and would walk the floor almost every night.

"I had three doctors and got no better, and life was a burden. I was advised to try Lydia E. Pinkham's Vegetable Compound, and it has worked wonders for me.

"I am a well woman, my nervousness is all gone and my friends say I look ten years younger."

Will not the volumes of letters from women made strong by Lydia E. Pinkham's Vegetable Compound convince all women of its virtues? Surely you cannot wish to remain sick and weak and discouraged, exhausted each day, when you can be as easily cured as other women.

HOSPITALS CROWDED

MAJORITY OF PATIENTS WOMEN

Mrs. Pinkham's Advice Saves Many From this Sad and Costly Experience.

Miss Luella Adams

It is a sad but true fact that every year brings an increase in the number of operations performed upon women in our hospitals. More than three-fourths of the patients lying on those snow white beds are women and girls who are awaiting or recovering from operations made necessary by neglect.

Every one of these patients had plenty of warning in that bearing down feeling, pain at the left or right of the womb, nervous exhaustion, pain in the small of the back, leucorrhœa, dizziness, flatulency, displacements of the womb or irregularities. All of these symptoms are indications of an unhealthy condition of the ovaries or womb, and if not heeded the trouble will make headway until the penalty has to be paid by a dangerous operation, and a lifetime of impaired usefulness at best, while in many cases the results are fatal.

The following letter should bring hope to suffering women. Miss Luella Adams, of the Colonnade Hotel, Seattle, Wash., writes:

Dear Mrs. Pinkham:—

"About two years ago I was a great sufferer from a severe female trouble, pains and headaches. The doctor prescribed for me and finally told me that I had a tumor on the womb and must undergo an operation if I wanted to get well. I felt that this was my death warrant, but I spent hundreds of dollars for medical help, but the tumor kept growing. Fortunately I corresponded with an aunt in the New England States, and she advised me to take Lydia E. Pinkham's Vegetable Compound, as it was said to cure tumors. I did so and immediately began to improve in health, and I was entirely cured, the tumor disappearing entirely, without an operation. I wish every suffering woman would try this great preparation."

Just as surely as Miss Adams was cured of the troubles enumerated in her letter, just so surely will Lydia E. Pinkham's Vegetable Compound cure every woman in the land who suffers from womb troubles, inflammation of the ovaries, kidney troubles, nervous excitability and nervous prostration.

Mrs. Pinkham invites all young women who are ill to write her for free advice. Address, Lynn, Mass.

Change of Life

These Women were Helped Through Woman's Great Crisis by Mrs. Pinkham—All Middle-Aged Women Should Read Their Letters.

Nine Years of Suffering

"DEAR MRS. PINKHAM:—When I first wrote to you, I was in a very bad condition. I was passing through the change of life, and the doctors said I had bladder and liver trouble. I had suffered for nine years. Doctors failed to do me any good. Since I have taken Lydia E. Pinkham's Vegetable Compound, my health has improved very much. I will gladly recommend your medicine to others and am sure that it will prove as great a blessing to them as it has to me."—MRS. GEO. H. JUNE, 901 DeKalb Ave., Brooklyn, N. Y.

Relief Came Promptly

"DEAR MRS. PINKHAM:—I had been under treatment with the doctors for four years, and seemed to get no better, I thought I would try your medicine. My trouble was change of life, and I must say that I never had anything help me so much as Lydia E. Pinkham's Vegetable Compound. Relief came almost immediately. I have better health now than I ever had. I feel like a new woman, perfectly strong. I give Lydia E. Pinkham's Compound all the credit, and would not do without your medicine for anything. I have recommended it to several of my friends. There is no need of women suffering so much, for Mrs. Pinkham's remedies are a sure cure."—MAHALA BUTLER, Bridgwater, Ill.

No woman is so healthy but at this crisis in her life she needs advice and help from the most competent source. Mrs. Pinkham will advise such women without charge on request.

Experienced Great Benefit

"DEAR MRS. PINKHAM:—I took Lydia E. Pinkham's Vegetable Compound during change of life and derived great benefit from its use."—MARY E. JAMES, 136 Coydon St., Bradford, Pa.

Mrs. Harrold Relieved of Pain

"I had pains in my head and back and could not stand on my feet without causing terrible pains in abdomen. I was short of breath and could not sleep. I tried several doctors but none helped me. I read of Lydia E. Pinkham's Vegetable Compound in a paper and before I had taken half a bottle I felt better than I had for months. I have taken several bottles and am now well."—MRS. R. E. HARROLD, Clinton, Ill.

The medicine that has cured a million women of serious female ills—an incomparable record—such is

LYDIA E. PINKHAM'S VEGETABLE COMPOUND

Sarah Remmi on steps of her home at 1507 Prince Street, Berkeley. Sarah was born Sarah Macleam in Scotland and came to America by ship. On the way over, the ship captain, Robert Remmi fell in love with her and they were married. Many ship captains settled in Berkeley. Courtesy of the Berkeley Public Library, South Branch, Vincent Dell'Ergo Collection, photo #sb000-575.

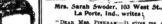

Woman on Ashby and Telegraph Avenues looking east. Circa 1900. Courtesy of the Berkeley Historical Society.

Woman on U.C. Berkeley Campus, looking east toward the Berkeley hills. Courtesy of the Berkeley Firefighters Association.

14. Human Interest

Sometimes news is too real, too close or too frightening. Touching or comical stories about everyday people are a welcome balance and special part of news reporting.

In the *Berkeley Gazette* we find dummy corpses, poison pastries and a rash of bottles stuffed with notes found washed ashore on local beaches. Here too are a reverend that cleaned steam locomotives for faith, a man arrested for taking his shoes off, and a classic, politically opinionated Berkeley juror. Let us not forget the railroad worker who unearthed a coffeepot full of old Mexican silver coins while digging up tree roots.

Exempt From Jury Duty.

F. A. Parsons Excused By Justice Edgar For Very Good Cause.

Many a business man has made strenuous effort in vain to get excused from jury service, but it did not take long for F. A. Parsons, a Berkeley carpenter, to successfully elude that public claim upon his citizenship in Justice Edgar's court today.

In common with a large and varied assortment of his compatriots, he was subpoenaed as a jury in the case of The People vs. Thos. G. Gibney, charged with malicious mischief. As usual, the justice administered the oath as to the answers to questions relative to the capacity of the prospective juror to serve in the case in contemplation, ending with the familiar exhortation "—so help you God."

"All but the 'God,'" replied Parson with distinct emphasis.

"What?" asked His Honor, with a suprised look on his judicial features.

"All but the 'God,'" repeated Parson.

"Oh, then you will 'affirm?'"

"Yes."

And when the regular juror's obligation was being put upon him, Mr. Parsons startled the court and spectators by declaring:

"Judge, I'm an Anarchist, and would not convict any person whatever!"

"Oh, you wouldn't, wouldn't you? Then you may be excused," said the court, and the natural friend of defendants in general made his exit to an accompaniment of titters throughout the room.

POTATOES AND ICE FIGURE AT WEDDING ANNIVERSARY

A sack of potatoes and a delivery clerk in the employ of the Oakland Express Company who was attempting to deliver the former were the disturbing element that nearly broke up the wedding party gathered Thursday afternoon at the home of Mr. and Mrs. Cyprian A. Barcelon, at 2119 Channing way. The Barcelons was celebrating the first anniversary of their marriage. The affair was not an elaborate one, but under ordinary circumstances would have gone into the social history of their lives as a pleasant event. But the arrival of the expressman with a sack of potatoes, in the midst of the celebration, gave the occasion a quick and almost fatal wrench that for a time made it look apphensive for both the party and the expressman.

James A. Hill, who is the father of Mrs. Barcelon and also resides at the Channing way home, had ordered the potatoes, and, as he claims, had paid for them. The expressman, however, having been instructed to collect the the price before he left the goods, refused to believe the assertions of Hill. A few moments of argument brought the matter to a climax. Hill, seizing a piece of ice that had been laid aside for use in the punch, hurled the cold missile at the head of the combative expressman. The intruder dodged and caught the ice with the back of his head, the impact felling him to the ground.

In the meantime the commotion between the two men had brought the rest of the wedding party to the scene. It was not large, numbering only fifteen. These led by Mrs. Barcelon, who ordinarily appears very peaceful and mild, advanced upon the prostrate expressman, driving him from the porch.

A score or more of neighbors, who were attracted by the noise coming from the Barcelon home, thinking some one was being injured, had rushed up to afford what assistance they could. The expressman had regained his feet and his sack of potatoes, but not his temper. In a loud, defiant voice he was daring any and all of the members of the Barcelon household to come forth and meet him in open battle. This challenge was accepted by Hill, Mrs. Barcelon and her husband. The driver of the express wagon suddenly changed his tactics. Without a word of explanation, without a parting oath, without the sack of potatoes, he climbed into his wagon and hastily departed.

The Barcelons and their guests returned to their celebration. They regained their composure, resumed their entertainment and to all appearances were as happy as before the exciting event. Mr. and Mrs. Barcelon were married a year ago yesterday in Cedar Rapids, Ia. Since their coming to Berkeley, Barcelon has been employed as photographer at Needham Brothers' art store.

July 22, 1905

A Reunion.

A Brother and Sister Meet After Years of Separation.

Mr. and Mrs. John Pickett of Missouri left Berkeley this morning for their home after a two months' visit to Mrs. Pickett's sister, Mrs. O. N Woods, 2424 Ellsworth street, and brother, Frank Groom. The latter came to California in the early fifties and has never returned to Missouri; at that time his sister, Mrs. Pickett, was but a little baby just able to walk, and therefore she was not even acquainted with her brother, now a venerable old gentleman in the seventies.

Their visit here was greatly enjoyed as it re-united that part of the Groom family that had for nearly half a century been parted.

Mr. and Mrs. Pickett will travel extensively through the southern part of California before returnig to their home.

September 6, 1900

NO MORE BLASTING AFTER 8

Acting upon the request of Marshal Vollmer the Spring Construction Company has discontinued blasting after 8 o'clock at night, at its quarry just north of the town line. Owing to the necessity of completing a large number of big contracts for street work before the rainy season, it became necessary for the Spring Company to operate both day and night shifts in its quarry. To get out rock for the day shift, blasting was done at all hours of the night, greatly to the discomfort of residents in the northern and eastern section of the town.

Many complaints were made at the Marshal's office on the night blasting, and the attention of the company was called to the complaints. Manager Creed immediately investigated and arranged matters so that blasting would not occur after 8 o'clock at night.

September 25, 1905

Carrots Studded with Gold.

Alameda, Aug. 1.—Pazzoni Bros., who conduct a vegetable garden near the borax works, think they have a gold mine in a patch of ground which they have been using to raise carrots. A bunch of carrots sold by them to Tallman Bros. in Oakland was found to carry traces of gold in the earth clinging to the carrots and now the owners of the garden are prospecting. They claim to have discovered flour gold in the surface earth, but as yet have not reached bedrock.

ANOTHER BOTTLE FOUND

West Berkeley has an epidemic of bottles with notes in them—large bottles and small bottles, new and old, corked and sealed, but all with the indispensible note telling of disaster and asking for aid. There is a strange similarity between all the notes—they are invariably written in indelible pencil on scraps of memoranda paper and are illiterate, which leads to the conclusion that all sailors use indelible pencils, carry memoranda books and spell and write poorly. It has been suggested that a museum be founded in the West End where the numerous bottles picked up on the bay shore can be kept as objects of curosity.

The latest tax upon the creduality of Berkeley people was discovered last Wednesday afternoon by Albert Anderson, a school boy of some fourteen years. It was a soda water bottle and contained a note purporting to have been written and placed in the bottle at the time the ill-fated gunboat Bennington sank in San Diego bay .That a sailor would have had time to write a note, put it in a bottle,

cork it and cast it overboard in the five seconds in which the gunboat blew up, is considered little short of the miraculous and stamps the note as a "fake."

Young Anderson was going for a row on the bay and climbed under the El Dorado Oil Works bridge to get his skiff, which he kept there. He noticed the bottle floating there and idly picked it up. He saw it contained a note and tried to open it, but the wires around the cork were rusted so badly that he was forced to break it before he could get the note. He carried his find to I. Wolff, 777 University avenue, who now has it.

The note read as follows: "August 2, 1905—This bottle was thrown overboard August 2th in San Diego harbor the time the Bennington blew up. I bing a salor jumped overboard. I guess someone will find my body some day here. Edward goodfellow." Immediately underneath this signature was another in the same handwriting, "N. J. Cronan."

Though the handwriting was passably fair, the mistakes in spelling and grammar would point to the author of the note being an uneducated man. Across the face of the note was the figures 2038 in ordinary pencil, while on the back of it, were several columns of figures in addition and check marks. The paper was pretty well saturated with sea water, which served to bring out the writing clearly, thus showing that an indelible pencil was used. There was a little water inside.

September 1, 1905

ANOTHER FAKE NOTE

A note in a sealed bottle found on the beach in West Berkeley yesterday by Eric Erickson of 2231 Bryon street, written supposedly at Cape Nome and thrown into the sea, has been handed over to Marshal Vollmer. From the nature of the note and the fact that the Japan current along the Pacific, runs from south to north, it is the belief of the Marshal that the note is a fake and was probably thrown into the bay by some one not well posted on the conditions along the Pacific Coast. The writer of the note has apparently read Jack London's story of the "Sea Wolf," as reference is made to that name and a feature of the story. The note found in the bottle follows:

"Meet me at the fair at St. Louis or at the Portland fair. If not there I am at the Lord's side in heaven or h—. I put the note in the bottle at Cape Nome bound for San Francisco, California. The sea is rough and I don't think the ship will hold out. If we sink, all right, I meet my death like a sailor. I am off the ship as the San Francisco call it the Sea Wolf. I meet her in Drake's bay. Our captain is a ———. He is a poacher on the seal rookeries of North Alaska. Maybe the ship will turn over. Yours as a friend, Harry Brown, Chic., Ill."

Erickson, who is a longshoreman, informed Marshal Vollmer that he found the bottle containing the note, lying on the beach in the West End. He opened it and upon reading the contents of the note, which was written on a thin strip of white paper with an indelible pencil, he reported the matter at once to the police.

DUMMY CORPSE IN BASEMENT

Laboring under the mistaken impression that he had discovered evidence of a dastardly crime including the corpse of a man laid low by assassins' bullets, E. F. Barry, a prominent Berkeley real estate man, called out the police, Morgue wagon and Deputy Coroner J. E. Streightif last night. Tremendous excitement reigned in usually quiet Berkeley after the news of the awful crime had been spread by Barry. Deputy Coroner Streightif was first on the scene, prepared to take the grewsome corpse to the Morgue where the cold slab lay all in readiness. But the corpse proved to be only a straw man prepared by practical jokers. Now the whole town is laughing at Barry's expense, but Barry hasn't time to take notice. He is looking for the villains who perpetrated the hoax.

The darkness of early evening was beginning to settle over the land last night when Barry left his home to stroll down Addison street, where the real estate broken has a house in course of construction. Barry resolved to inspect the house and note the transformation wrought by the workmen's hammers.

He walked into the basement. But he started back in horror, his blood freezing and each individual hair stirring at the root. There before him in the dim light of the basement lay a dead man. A terrible murder had been committed. There could be no doubt of it. A handkerchief even was thrown over the face of the corspe to conceal the ghastly features.

The real estate man, brave as he is in the face of tangible danger, fled precipitously from the scene. Bodies of murdered men were outside his field —such things were matters for the coroner and police. So to the Coroner he went.

Streightif beat the police to the scene of crime. He walked boldly into the dark basement and with the coolness of a man long used to such little affairs he leaned over the dead man and removed the face cloth. Then merriment shook his patriarchal beard. Then more merriment. Then little silvery notes of laughter, which gathered into a long, loud merry ha ha that smote heavy upon the tense silence of the outer darkness. For at the feet of the Coroner lay an innocent man of straw instead of the murdered human reported by Barry.

Barry is still looking for the jokers.

February 2, 1905

PAINTER PAYS PRETTY PENNY FOR "PACKAGE"

When W. C. Schwartz, a South Berkeley painter, returned from San Francisco, the other night, he brought back something he had not taken with him. The package Mr. Shcwartz carried was a prize bundle which he had collected in several places of amusement. As a result the decorator of dwelling rode through to the Berkeley station. The walk home proved too much for him and upon reaching the public library he lay down on the sidewalk and was soon asleep.

Unfortunately for the painter, he was discovered by a policeman and arrested for being intoxicated. This morning Justice Edgar put on the finishing touches by fining Schwartz $10, after he had pleaded guilty.

WOMAN LOSES PURSE AND A VALUABLE PIN

While walking from the Sixteenth-street station in Oakland yesterday Mrs. Thomas Orchard of 2138 Center street, this city, lost her pocketbook containing some $5 in silver. She believes the pocketebook was removed from the front of her dress by a man who staggered against her as she left the station. She remembered having the purse while on the train, but upon boarding a street car near the station, she could not find the purse. She recalls having been jostled by a man and believes that he secured her money. The purse also contained a silver class pin.

September 7, 1905

IS NOW ENGINE WIPER

Attired in blue overalls and jumper and with a bunch of waste in his hand, the Rev. Dwight E. Potter, pastor of the Union Street Presbyterian Church of Oakland, began work last Friday night as an ordinary engine wiper in the West Oakland railroad yards.

The Rev. Potter's purpose in doing this is to familiarize himself with the trials, tribulations and temptations of the railroad men. Mr. Potter sympathizes with the railroad men who work with their hands, and wants to live and work with them so that he may reach them in a spiritual way.

In order to accomplish this study, Mr. Potter decided to make application to Division Superintendent Scott for work in the yards. It took some little correspondence between Scott and General Superintendent Palmer, but the order was finally issued for his employment. He desired to be permitted to work in every department for a short time, and so choose the humble position of engine wiper to begin with. He also wanted to be treated as though he were the newest and greenest hand on the road, so he was told to report on night duty.

When night came Mr. Potter began his work, crawling over and around the big locomotives, until he was hot, dirty and thoroughly tired. But he did not falter, and despite the unusual weather he remained with his shift all through the night.

When morning came, instead of going to his own room the pastor took a small room in a West Oakland lodging house, where many railroad men make their home. He carried his midnight luncheon in a small basket, and when it was time to eat he sat on the side of the engine pit in the roundhouse. His breakfast was eaten in a small restaurant which the railroad men frequeunted.

This close communication with the railroad men is not new to Mr. Potter because for several months he has been rooming close to the yards and taking his meals in a small restaurant in West Oakland. This did not satisfy him, so he now proposes to work among them and share their daily toil.

The young minister will work his way through the yards in every department and will learn to be a switchman, how to work in the car department, how to beat out 1⸍ and carpets in the Pullm⸍ ⸍⸍⸍⸍⸍⸍⸍, and how it feels to be the "green man" in all departments. Mr. Potter said Friday:

"I have already been working through the railroad yards for some time, and I have found the men who play so important a part in the affairs of the country as the railroad operatives to be sympathetic, earnest and sincere. Some of the best friends I have are among the railroad men, and now I propose to see just exactly what their daily toil is like. I want to know about their daily life, their trials and troubles, and so I have decided to work with them as long as I can remain upon this coast. I shall be compelled to go East shortly, and so the development of my plan has been hastened a little.

"I originally expected to go to Sacramento and seek employment in the shops there incognito, but this was thwarted by the hastening of my departure for the East. I shall now work through the various departments in West Oakland as a green hand, and try to find out just what it is like to 'break in' for the railroad service. There is a small army of railroad men in Oakland, and if there is any chance I propose to reach them."

July 14, 1905

FIND MEXICAN INDIANS WHO SPEAK TURKISH

CITY OF MEXICO, August 29.—An important ethnological discovery has been made by students at the University of Campeche, the principal educational institution in the city of Campeche, capital of the Mexican state of the same name. It is that the language of the Indians of Campeche and the Turkish language are almost identical. Turks coming directly from their country to Mexico find no difficulty in making their wants known to the Indians of Campeche, and within a few weeks they are able to talk the language of the Indians fluently.

Ethnologists of this capital have now decided to attempt to establish a relation between the Indians of Campeche and the Turks. It looks to be as difficult a problem as that of explaining the discovery in the state of Oaxaca of Egyptian and Chinese idols. The discovery was made a short time ago.

August 29, 1905

WAS ONLY COOLING HIS FEET

Residents in the vicinity of Magee avenue and Blake street became very much alarmed yesterday afternoon over the actions of a stranger. In fact they became so alarmed that the Marshal's office was called upon to investigate the case and protect the people from what they supposed was a maniac—and all because the man was so thoughtless as to sit down on the edge of the sidewalk and remove one of his shoes.

In response to an urgent request to go immediately to the corner of Magee avenue and Blake street, Deputy Marshal Moran went in hot haste to capture the supposed insane man. Instead, however, of finding a raving maniac, Moran found the suspect to be a young man from Yuba county. He gave the name of William E. Kriski.

"You may be sane, enough," said Moran, after being assured by Kriski that such was the case, "but why do you sit on the street corner and remove one of your shoes? Don't you know that your most extraordinary behavior has frightened all the women in these houses around here; don't you see that your thoughtlessness has in a measure upset the police department—and all because you removed a shoe?"

The man from Yuba looked coolly at the man in police uniform and said: "I have chilblains and took off my shoe to cool my foot. Have you any laws in your college town preventing a man from cooling his feet?" Moran admitted that even Blackstone had not treated of the subject and made no arrest.

Thirty Days for Johnson.

When "Shoestring" Johnson, a notorious character in this section of the State, dropped into Berkeley yesterday afternoon, he carried a load that would have staggered an ordinary individual, but Johnson is no ordinary person and he managed to navigate with little difficulty. Marshal Vollmer, however, chanced to meet Johnson, and realizing that gentlemtn's condition, took him gently by the arm and led him to the police station. On the way the notorious "Shoestring" explained confidentially that he had just put away two alcohol cocktails, which he believed had been his undoing.

This morning he appeared before Justice Edgar for the sixth time and although he promised solemnly never to touch another drink, he was sentenced to serve thirty days in the county jail.

July 16, 1905

PASTRY POISONS FAMILY

That Mr. and Mrs. E. Hughes and their 4-year-old son of 1811 Addison street did not die early Monday morning as a result of being poisoned through eating cream puffs in an Oakland restaurant the previous evening, was due to the timely arrival of Dr. J. J. Benton who was compelled to resort to heroic measures to save their lives. Although Mr. and Mrs. Hughes and their child are now out of danger, they are still in a weakened condition and will be confined to their home for some time. The father was the most seriously affected of the three, and is still quite low.

Sunday afternoon the Hughes family went to Oakland, where they remained until late that evening. Before returning to Berkeley they visited an Oakland restaurant where they had a light meal, including cream puffs of which they ate freely. Upon reaching their home in this city, both Mr. and Mrs. Hughes complained of severe pains. Thinking that it amounted to nothing they retired. Toward morning, however, Hughes was aroused by sounds of moaning, and upon investigation found his wife suffering great pain. At about the same time the child was taken ill and Hughes experienced great difficulty in assisting his wife and child on account of his condition which continued to grow worse.

In a short time Hughes was almost doubled with the pain and was hardly able to call for aid. He finally aroused a neighbor who summoned Dr. Benton. When the physician arrived on the scene he found the family in a precarious condition, and it was only after several hours' work that the sufferers could gain relief. Not until to-day were they pronounced out of danger, and the physician expresses great surprise that they recovered so rapidly, the cases being of such unusually severe nature.

August 4, 1905

FIVE POISONED IN OAKLAND FROM PUFFS

Dr. J. J. Benton was notified Saturday by Dr. Smith of East Oakland that he had a case of poisoning from stale cream, similar to that of the Hughes family of Addison street. In this instance a family of five were effected from eating chocolate eclairs, obtained in the same restaurant in Oakland that the Hughes' ate in.

August 7, 1905

Condemned Flour Nipped.

The San Francisco Board of Health discovered yesterday that an attempt was being made to ship 42,000 pounds of condemned flour to Berkeley. In some mysterious manner the flour had been secured after it had been pronounced deleterious to health and the plan to secretly get it out of San Francisco was almost successful.

The scheme to ship the flour to this side of the bay was nipped in the bud by Policeman Butterworth

The condemned consignment will now be saturated with coal oil, so as to make it entirely unsalable.

July 14, 1900

U. S. MAIL HAULED BY ELEPHANTS

New York, Sept. 21.—But for the strength and courtesy of four huge elephants, a two-ton batch of mail stuck in the mud at Sixth avenue and Forty-second street, would have missed its train at the Grand Central depot last night.

The trouble began when a large mail wagon, loaded to the top, swung down Sixth avenue and ventured a sharp turn at the corner, where street repairs had left a strip of soft earth turned to sticky mud by recent rains. A new driver, employed in place of a striker, was on the wagon and was accompanied by a policeman. He urged the horses into the trap and the wheels sank to their hubs. A crowd gathered and broke three heavy ropes in their efforts to help the horses.

Then the policeman had a happy thought. He sent a messenger to an amusement house near by and asked for the services of the performing elephants. Four were hurried to the scene in charge of their keepers. They were harnessed to the sides of the wagon and jerked it out of the mud with indescribable ease while the crowd cheered.

September 21, 1905

EIGHTEEN YEARS TO DELIVER A POSTAL CARD

Uncle Sam's mail has been making some records which for slowness would put he snail to shame in Santa Clara county. On January 16, 1887, a postal card was mailed in San Jose, to the M. M. Alvarez Cyclery at Los Gatos. Although the distance is only ten miles, the card did not reach Los Gatos until a couple of days ago. It was then sent to Alvarez, who had removed from Los Gatos. The card traveled the ten miles in 18 years. A postal card, mailed in San Francisco in November, 1895, by the San Francisco News Company reached E. P. Davis in San Jose last Saturday. In this instance the distance of fifty miles was covered in ten years.

In both of these cases it is apparent that the postal cards had become caught in the mail boxes, and were only dislodged when the boxes were examined. The postal card from San Francisco bore the stamp of July 28, 1905, at that office and was received in San Jose the same day. It had evidently remained in a San Francisco mail box for ten years.

September 21, 1905

Berkeley mailman Vollmer. I believe this man is August Vollmer, who went on to become Berkeley's police marshal a short time later. Courtesy of the Berkeley Firefighters Association.

DYING MAN MAKES PLEA FOR DOG

Unfortunate Man Stealing Ride Is Mortally Wounded.

Waterbury, Conn., Sept. 26.--Patrick Ryan, very ragged, not overclean and in every way a thorough representative of the tramp type, tried to steal a ride to Bristol on a Highland division freight train yesterday. In his arms he carried a fox-terrier puppy, whose white coat was as immaculate as Ryan's garments were slovenly.

"Oh, let me and the pup ride," pleaded Ryan from the bumpers when the brakeman discovered the pair. "We're mighty tired and the pup ain't feeling right."

The brakeman let them alone.

Half way to Bristol the motion of the train made the terrier ill. He licked Ryan's grimy hand and whined piteously.

"All right, doglums," said Ryan; "if you can't stand it we'll get off."

Ryan edged his way out to the end of the brakebeam, holding the terrier carefully in his arms. Then as the train slowed at the Terryville switch he leaned far down toward the ground and dropped the little animal on a spot of grass. The terrier yelped in fear.

"It's all right, I'm coming," cried Ryan, and leaped.

His foot slipped, caught in the brake ladder, and he pitched under the wheels. When they picked him up his right arm was cut off, his left leg crushed and his head a mass of bruises. The terrier crouched beside him, licking his battered face. The tramp is dying at the Waterbury hospital. He regained consciousness for a moment this afternoon.

"Has anyone remembered to feed the little dog?" he asked.

Worshiping a Turtle.

At a place called Kotron, on the French Ivory Coast, the natives believe that to eat or destroy a turtle would mean death to the guilty one or sickness among the family. The fetich men, of which there are plenty, declare that years ago a man went to sea fishing. In the night his canoe was thrown upon the beach empty. Three days afterward a turtle came ashore at the same place with the man on its back, alive and well. Since that time they have never eaten or destroyed one of that species, although they enjoy other species.

If one happens now to be washed ashore, there is a great commotion in the town. Firstly, the women sit down and start singing and beating sticks; next a small piece of white cloth (color must be white) is placed on the turtle's back. Food is then prepared and placed on the cloth, generally plantains, rice and palm oil. Then, amid a lot more singing, dancing and antics of the fetich people, it is carried back into the sea and goes on its way rejoicing.

Could not go to a Picnic so Drowns.
Missoula, Mont., Aug. 8.—Miss
Georgia White, aged 17 years, wanted
to go to a picnic, but her mother said
she could not do so. The girl became
despondent, threw herself into a
stream and was drowned.

August 8, 1905

A Noiseless Ring Game.

The small rubber rings that are used
in every household with which to seal
preserve jars may be made the means
of much amusement when a lively
game is desired for the amusement of
friends. First obtain a smooth head of
a flour or sugar barrel and see that the
pieces are all fastened together, forming a circular board, or any smooth
board about a square foot in size will
serve the purpose.

Procure ten coat hooks of medium
size and secure them into the board
and mark above each hook its number,
ranging from No. 1 to No. 10. A hole
may be made in the upper end of the
board or a screw eye inserted by which
to hang it upon a nail in the wall.

No. 10 is a sort of a "bullseye," and
each player, having three of the rubber
rings, takes turns in throwing them
from a position about ten feet away
endeavoring to "hook" as many on the
board as possible. A score is kept of
the points gained by each player, the
one first getting 100 points being the
winner. However, exactly 100 points
must be made. For instance, if a player has 99 he has to work for "hook No.
1," as any other hook would carry him
over the mark. This difficulty adds to
the interest of the game.

An advantage of the game is that no
noise is made nor damage done by the
rings, and it may be improvised by any
boy or girl.—New York Sun.

Found Buried Treasure

William Britt, a cabinetmaker in
the Southern Pacific Railroad shops,
while at work about his place at
Oak Park, near Sacramento, discovered an old coffee pot underneath
the roots of a swamp oak which had
been overturned by the wind, containing about $700 in Mexican sil-
ver coins. The coins are all dated
more than fifty years ago, and,
judging from the condition of the
tree under which they were found,
had been in the ground fully that
length of time.

Britt cut the roots of the oak
several days ago and so weakened
its support that it was overturned
by the next high wind. On Sunday, while converting the tree into
firewood, he discovered the treasure. The money had evidently been
buried at the base of the tree. It
is believed to have belonged to some
Mexican, who, on leaving Sutter's
Fort for the mines, buried his
money in this spot and either died
in the diggings or was unable to
discover the hiding-place upon his
return.

January 19, 1900

AERONAUT TO BLAME.

Father Bell Thinks Maloney Upset The Machine.

San Jose, July 20.—The funeral of
Daniel Maloney, the aeronaut, who lost
his life in the collapse of Professor
Montgomery's aeroplane, at Santa
Clara, Tuesday morning, took place
yesterday from the chapel of Santa
Clara college. At 10 o'clock the remains were conveyed from Fleury's undertaking parlors to the chapel, followed by the sorrowing friends and relatives of the unfortunate young man.

The inquest held by Coroner Kell developed evidence that Maloney had
determined upon making a flight Tuesday even under adverse conditions.
The cries of fake which have been
raised repeatedly of late over the failure of the aeroplane to meet expecta-
tions had rankled in Maloney's mind,
and he stated to a number of friends
that he would "fly or break his neck."
The jury exonerated Professor Montgomery of all blame for the accident.

FORESTS WILL BE DEPLETED

Uncle Sam Will Cut Fifty Million Feet of Timber.

Washington, July 5.—The bureau of
forestry has received an offer of
$20.50 a thousand feet for 50,000,000
feet of lodge pole pine and Englemann
spruce in the Big Horn forest reserve,
Wyoming. The timber will be advertised for sale and if no higher bid is
made the offer will be accepted. The
exportation of the timber from the
state where the reserve is located has
been made possible by recent congres-
sional enactment. The 50,000,000 feet
will be cut strictly under the new regulations, which provide that only the
dead mature timber shall be used.

July 5, 1905

15. Love and Marriage

Five years in San Quentin for a soldier who broke his promise to marry Miss Mary Schaffer of West Berkeley! He married another! Justice was severe in 1900. Bigamists disappeared. First cousins married and kept their marriage secret fearing ostracism by family and community.

1900 Berkeley had it all: Reno weddings, elopements and divorce battles over a husband not bathing.

The Hicks family circa early 1900s. **Standing:** *Roberta, Hernando, Milton.* **Seated:** *mother Martha Evelyn, with Whitelaw, Irving, Ethel. Ethel was six or seven years old in the photograph. She went on to marry Fred Tillman and has been a longtime Berkeley resident. Pearlie Tillman says that like most fathers, Mr. Hicks was the one elected to take the photograph. (Thanks to Pearlie Tillman for her help.)* Courtesy of the Berkeley Public Library, South Branch, Fred and Ethel Tillman Collection, photo #sb000-662.

MAN OF MYSTERY MARRIES

Thorrington Chase, detective, Government scout, astrologist, mental telepathist, violinist, ad solicitor and for a brief time U. C. student, is married. At least, it is presumed he is from the following dispatch received by the Gazette: "Neosho, Mo., Aug. 7, 10 words paid, Gazette, Berkeley, Cal.— Thorrington Chase married here to-day Aida Louise Snively father's ward. T. C."

The "man of mystery" left here some three months ago, and his friends were in doubt as to whether he had received a message from Mars or was simply going to do some ranch work and attend to the live stock on his father's farm at Neosho in the "Show Me" state.

Chase while here went by the name of Thorrington Clarke Chase and frequently regaled his friends with weird tales of his adventures by land and sea and his communications even with the stars.

His first advent at the University was marked by the now famous "Crocodile" advertising which was the freakiest ever seen in the State. Many business men who know him by no other name will remember him as the "Crocodile man." He was a fine violinist and organized a class at one of the U. C. cottages.

Several months ago he left Berkeley with the announcement that he was going to South America, called by some great detective mission from the Government. It subsequently developed that he had gone to Mare Island and was in some employment in the naval department.

Chase made a number of friends here who will be pleased to know that he has married and hope he will settle down and cut out the mythical and mysterious.

August 8, 1905

Chester C. Post, a clerk in San Francisco, and his wife, Jeannie, with their baby Chester Jr. at Russell Street and Claremont Boulevard waiting for public transportation and an outing probably over the hills. December 1900. Courtesy of the Berkeley Historical Society, catalog #1471.

FROM WORK TO WEDDING

Desirous of avoiding the usual publicity attendant on pre-arranged weddings, James Mathieson, a lineman, climbed down from a telephone pole on Center street near Shattuck avenue, at 5 o'clock Saturday evening and, in company with Frances Bender, who had just closed her typewriter in a local real estate firm, walked to the house of Rev. W. R. Hodgkin, curate of St. Mark's Episcopal Church, where they were made husband and wife. Mathiesen did not even stop to remove his "climbers" from his legs or his belt of tools, while the bride was dressed in her ordinary office clothes.

Then the principals in the exceedingly unconventional marriage, purchased the materials for a wedding supper and proceeded to the home of the bride's parents 1334 University avenue.

Though the young people had been engaged for some time, the wedding was a surprise to Mr. and Mrs. Frederick Bender, but the parental blessing was quickly given. Mrs. Mathiesen has been employed for some months as a stenographer by M. P. W. Albee.

The couple left late Saturday evening on an extended honeymoon trip.

1300 block of Spruce Street. Circa 1900. Note the water tank in the background. Courtesy of the Berkeley Historical Society, catalog #1472.

St. Marks Episcopal Church, Berkeley. Courtesy of the Berkeley Firefighters Association; photo from *Berkeley Reporter*, December 1906.

Cost Him Five Years.

Goodwin Betrayed Mary Schaffer of West Berkeley.

Judge Greene has sentenced Charles Goodwin to five years in San Quentin for the betrayal of Mary Schaffer of West Berkeley. It appears that Goodwin met Miss Schaffer about two years ago, while he was a soldier on the way to Manila. He promised to marry her on his return from Manila, and correspondence established the fact, as well as other testimony; but instead of doing so Goodwin took another wife.

Goodwin took his sentence coolly, but his young wife, whom he had married one day before he was arrested on the charge of which he was convicted, broke down and wept violently. A stay of execution for ten days was granted, but finally withdrawn by his attorney, Edward Sweeney.

Deputy Sheriff Welch started for San Quentin this morning with Goodwin where he will enter service on the sentence of the court. The case has caused considerable comment from the fact that few betrayers are brought to justice so successfully as Miss Schaffer has done with Goodwin. The courts are growing more strict in the enforcement of laws relating to matrimony and are inclined to allow cupid to change his mind only by mutual consent.

March 29, 1900

The Divorce Mill.

Two Husbands Claim That Their Wives Have Deserted Them.

Edward Frick brought suit for divorce yesterday on the grounds that his wife had deserted him. Frick and his wife have been living in Alameda. A few days ago Mrs. Frick quietly packed her belonigigs and moved to the home of her parents, Mr. and Mrs. J. P. Haines, who live on the corner of Lorina and Russell streets in South Berkeley. Frick says that his wife left him because he was too good. He claims that he never smokes, drinks or swears, and that Mrs. Frick objected to his habits of sorbriety.

Mrs. Frick could not be seen, but Mrs J. P. Haines, the mother-in-law in the case, said that her daughter came home ill from nervous prostration as the result of the treatment she received from Frick.

Frank Lockyer the well-known druggist who resides at Dwight way has also brought suit for a divorce from his wife on the ground that she deserted him.

December 11, 1900

LICENSES ISSUED.

The following marriage license was issued yesterday by the County Clerk, James F. Frisbee, 75, Pomona, and Ida J. Haight, 49, Berkeley. Edmund O. Pullen, 26, 2217 Pine street, San Francisco, and Lillian Davis, 23, Berkeley, took out a marriage license in San Francisco yesterday.

Accused Bigamist Runs Away.

San Francisco, July 11.—George D. Collins, at one time one of the most prominent attorneys of this city, but now charged with bigamy, has jumped a $3000 bail bond and in company with his bigamous wife, Miss Clarice Mc-Curdy, is believed to be well on his way to Canada, if not already within that country. Collins leaves a wife and three children in this city.

July 11, 1905

An Eloping Girl Arrested.

San Jose, July 31.—Hazel Melbye, 16 years old, who disappeared from her home in this city a month ago, was arrested yesterday at Sacramento, with Roswell E. Brown, a 19-year-old messenger on the Southern Pacific trains out of that city, with whom she eloped The boy will be prosecuted.

July 31, 1905

Sold His Wife.

Wilkesbarre, Pa., July 11.—Ige, Vino, a young Italian of Pittston, who sold his wife for $5, was arrested yesterday and arraigned before Alderman Redding because the wife refused to fulfill her part of the bargain. Vin was married a few months ago, bu soon tired of wedded life and bargained with John Sandy, who was in love with his wife, to give him the woman for $5. Sandy paid the money last week, but Mrs. Vino refused to be sold and Sandy had Vino arrested to get the money back. At the hearing Vino gave the $5 back and paid the costs.

1905

DANDY DRESSER DECAMPS

When James Graham, erstwhile proprietor of the Pantorium, disappeared from Berkeley last week, leaving a seventeen-year-old wife and a long list of creditors, it was given out that the tailor was going to Paris to prepare for the operatic stage. It is supposed that Graham gave out the information of his intended departure for the French capital to deceive the newspapers that published the story. It has since been learned from the young wife and her relatives that Graham left without informing them of his intended departure. They discredit the story of his alleged musical career, claiming that so far as they knew he didn't have enough money to pay his fare to San Jose.

Graham was a "sport" of the aggravated type, and for many months prior to his sudden disappearance, he was a familiar figure on the streets, attired in a well-padded, swallow-tail coat of loud pattern. On the strength of his family connections, having married the daughter of A. H. Broad, the well-known contractor, the dandy tailor managed to secure considerable credit among the business men about town. When creditors began to press him Graham slipped quietly away.

R. R. Graham, father of the wayward tailor, arrived here yesterday from Vallejo to ascertain if his son had actually started for Paris as had been announced in certain papers. He found the Broad family in a state of agitation as a result of the action of his son. Mrs. Graham, the wife, is heartbroken over the behavior of her husband stating that she did not know of her husband's departure until she saw his picture in a San Francisco paper.

Broad, the father of the deserted wife, is thoroughly indignant at the sneaking manner in which the dandy tailor left and he is not choice in his language when speaking of the disreputable conduct of young Graham.

September 13, 1905

MARRIAGE OF EDNAH ROBINSON

First of the romances of that unique organizations, the Sequoia Club, is that of its founder, Miss Ednah Robinson, and its president, Charles Sedgwick Allen, which was culminated today before the altar of Trinity Episcopal Church of San Francisco. The bride resided for some years with her family at the corner of Channing way and Piedmont avenue.

The marriage took place early this afternoon. The only guests present were Miss Robinson's father, Cornelius Preston Robinson, her sisters, Mrs. George Beardsley and Miss Helen Robinson and Miss Aiken, the sister of the groom. Mrs. Robinson, the bride's mother, who has been so seriously ill, was not yet well enough to attend the wedding, which was the reason of the extreme quietness of the affair.

The bride wore her going-away gown and the entire absence of formality was further marked by the fact that there were no attendants for either bride or groom. They left immediately after the ceremony to spend their honeymoon at Del Monte, and on their return to the city, will live on Chestnut street, near Hyde, where they have already fitted up a delightful apartment.

The bride is a charming girl and very clever, having written many excellent short stories and verses. She comes of the oldest and best-known Southern families in the city, being a niece of the late Mrs. Monroe Salisbury and of Mrs. John R. Jarboe. She is also related to the Thornton and Crittenden families.

Mr. Aiken occupies an enviable position, both socially, among clubmen and in the world of letters. For many years he was actively and prominently engaged in daily newspaper work, leaving that field to take charge of the Southern Pacific literary bureau and to edit Sunset, the railway's interesting and prosperous magazine.

WED ON SHORT NOTICE

Miss Edith Faulds Crawford and Theodore Johnston Ludlow were married hastily Tuesday evening at the home of the bride's mother, Mrs. John Crawford, 2435 Piedmont, after only a few hours' preparation. The haste with which the wedding was arranged and carried out, was due to a sudden call for the groom to go to Alaska, where he will engage in a large mining enterprise. Receiving word on Tuesday that it would be necessary for him to leave for the north on a vessel that sails to-day from Seattle, and, as the couple were to be married the latter part of this month, it was decided to rush preparations and have the ceremony performed in order that they might leave for Seattle on the evening train of the same day.

Friends were informed of the arrangement by telephone and in a short time the house was filled with young women eager to assist in preparing for the wedding. In less than an hour the residence was beautifully decorated in pink and green. A bower of feathery bamboo and masses of pink geranium was arranged for the ceremony. In the mean time, the prospective groom secured a marriage license and Rev. William H. Hopkins, pastor of the First Congregational Church was informed. By evening everything was in readiness, even to the guests, who had been summoned by telephone.

At the appointed hour Rev. Hopkins arrived at the Crawford residence and the ceremony was performed. Miss Eliza Lee Crawford attended the bride, her sister, while Richard F. Monges supported the groom. The pair departed almost immediately after the wedding, taking the train for Seattle.

The bride is well known in Berkeley, where she had resided for some time, while the groom is a graduate of the University of California with the class of '04. He is a mining engineer.

August 3, 1905

Matrimonial Troubles

Of a Former University of California Student.

The story of a strange divorce suit, involving Mr. and Mrs. William Hickox, the former an ex-student at the University of California, comes from Stockton. It seems that the marital woes of Mrs. Hickox consist of her husband's laziness, for the complaint that was filed in the case recites that Hickox went for weeks without washing his face and for months without bathing. She further alleged that she was made to attend to his horse even when she was ill.

The suit for a divorce was thrown out of court by Judge Budd who held that the infrequent ablutions of Hickox were not grounds enough for the granting of a divorce.

September 11, 1900

JOHNSON TENDERED BANQUET

Harry H. Johnson, the popular Town Attorney, will be married next week and in honor of the event about twenty-five of his friends tendered him a banquet at Bruel's last night.

The affairs was a most enjoyable one. Redmond C. Staats, Trustee from the Fifth Ward, was toastmaster, and presided with dignity and tact. To his right sat Attorney Johnson, the bachelor.

The meal was a sumptuous one and was done full justice. The menu was as follows:

Soup Thomasina,
Cracked Crabs a la Checkermills
Artichokes cold Secondward
Sweetbreads with puns by Merrill
Broiled Chicken, Onion club
Potatoes au Deasy-heater .
Green Corn from Cloverdale,
Ice Cream Coffee Nuts Fruits
Cheese Mineral Water

After the feed, Toastmaster Staats, in his most happy and facetitious manner called for remarks from those present. His witty sallies were the feature of the evening. All joined in wishing Harry Johnson a happy and a strenuous life with many "little troubles." Mr. Johnson replied in a very pleasing manner and after Chas. Mills had sung the "Holy City" in his best style the happy party adjourned.

Those present were: Redmond C. Staats, John W. Havens, John M. Foy, G. A. Wanger, C. B. Mills, Wm. Schmidt, F. W. Richardson, T. Donahue, C. E. Dunscomb, Robert Greig, Walter P. Woolsey, W. K. Weir, Walter Gompertz, C. S. Merrill, S. S. Quackenbush, E. L. Coryell, Thomas Turner, Charles E. Thomas, E. L. Brock, L. W. Kerr and Harry H. Johnson.

WEDDING IS KEPT SECRET

Without dropping the slightest hint to their friends and relatives, Stuart G. Masters and Miss Grace I. Shaw went to San Rafael on July 3 and were married by Rev. J. Ulrich, the Methodist minister in that town. On account of the absence of many of the relatives of both contracting parties the young people decided to have a quiet wedding, and they kept the fact a secret for over two weeks. They leave to-morrow evening on a wedding trip for two weeks.

Masters is the son of the late Rev. F. J. Masters, D.D., formerly superintendent of the Methodist Episcopal Chinese missions on the Pacific Coast. His mother and sister are now traveling in the British Isles. During his college career he edited the 1900 Blue and Gold and the Occident. Since his graduation he has been connected with a San Francisco morning paper.

His bride is the youngest daughter of Mr. and Mrs. Lent Hamline Shaw of 2224 Dana street. She is a graduate of the Berkeley High School with the class of 1905.

KEPT SECRET OF MARRIAGE FOR YEARS

It leaked out yesterday that Genevieve A. Peladeau of Emeryville and John J. Brennan, a well known business man of Berkeley, have been husband and wife for nearly three years. They were married November 9, 1902, and ever since that time have kept their secret safe from relatives and friends.

The fact that the young people are first cousins was the objection urged against their proposed marriage three years ago, when they told their relatives that they were engaged. They did not listen to these objections, however, but sent for a special dispensation from the Pope, which is necessary in the Catholic church, before cousins can marry. This obtained, they were married in St. Patrick's Church, San Francisco, by the Rev. Father Heslin. The bride then returned to her home, where she has remained ever since.

August 22, 1905

The Allen family of 1432 Walnut Street in front of their home. Charles Allen and his Rambler with Mrs. Belle Richards and Mrs. Allen. Circa 1910. Courtesy of the Berkeley Historical Society, catalog #1486.

16. The Bay Area and the Poor

How to assist the poor was a challenge as pertinent in 1900 as it is today. Private endeavors, often led by charitable women, offered temporary relief to the poor. Though the number of poor people was clearly a major issue, there were no articles in the *Berkeley Gazette* outlining government policy.

Gazette writers believed that the poor would be best helped if they worked for what they received. Inmates at the Marin County Poor Farm were made to work for their meals. Fields were established in San Francisco for poor people to plant and harvest their own potatoes.

Spuds for the Poor.

Potato vines may soon be growing in the vacant lots of San Francisco Philanthropic women looking to extend their charitable work have taken up the "Pingree potato-patch plan," and a big entertainment will be given to raise the necessary funds. The adoption of the project at this time is not the outcome of necessity, as was the innovation of Pingree of Detroit, but is due to a conclusion that those who need help can best be helped by allowing them to work for what they receive.

The social science section of the California Club will direct the venture. It is estimated that the potatoes saved the Poor Commissioners of Detroit $30,000 in one year.

October 3, 1900

The Famine Fund.

The following amounts have been added today to the fund collected by the Bay cities for the famine sufferers of India:

Total for today........ $23 15
Previously reported....... 928 10

Total $592 35

Whilst public interest is turning Indiaward in the time of her terrible need, we would like to call attention to the little boxes placed in the different banks at their main counter windows for contributions. All money placed in them will be forwarded weekly to Rajputana, the very heart of the famine district, where Miss Lillian Marks, a native Californian, the sole American representative engaged in relief work in that particular district, is located.

A box has been placed in the First National Bank of Berkeley for contributions from Berkeley citizens.

July 16, 1900

Paupers Must Work in
Marin County

The inmates of the Marin County Poor Farm are no longer to be allowed to eat at the county's expense and do no work for their daily bread Hereafter, says an ordinance passed by the Board of Supervisors, it is to be one of the conditions for entering and remaining at the poor farm that the inmates consent to perform any work set them by the superintendent. The ordinance also states that no pay is to be demanded for such work.

March 2, 1900

Her Holy Crusade.

Mrs. Charlton Edholm to Speak at Friends Church on Rescue Work.

Mrs. Charlton Edholm will again address a Berkeley audience in the Friends Church on Haste street tomorrow morning, her subject being, "Rescue Work." She is meeting with great success in her

MRS. CHARLTON EDHOLM

"Help-in-Time" effort to provide homes for the poorly-paid self-respecting factory girls of San Francisco. Last Sunday Mrs. Edholm addressed a congregation at Golden Gate and in the evening at Lorin. At both places the people were greatly stirred by her touching appeal. The Ladies' Aid Society of the Golden Gate M. E. Church will furnish a room in the home. Recently a wealthy lady of benevolent instincts has completely furnished the two large parlors of the new home, and help is coming from the most unexpected sources. One gentleman contributed $10 per month toward the support of the excellent enterprise.

Mrs. Edholm's time for the coming month is being rapidly taken by the various churches. Her coming always draws a large audience, and the effect of her inspiring words is to impel her hearers to a deeper consecration to Christian effort, especially in a practical work, for which she stands.

That Mrs. Edholm's work is beginning to have wide spreading effect is evidenced in the sale of her great book, "Traffic in Girls and Rescue Missions." They are sold everywhere. Twenty thousand have already been disposed of, and the demand is constantly increasing. No book has yet been written that is so much needed as a warning to the young people. Young men should read it just as well as young women. Thousands of poor girls are being saved from bitter mistakes in life by this timely volume, and ...

January 13, 1900

To Aid the Poor.

The school children of Berkeley are taking a great deal of interest in the boxes which have been placed in the schools for a Thanksgiving offering to the poor of Berkeley, and if parents will encourage their children in this work the Berkeley Benevolent Society will receive such a liberal donation as to enable it to make many a heart happy on Thanksgiving day. The boxes will be collected after school opers Wednesday morning.

January 3, 1900

Not Insane: Only Hungry

Miss Luzia Suquiera, the Portuguese woman who was taken to the Receiving Hospital from her ranch near Hayward on a charge of insanity, was ordered discharged from custody after an examination by the Lunacy Commissioners yesterday morning. Judge S. G. Nye testified on behalf of the woman that her dementia was caused by privations. He said that she was annoyed by her neighbors, who were trying to secure her small farm.

Died of Starvation.

William Kenyon Expires Alone While in a Hovel

Late yesterday afternoon Mrs. Stephenson of West Berkeley notified Marshal Lloyd that William Kenyon of Third and Gilman streets was sick and in need of assistance. The marshal lost no time in hurrying to the premises, Deputy Preston accompanying him. When the officers reached Kenyon he had expired, but the body was still warm. The shack in which the deceased had been living was in a horribly filthy condition. Adjoining the habitation was a chicken house. No food was found on the premises, but it is thought that the old man must have been demented, else he would have killed the chickens and used them for food.

Miss Stephenson stated that she had administered hot drinks to the old man in the hope that his pain would cease. When he became worse she notified the Marshal. When found, Kenyon's body was resting against his bunk. The remains, which were emaciated, were removed to the morgue.

The deceased, who has been a resident of Berkeley for the past ten years, dug clams for a living. He used to tell his intimate acquaintances of a prosperous life in his earlier days. He came to California from Indiana at the outbreak of the gold fever and the fortune which he acquired at that time was eventually lost.

This afternoon Marshal Lloyd and Deputy Coroner Streightif made an investigation of the premises, but could find no food upon which Kenyon could have subsisted. A letter, dated 1896 was found, which may throw some light as to where the deceased's relatives are located. It was also learned that some of Kenyon's neighbors knew of his destitute condition but failed to help him.

17. Neighborhoods Are Developed

The number of real estate advertisements and photos of Berkeley at the turn of the century illustrates one of Berkeley's huge growth surges. Mason-McDuffie, a powerhouse real estate company in 1900, developed entire neighborhoods, employing high-minded concepts such as curving streets and innovative landscape design. One of their lots in Berkeley Heights could be bought for twenty-five dollars a month with no interest or taxes due until 1911. In Schmidt Village, a suburban neighborhood, a lot sold for $150-$400. Payment on a five-acre tract was ten dollars a month. A neighborhood was considered suburban if the train didn't stop there.

The Newell Hendricks Company advertised land in Thousand Oaks around the Great Stone Face Rock. To attract buyers, it touted the area as an old Indian burial ground.

One ad summed it up well: "We Sell the Earth."

By 1900 Berkeley had evolved from a frontier to a town.

The Claremont tract is in the area between Russell to Webster Streets, and College to Telegraph Avenues.

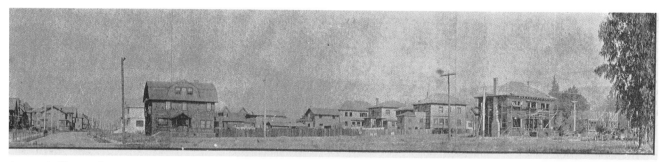

A view in the Claremont District. All these houses were built within twelve months during 1905-1906. Courtesy of the Berkeley Firefighters Association; photo from *Berkeley Reporter*, December 1906.

"And, as one splendid building after another is added to the noblest college site in all the world, although I am Berkeleyite and Californian only by adoption, and although my years and sex forbid me to voice my enthusiasms, in my heart I am shouting with the loudest of them: Rah! Rah! Rah!"

—Mrs. Alice Chittenden, *Berkeley Reporter*, December 1906

"What impresses strangers visiting here, is the artistic houses, as one lady exclaimed 'why even the rich have good taste.'"

—Mrs. Cleon Kilborn, *Berkeley Reporter*, December 1906

"Very few cities have so complete a system of improvement clubs as Berkeley. Their existence is attributable not so much to dissatisfaction with our municipal boards, but to the conformation of Berkeley as a city, spread out in separate stations, each with its business center and its own peculiar internal needs."

—Mrs. Elinor Carlisle, *Berkeley Reporter*, December 1906

Those Horrid Bills

For rent should cause every one to shrink with horror. After years of paying rent you have nothing but receipts. Why not build a home on those choice lots in—

BERKELEY HEIGHTS

MASON & McLENATHEN

Adjoining Post Office   **BERKELEY**

"It is indeed wonderful. Who would ever have thought to see the houses climbing to the very hill tops. I feel that it is a privilege to have witnessed such a growth and when I compare the Berkeley of today with that of yesterday, I am filled with astonishment at the result."

—"An Old Settler," *Berkeley Reporter*, December 1906

View of Berkeley Heights development as it went on sale. Courtesy of the Bancroft Library, University of California, Berkeley, photo #PIC 1989-055 D9-8.

BERKELEY HEIGHTS.

Otherwise known as Hopkins' Terrace.

THIS FINE tract, situated at the extreme northeast end of Berkeley, without doubt the very best portion of North Berkeley, having been placed in our hands for sale, we take this opportunity of calling attention to some of its extraordinary features.

Being at an elevation of 350 feet and commanding a view of every part of the bay of San Francisco and surrounding country, the outlook surpasses any scenery on the Pacific Coast.

It is only two short blocks from Berryman Station. The Oakland Electric Railroad has extended its line right to the property.

Two-thirds of the tract front on streets already graded, sewered and macadamized; and though so high there are no steep hills to climb.

For prices, maps and other information call upon

MASON & McLENATHEN

Adjoining Post Office   BERKELEY

Berkeley Heights was also known as Hopkins Terrace. It was located in the area between Summer and Rose Streets, and Spruce Street and the Rose Garden.

Panoramic view of West Berkeley. Many of the houses in this photograph were built within eight months around 1906. Courtesy of the Berkeley Firefighters Association; photo from *Berkeley Reporter*, December 1906.

"Simplicity seems to be the key note, and the glory of life here is to be able to go out in the dirt all day long with your oldest clothes on, free from restraints of fashion and getting the best out of life. Everything grows, thrives and prospers. It is astonishing to see with what luxuriance things grow. All of us can have a little patch of ground to make beautiful, to help us to better health and strength and so to contentment.

"But it was not a sermon I was asked to preach—only my impression—it is that this is the loveliest place in all the world to live."

—Mrs. Cleon Kilborn, *Berkeley Reporter*, December 1906

Schmidt Village is located approximately between Rose and Vine Streets, and Holly and Edith Streets.

Children playing in the Berkeley hills. Note the back of the arrow sign, which makes it likely they are in the Northbrae or Berkeley Heights developments. Courtesy of the Bancroft Library, University of California, Berkeley, photo #PIC 1989-055 D7-8.

View of Southern Pacific train on Shattuck Avenue near Cedar Street looking east from below Shattuck Avenue. Courtesy of the Berkeley Historical Society.

North Berkeley from the Cragmont area. Courtesy of the Berkeley Historical Society, catalog #1473.

"There is another practice recently introduced in building in North Berkeley which must in time prove disasterous to the commercial instinct that prompted it. This is the practice of crowding several building on the space formerly devoted to one. It may readily be seen that crowded dwellings, aside from implanting a city tenement district appearance to the neighborhood, are surely deprived of air, space and sunshine...."

—Victor J. Robertson, *Berkeley Reporter,* December 1906

Are You an Admirer of the Beautiful?

Where, in all creation can you see a more beatiful sight than the sunset at the present time of year? And where better seen than from the—

HOPKINS TERRACE

At North Berkeley.   REMEMBER—

First—Hopkins Terrace is only 800 feet from Berryman Station.

Second—The Telegraph Avenue Electric R. R. runs to the property.

Third—There are no back breaking climbs to reach Hopkins Terrace.

Fourth—Lots are for sale at reasonable prices, and on easy terms, by—

MASON & McLENATHEN

Sole Agents.

Adjoining Post Office   **BERKELEY**

Panoramic view of the predeveloped area around Stoneface Park near Thousand Oaks and San Fernando Streets. Courtesy of the Berkeley Firefighters Association. Photo from Berkeley Chamber of Commerce election pamphlet for proposed new park, 1908.

Marin Avenue below Arlington Circle, with trolley. Circa 1912. Courtesy of the Berkeley Historical Society, catalog #1499.

McKinney home on Alcatraz Avenue. Circa 1902. Courtesy of the Berkeley Historical Society, catalog #1483.

Ashby and Telegraph Avenues looking east on Ashby. Circa 1901. Courtesy of the Berkeley Historical Society, catalog #1507.

The roadbed of College Avenue before paving, looking northeast from Derby Street. Circa 1885. The white material is from the local Native American shellmounds, which was often used as roadbed or fertilizer. What is disturbing is that the local shellmounds are still being destroyed or threatened by current developments in the East Bay. Courtesy of the Berkeley Historical Society, catalog #1501.

Trinity Methodist Church at Fulton Street and Allston Way. Courtesy of the Berkeley Firefighters Association; photo from *Berkeley Reporter*, December 1906.

Creed's Farm between Rose and Cedar Streets and a street called Cypress. Courtesy of the Berkeley Firefighters Association.

Houses and farmed fields mix, as residential development begins to overwhelm the farming community. Circa 1890. This is the northeast corner of Dwight Way and Bowditch Street. Courtesy of the Berkeley Firefighters Association.

Snow covering the Berkeley hills in 1885. The view is looking east on Durant Avenue. Note the First Congregational Church at Durant and Dana Streets in the upper mid-right of the photo. Courtesy of the Berkeley Historical Society.

Looking north across University Avenue at the Santa Fe rail tracks. Courtesy of the Berkeley Firefighters Association.

New residences on Grant Street built around 1906. Courtesy of the Berkeley Firefighters Association; photo from *Berkeley Reporter*, December 1906.

Panoramic view of the Magee Tract in 1906 showing the hundreds of houses built within eighteen months. Courtesy of the Berkeley Firefighters Association; photo from *Berkeley Reporter,* December 1906.

"Where is the old McKee ranch? Where is the farm of the Poiriers? Where are the rabbit patches of this section? The answer is, gone, gone all gone and in their places are fine streets and homes. Homes, that is the word, homes...."

—P. F. Bradhoft speaking of South Berkeley, *Berkeley Reporter,* December 1906

"Where was only plowed fields and acres of pasture, are now beautiful streets and drives, lined on all sides with splendid homes, churches and schools, and nowhere in Berkeley is this change so marked, as in South Berkeley the 'Gateway'."

—P. F. Bradhoft, *Berkeley Reporter,* December 1906

The Magee Tract is approximately between Martin Luther King, Jr. Way to California Street and Addison Street to Dwight Way. Today McGee Street (note change of spelling) runs through the center of the area.

The Northbrae Development. Courtesy of the Bancroft Library, University of California, Berkeley, photo #PIC 1989-055 D9-6.

LA LOMA IS NOT IN IT!

BERKELEY HEIGHTS have the finest view in Alameda County. Only 5 minutes walk to R. R station and no back-breaking climbs to get there. Lots 50x135 $500; ⅓ cash, balance in 1 and 2 years. Only one block to be sold at this figure.

Apply to—

MASON & McLENATHEN

Adjoining Post Office   **BERKELEY**

"North Berkeley is next on the list. The Syndicate is soon to throw that property on the market. There will be a merry scramble, no doubt, when such is the case, for there are many beautiful building sites in that locality. How I wish I were young again and in the midst of this great activity! But, without drinking of the fountain of health, I hope to live long enough to witness the improvements the Syndicate still intends to make, for these are to be in the very near future; and in consideration of all that their coming has meant and will mean to Berkeley, I invite the inhabitants of our city to join me in giving three cheers and a tiger for the Realty Syndicate."

—"An Old Settler," *Berkeley Reporter,* December 1906

New houses on Shattuck Avenue in North Berkeley. Courtesy of California Prudential Realty, photo #G-2-I.

"But with all these natural advantages it is a source of wonder and regret that we have done so little to make Berkeley worthy of its setting. The early residents planted some street trees and developed extensive gardens about their residences.... The commercial spirit has taken hold of this academic village and great numbers of houses, with little or no garden adorn- ment, have been put up to rent and to sell. Every house shuts off the neighbor's view and many of our streets are adorned with gaunt white telegraph poles instead of trees.... There are no parks, no school play grounds worthy of the name, no boulevards, no concerted street planting movements."

—Charles Keeler, *Berkeley Reporter,* December 1906

5 Acre Lots
Berkeley Villa Tract.

Near San Pablo Avenue and about 20 minutes drive from the State University.

Prices Exceptionally Low.

For Maps, etc., apply to——

The E. P. Vandercook Co.
1016 Broadway   Oakland.

The Berkeley Villa tract was located approximately between Martin Luther King, Jr. Way and Spruce Street, and Eunice and Rose Streets.

Thousand Oaks area, now Solono Avenue, looking east around 1912. The large building on the north (left) side of the street is the North Berkeley Substation for the Southern Pacific electric rail line. This station ran one-third of the whole system. The Northbrae Tunnel built for the trains is now known as the Solono Avenue Tunnel and is utilized by automobiles. The neighborhood was subdivided in 1909 by John Spring. The Northbrae neighborhood, by Mason-McDuffie, developed on the southern edge of Spring's holdings. Development began only with the coming of these train lines. Courtesy of the Berkeley Historical Society.

The North Berkeley hills. The roads show rutting from wagon wheels. This view is from Marin Avenue and Spruce Street, looking north. Courtesy of the Berkeley Historical Society, catalog #1502.

ANOTHER BIG LAND DEAL CONSUMMATED IN BERKELEY TODAY

One of the most extensive deals in unimproved real estate that has been consummated in Berkeley for some months was closed this morning when a large portion of the University Terrace Tract was sold to Hansford B. Griffith and Henry H. Haight for $10,-000. Both of the purchasers are well known, active citizens of this city. Haight is a son of ex-Governor Haight, while Griffith is a prominent attorney and a power in local politics.

It is the intention of the two men to grade and level the tract and then subdivide it into ten or twelve residence lots. The parcel will then be placed on the market. In making the purchase Haight and Griffith have kept in mind the trend of home building at the present time. The University Terrace Tract, which is situated to the northeast of the University grounds and almost adjoining the Deaf, Dumb and Blind Institute, is hemmed in on all sides by new residences and scores of homes in the process of construction. The neighborhood is the special stamping ground of faculty members from the University and retired army and naval officers. The tract lately purchased is on an elevation commanding a sweeping panoramic view of Berkeley and of San Francisco bay.

There has been a great tendency since the beginning of the year to develop new residence districts. A few months ago Mason-McDuffie placed on the market a large number of lots in the Northlands tract, which they had recently improved and subdivided. The tract is situated in the northeastern portion of the town. In North Berkeley beyond Berryman station a large tract was opened last month. The Realty Syndicate is continually opening new residence sections in the southern part of the city and the same is being done in West Berkeley although in a much smaller degree. It is evident therefore that all portions of the town alike are being affected by this impetus of residenc building which is steadily widening the limits of this city.

"The simple houses of shingle, plaster and brick which have been built in various sections of Berkeley, and more conspicuously on the north hillsides, are a notable contribution to American architecture."

—Charles Keeler, *Berkeley Reporter*, December 1906

"In choosing a permanent home we seek that place above all others which promises abundance of life, stimulus, interests that postpone as long as possible the inevitable apathy of old age. Where do we find this precious boon more abundantly than in Berkeley?"

—May L. Cheney, *Berkeley Reporter*, December 1906

"Winding streets conforming to the hill contours, park areas, street trees, larger lots and building restrictions making congestion impossible, will develop the hill country to the north and south of the settled section in a manner to realize to the full the latent charm of the site."

—Charles Keeler, *Berkeley Reporter,* December 1906

"The Berry-Bangs, Hillegas Tract, Fairview Park, Elmwood Park, Claremont Park, Claremont Heights, Colby Tract, Oaklawn and Rock Ridge Park, are all graded, sewered, macadamized, curbed, sidewalked and otherwise beautified, and there is hardly an engineer, architect, or landscape gardener 'about the bay' that has not been called upon to 'give the best that is in him' in the effort to do justice to Nature's setting."

—P. W. Rochester, *Berkeley Reporter*, December 1906

————◆————

"The best Eastern architectural critics who have visited California recently consider these Berkeley homes amongst the most distinguished examples of simple domestic architecture in America."

—Charles Keeler, *Berkeley Reporter*, December 1906

One of the two offices of H. D. Irwin of South Berkeley, 3264 Adeline Street, Lorin Station. Courtesy of the Berkeley Firefighters Association; photo *from Berkeley Reporter,* December 1906.

"The landscape takes on a new look every day. It seems to be playing a game of now you see it and now you don't. Only there is nothing tricky in mother earth's anatomy, and the public are not having dust thrown in their eyes—unless it is gold dust—and the property owners seem to be getting a goodly share of that."

—"An Old Settler," *Berkeley Reporter,* December 1906

New homes being built on Deakin Street around 1906. Courtesy of the Berkeley Firefighters Association; photo from *Berkeley Reporter,* December 1906.

REALTY MEN REPORT
MANY SALES AND AN
ADVANCE IN PRICES

Although the past week has not been noticeable for any unusually large sales of Berkeley real estate, the market is steady and in many ways in advance of the business transacted during the previous week. The attention of buyers has been directed from unimproved property to houses. The great demand for residences and flats, both by renters and buyers, is the most pronounced feature in the local realty market, indicating a large influx of new families, due no doubt to the opening of the fall semester at the University.

There has been no lull in the demand for lots in the North Berkeley residence tracts. In Northlands the Mason-McDuffie Company have negotiated the sale of six lots during the past ten days. On two of these, houses will immediately be erected. In Hopkins Terrace No. 4, nine sales have been closed by the same company. In all cases the buyers were from San Francisco and several of them intend to build before the rainy season sets in.

Some time ago the Berkeley Development Company announced its intention of parking Bay View place. This work is now nearly completed. Enormous pillars of honeycomb rock have been erected at the entrances of the place, and sidewalks laid along its entire extent. As soon the rains commence, the parking proper will be done. This particular section of Hopkins Terrace now bids fair to become the choicest in all North Berkeley.

One of the notable sales of the week was that made by the Mason-McDuffie Company of the nine-room house owned by Kidder & McCullough on Hillegas avenue.

Demand for Hill Property.

Juster & Baird report numerous sales in the University Terrace Tract, five lots having been disposed of this week. In speaking of the general conditions R. B. Baird said, to-day:

"Hill property is demanding good prices and there is an unusual call for lots in the highest sections of Berkeley. We have disposed of several lots in the University Terrace during the past week and have several deals under negotiation. Another Santa Fe Trace, known as Number 15, has been opened in the southern section of town which promises to sell rapidly owing to the reasonable prices and good location. Its convenience to the Key route ferry line and the street cars makes it a desirable location for homes. The demand for five and six roomed cottages cannot be supplied. Every day we are besieged with inquiries for houses of that character but the supply has been exhausted."

Reports Large Sale.

Philo Mills, the real estate man, reports the sale of property on the northwest corner of Telegraph avenue and Dwight way. This property was purchased by Mills six months ago and its sale price was considerably in advance of the purchase price. "This shows a steady growth in prices," said Mills to-day. "We don't want a boom, but we do want prices to keep going ahead at a reasonable rate. Investments are good and general conditions in the realty market are favorable.

"We are practically assured a low tax rate this year," continued the real estate man, " which will have a good effect in all lines of business and will induce many more outsiders to purchase Berkeley property. We have many inquiries for home property. Some people say we have too many houses in Berkeley, but I have been unable to find enough, the demand for rentable places is so great."

Sales Are Good.

In an interview this morning Francis Ferrier said: "Sales have been good during the last few weeks as is evinced in the sale of lots in the McGee Tract, which is now almost disposed of. The Mathews Tract is also going rapidly and the Northlands Tract No. 1 is all sold with the exception of two blocks and a few scattered lots. We now have a good offer for one of these blocks, which is still pending. Several properties on Bancroft way and Durant avenue are being negotiated for. In fact on all sides there are signs of a steady growth. With the advertising Berkeley should received throughout the East, however, we would not be able to wait on the buyers. A good investment in Berkeley at the present time would be the erection of a large number of cottages of five and six rooms for renting. Demands for such houses are constantly being made and the real estate men are unable to meet them on account of the scarcity of houses."

VALUABLE BUSINESS SITE PURCHASED BY WEALTHY NEVADAN

"Berkeley has not been boomed. But little property is held for speculation. Purchases are mostly made for immediate use. …this growth rests upon a sound foundation. The writer, for one, does not want a boom nor does he want speculators to buy. The kind of investors that Berkeley wants are those that will invest themselves and their families as well as their capital, and to these it offers abundant opportunities."

—W. A. Gates, *Berkeley Reporter,* December 1906

Through his attorney Redmond C. Staats, Enoch Merrill, a wealthy Nevadan, has purchased a large piece of property on the southwest corner of Addison and Oxford streets, which it is understood he will have a fine business block erected. It is stated that more than $100,000 will be expended in improvements on this valuable piece of property. The land brought something in the neighborhood of $25,000, constituting one of the largest sales of local business property. It was purchased of Frank M. Wilson.

The land was secured by Attorney Staats, the deal being closed Saturday, after several weeks of negotiation. The property consists of 125 feet on Oxford street by 150 feet on Addison street. It is in one of the most desirable locations, being convenient both to the University and the business section.

Although it has not been definitely announced by the purchaser of this valuable piece of property, it is understood that he will soon have a handsome three or four-story business block erected on the corner, the building to cost in the neighborhood of $100,000. The plans for this undertaking, however, have not been prepared and Attorney Staats refuses to discuss the matter.

Although Morrill has been a resident of Berkeley but a short time, coming here from Nevada, he has already purchased considerable property. The future of the town he believes is very promising and has taken the advantage of opportunities to secure several valuable properties.

Looking east up Gilman Street from Eighth Street. Note the Peralta Park Hotel in the distance on the right. Courtesy of the Berkeley Historical Society.

Looking east on Hearst Street at Oxford Street. Circa 1890. Courtesy of the Berkeley Historical Society, catalog #1500.

18. Saloons and the Temperance Movement

"Berkeley, being a scattered community, has developed as many as four or five business centers—Berkeley proper at the western entrance to the University grounds; North Berkeley, Dwight Way, the corner of Telegraph Avenue and Bancroft Way, and South Berkeley. The conspicuous absence of saloons renders any of these places safe at any hour of the day or evening."

—Kathrine O. Easton, *Berkeley Reporter*, December 1906

"Now and then we find some one who is far enough behind the times to assert that beer is not harmful in its effects, and indeed quite a healthful drink."—Berkeley Gazette, 1905

Scientists joined the temperance cry against beer. They reported that daily indulgence in beer would result in a mental state akin to criminal insanity and cautioned that beer was the first step towards the use of stronger alcohol.

Temperance had gained momentum at the new century. In 1899 Berkeley residents voted to make their city an alcohol-free zone. Scholars and religious leaders spoke vehemently of the dangers of alcohol. They depicted saloons as crime incubators and were convinced the most dangerous ruffians in our large cities were beer drinkers.

Osbourne's Saloon, located at the southeast corner of Marin Avenue and Spruce Street, in the area where the John Davis farm was located. Courtesy of the Berkeley Historical Society, catalog #1476.

Saloon owners countered that their establishments were meeting places for poor and working men. They argued that those with means hoarded liquor in their homes and privately partook, while those with less means had to hide their public drinking from the authorities. This sometimes included the use of secret rooms in hotels. While there was no outcry against private drinking, it was considered a blemish on the city to allow drinking in public. A steady traffic of patrons came from San Francisco to West Berkeley where the saloons were highly concentrated. Those who lived near the saloons consistently complained of inebriated men prying at their door locks and urinating in their doorways.

Young men were the most likely to engage in drinking and young women were especially encouraged to join the temperance brigade. "If our girls could be made to realize the almost omnipotent power of their influence, it would surely cause them to pause and consider whether they are not, in a large measure, their brother's keeper."

While some Berkeley residents claimed temperance would destroy the economy, others penned long articles that touted the California cities that had adopted temperance asserting that they had quadrupled their economies.

Berkeley was a town with a mission. As the Reverend C.K. Jennis sermonized, "In our emphasis of the claims of the individual, we have lost that very valuable belief in social solidarity and social responsibility which we should have preserved as the best fruitage of the civilizations of antiquity....We teach a man that the city exists for his convenience, and as a consequence he does not make it the serious purpose of his life to serve his city."

While pro-temperance forces were given space to publish their views in the *Berkeley Gazette,* the opinions of those in opposition, most notably restaurant owners and barkeeps, were less represented. Occasionally the *Gazette* would publish a quote from a barkeep or restaurant owner, usually procured as he was being arrested for serving alcohol in his establishment.

EFFECTS OF BEER DRINKING

Now and then we find some one who is far enough behind the times to assert that beer is not harmful in its effects, and indeed quite a healthful drink.

For some years there has been a tendency toward praising it as a substitute for whiskey and other stronger alcoholic drinks—but the voice of science declares otherwise.

Up-to-date physicians are uncompromising upon this point—and declare that the use of beer is found to produce a species of degeneration of all the organs; profound, and deceptive fatty deposits, diminished circulation conditions of congestion and, perversion of functional activities, local inflammation of both liver, and kidneys are constantly present.

In appearance the beer-drinker may be the picture of health, but in reality he is most incapable of resisting disease.

Says the Scientific American: "A slight injury, a severe cold, or a shock to the body or mind will commonly provoke acute disease, ending fatally. Compared with inebriates who use different kinds of alcohol, he is more incurable, and more generally diseased.

"The use of beer every day, steadily lowers the vitality. It is our observation that beer drinking produces the very lowest kind of inebriety, closely allied to criminal insanity. The most dangerous ruffians in our large cities are beer drinkers."

The claim of Kendall, the national president of the Brewers' Association, that "the brewers have done more for temperance than all other agencies combines," sounds like the usual bombast from such sources, and holds about the same modacum of truth as their assertions usually do.

In refutation of this, hear the noted chemist, whose name is almost a household word, Baron Liebig, as he writes: "The whole purpose of brewing is to get rid of the blood-forming elements of the grain, and to trans-

mute the useful sugar into alcohol. We can prove with mathematical certainly that as much flour as can lie on the point of a table knife, is more nutritious than eight quarts of the best Bavarian beer."

The Chicago Daily News says: "The fact is, that the use as a temperance beverage is a delusion and a snare. It is the first step to indulgence in stronger liquors."

Henry Bach in 1830 England tried the experiment of "beer temperance," but found it a sad failure.

The attention of New York hospital surgeons has been called to the large number of bartenders who have lost several fingers of both hands within the last few years. Says the New York Mail and Express: "The first case was that of an employe of a Bowery concert hall. Three of his fingers of the right hand and two of his left, had literally dropped away, and he called at Bellevue one day and begged to know the cause. He said his duty was to draw beer for the thousands who visited the gardens nightly. The man seemed otherwise to be in good health. After consultation the surgeons told him it was the beer that had litertlly decayed the flesh of his fingers. Other cases of a similar nature often came after this, and today there are many patients of this kind whose fingers have been ruined by the acid and resin in the beer.

"Said a head bartender of a well known saloon: 'Beer will rot iron, I believe. I know and every bartender knows, that it is impossible to keep a good pair of shoes behind the bar. Beer will rot leather almost as acid will eat iron. If I were a temperance orator I would ask, What must beer do to men's stomachs, if it eats away men's fingers and their shoe-leather? I'm here to sell it—but I don't drink it —not much.' "

That beer shortens life, causes rheumatism, dropsy, makes one peculiarly susceptible to pneumonia and Bright's disease, and that beer-drinkers are the most unpromising patients—and the worst risks that insurance companies have to deal with, is testified to by surgeons innumerable, both at home and abroad.

Says Dr. S. H. Burgen, a practitioner of twenty-five years in Toledo, "The only safe course is to let it alone. I have told you the frozen truth—cold, scientific facts, such as the profession

recognizes everywhere as absolute truths. I do not regard beer drinking as safe for any one. It is a dangerous, aggressive evil that no one can tamper with with any safety to himself. There is only one safe course, and that is to let it alone entirely."

Surely the warnings of unprejudiced science should be enough to prevent any one from indulging in this so-called "harmless temperance drink."

M. H. C.

September 4, 1905

The Need of Young Women in the Temperance Work.

One of the greatest needs in all reform work, and especially in temperance reform, is the active co-operation of young women.

If our girls could be made to realize the almost omnipotent power, of their influence, it would surely cause them to pause and consider whether they are not, in a large measure, their brother's keeper. As one has said, we are all sowers, and "Every sower must one day reap From the seeds that he has sown.";

What then will the harvest be?— is the question which should interest us to an extent that will each day increase our desire to sow only that which will cause us gladness in the day of reaping. Surely we all want to see the time hastened when public opinion shall so support the temperance sentiment, that saloons and like evil resorts shall be forever closed. What seed are we sowing in order to insure that kind of harvest? We want the same standard of purity and temperance virtues held aloft and lived up to for brother man—and woman: this is what our Union stands for, is constantly working for, and will steadfastly continue to strive for, until

the end in view is reached, but all these so much-to-be-desired conditions can only be ushered in by careful sowing. And the field is so wide-spread, it takes many hands to be diligently engaged in casting forth the seeds! And in the hands of our young women is, in an almost unlimited degree, this responsibility placed. Your thoughts along these lines, your words and acts, your very looks when these subjects are introduced in conversation may,—yea will tell for all eternity upon the youths whose characters are in that formative state when they are most easily biased toward the right or wrong.

Wherever a Y. W. C. T. U. has been organized, and the young women have entered with any degree of enthusiasm, into its life, the community has been benefited, and a higher moral tone has prevailed. A young woman who wears our white ribbon badge and lives up to the sentiment it represents, creates a purer moral atmosphere wherever she moves, and unconsciously exerts an untold influence over the young people with whom she associates. Don the white ribbon then, dear girls—stand by us older workers in the field—bring into the work the life of your enthusiasm....

January 20, 1900

Anti-Saloon Mass Meeting.

The First Presbyterian Church was well filled last evening by those interested in the Anti-saloon League and its efforts to close the saloons of Berkeley. All other churches were closed in order to allow their members to attend.

Town Attorney Hayne in his talk upon the legal aspect of the prohibitory ordinance said:

"You probably know of the mile limit law which has existed since 1876 which provides protection for a territory surrounding the University. This left out a large portion of the town and about eight or nine months ago the people in response to a call voted to pass a prohibition law covering the whole town. But at that time funds to the amount of $2500 had to be met in order to carry on the municipal machinery of the town. To meet this some of our citizens came forward and offered to make good to the treasurer this amount.

The ordinance then went into effect. The people most effected by it were those in the west and who announced that they intended to sell wide open. For three weeks they run the saloons.

Evidence was obtained in a systematic manner and some twenty arrests were made. There are about eleven who have not yet been tried. The Supreme Court, after some attacks being made on the ordinance decided in favor of the validity of the ordinance and our court.

The State Constitution says "All towns and counties in the State of California shall have power to pass such local, police and sanitary laws as are not in conflict with any general law. Mr. Hayne cited the Pasadena case, which was stronger than ours, but which was sustained by the Supreme Court. It is a question now what the Supreme Court will do with the Berkeley ordinance. It is probable that it will be decided speedily, although there is a probability that it might remain a year in

First Presbyterian Church of Berkeley, one of the earliest churches in Berkeley. Courtesy of the Berkeley Firefighters Association; photo from *Berkeley Reporter*, December 1906.

the court. The storage law is along the same line, prohibiting the storage in any public place of more than one-half gallon of alcoholic liquor.

Prof. Lloyd then spoke upon the financial side of the question and urged those present to lift the debt of $250 now resting upon them, the debt which had been assumed by others to help rid Berkeley of the terrible curse of the saloon.

April 9, 1900

IN DOUBT WHO TO ARREST

None of the members of the firm of Goldberg, Bowen & Co. or their drivers have as yet been arrested on the complaint of Detectives Jamison and Parker for selling liquor in violation of the mile-limit law.

The detectives secreted themselves at the home of E. L. Coryell and caught a driver of Goldberg, Bowen & Co. in the act of soliciting for the sale of liquor and the next day detected another driver in the act of delivering the liquor sold. The Marshal's office thinks the case is a good one and have presented the evidence to the District Attorney and asked for a warrant.

The first question involved is, Who shall be arrested? The driver who took the order, the driver who delivered the order, the manager of the liquor department of the firm of Goldberg, Bowen & Co., or a member of the firm. This is an intricate question.

Another question involved is as to whether the sale was consummated in Berkeley or Oakland, and District Attorney Allen says that is a difficult question. The State law provided that it shall be unlawful "to sell, give away or expose for sale" liquor of any ...

TWO MEN ARRESTED FOR BEING INTOXICATED

Frank Manto, a Japanese who resides at 2118 Durant avenue, and William Davis of Golden Gate, were arrested yesterday for being intoxicated. Both were severly reprimanded by the Marshal and were dismissed as they had caused no disturbance.

Four Arrests Made.

Liquor Dealers Held for Violating the the Town Ordinance.

Another crusade against the liquor dealers began this morning when the officers arrested four of the liquor dealers for violation of the prohibition ordinance. Those taken in charge come from all parts of the town. They are Charles Wieman of South Berkeley, Mrs. Mary Thompson of the Thompson Hotel, North Berkeley, Charles Hadlen of West Berkeley, and James Landergan of the California Hotel in East Berkeley. Two of these are within the mile limit.

The complaining witnesses were A. L. Woodard and H. T. Reeves. They were released on giving bond for the amount of $250.

There may be other arrests following these

The cases were set for hearing on Saturday.

Raspiller Brewery, at San Pablo Avenue and Delaware Street in Berkeley, started by Frenchman Joseph Raspiller. Note Franklin School in the background. Circa 1914. Courtesy of the Berkeley Historical Society, catalog #1477.

PRESENT UNASSAILABLE FACTS IN REGARD TO THE "NO-SALOON" TOWN

While the question of license, or no license; saloon or no saloon is a general subject of conversation, is in the air so to speak, it seems not to be out of place to present a few facts in regard to some localities wherefrom all saloons are banished—and to consider whether it is not a good time to say the "saloons must go" from all of Berkeley.

Of course, we are all familiar with the cry of saloon men, and their patrons, that "prohibition kills a town" and this oft repeated falsehood has influenced many voters, who ought to be wiser in this day and generation than to lend their ears to any such falacy.

Now, figures cannot lie, so let us examine a few items along this line taken from official statistics of the Census Bureau.

"Nine counties in California lost in population in the preceeding years, every one of them a saloon county. Seven cities suffered a decline in population, every one of them a saloon city." The average gain of the whole State during the decade was not 23 per cent. The average gain of the prohibition cities was over ninety per cent, or nearly four times the average of the whole state.

The county of Los Angeles has a precinct option law that has swept the saloons from a majority of the precincts, and only three towns outside of Los Angeles have saloons. The city of Los Angeles has limited the number to 200—one for every 600 inhabitants. San Francisco has one to every 85 inhabitants.

The relative growth of these cities is shown in the following figures:

San Francisco, 1890, 298,997; 1900, 342,782; precincts, 15.

Los Angeles, 1890, 50,395; 1900, 102,-479; precincts, 103.

Our two prohibition counties are Riverside and Sutter. The city of Riverside adopted prohibition in 1894. The population in 1890 was 4645; in 1903, 12,000. Prosperity ever since steadily increasing.

Pasadena banished saloons in 1887. Value of buildings in one year, $1,200,000. The growth of Redlands has been phenominal. The other prohibition cities of Southern California have no show at all in our town. Twenty-five per cent of our residents are emphatic in their declaration that our business relations are on a surerbasis, and developed to a greater extent than would have been under the license system."

Another says: "The saloon had no sooner been voted down than the conditions were bettered in every respect, value of properties increased in six months more than fifty per cent."

From Riverside comes the same refrain: J. G. Rassiter, attorney of Pasadena, March, 1905, sends the following: "Pasadena has 16,000 people, among whom but few could be found who would tolerate the return of the saloon. That infernal institution was banished seventeen years ago, and today I do not believe that fifty people here would favor its return upon any basis."

Dr. H. A. Reed writes: "For years past business has been very prosperous. The same is true of Riverside, Redlands and Long Beach, all no saloon towns, while San Pedro, Santa Monica, and Santa Barbara—all saloon towns, are still troubled with the ailments of chicken-pox, measles, and rum-rule blindness."

Had we unlimited time at our disposal, such testimoy might be sought for and obtained from the 174 no-saloon towns of our State, but it seems unnecessary in the light of what we have.

The question that we are morally interested in and that is worthy of the best thought of the Berkeley citizens is this: It is not time that the saloons should all be banished out of this town?

Has not the license-ordinance been tested quite long enough? Can it be stated with any shadow of truth that Berkeley's twenty-three saloons is or has been of the slightest benefit to the city?

If, as has so often been proved, one saloon is too many for the benefit benefit of any community, and in an especial measure of a university town, why not make a clean sweep of all the nuisances at once?

The best way to get rid of a noxious and dangerous beast is (not to cut off its ears exactly) but to "cut off. its head, just behind its ears."

July 28, 1905

NORTH BERKELEY CLUB UNANIMOUSLY RESOLVES TO ELIMINATE SALOONS

A large meeting of the North Berkeley Improvement Club was held last night at the fire house. Victor Robertson presided and Professor M. E. Jaffa acted as secretary in the absence of H. A. Squires. Two new members were admitted last night: William H. Wheeler of 1418 Le Roy avenue and Dr. John Ginno. In behalf of the conference committee Victor Robertson reported that that body had taken action in connection with the cutting up of the streets by heavy wagons.

The speaker stated that the loads on the teams had been lightened but that the condition of the street had not been improved. Euclid avenue according to Robertson was being cut up in such a manner as to make night traffic perilous. The conference committee also considered the plan of advertising Berkeley at the Portland fair; also the "Knowles Tuition Law."

Bad Condition of Street.

The attention of the club was called to the condition of Hearst avenue, near Euclid. It seems that a sewer had just been constructed for a new house and the contractors in filling in the ditch had put in soft earth only, causing a sagging and sinking, making it a dangerous crossing.

Saloon Question.

A letter was received from the W. C. T. U. of Berkeley, through Mrs. M. H. Cartwright urging the club to work for a temperance clause in the new charter. At the conclusion of the reading, Dr. J. T. Farrar presented the following resolution:

✳ **Whereas the saloon element** ✳
✳ **has always been a disturbing ele-** ✳
✳ **ment, a positive hindrance to the** ✳
✳ **progress and prosperity of any** ✳
✳ **municipality, depreciating the val-** ✳
✳ **ue of real estate wheresoever lo-** ✳
✳ **cated, and whereas Berkeley is** ✳
✳ **a city of homes, education and re-** ✳
✳ **finement, therefore be it,** ✳
✳   **Resolved, That the North Ber-** ✳
✳ **keley Improvement Club most** ✳
✳ **earnestly requests those intrust-** ✳
✳ **ed with charter revision to elim-** ✳
✳ **inate forever the saloon from** ✳
✳ **any part of our city.** ✳

Victor Robertson thought that the organization should think deeply before asking the charter committee to insert the desired clause. Personally he stated that he was opposed to the saloon but he did not believe that North Berkeley should interfere in the affairs of West Berkeley. The desirability of saloons was a matter of local option, said the speaker.

Dr. Farrar moved that the resolution he adopted as the sense of the North Berkeley Improvement Club.

West End Should Act.

J. C. Wright believed that the agitation against the saloons should begin in the West End. If the West End wants saloons it was their business and no other portion of Berkeley should interfere in the matter. He feared that the insertion of the temperance clause might cause the rejection of the entire charter by the people at the general election. He believed that there was a strong element in West Berkeley against the saloon and it was up to this portion of the citizens to agitate the anti-saloon laws. It was suggested that the liquor question be submitted to the people, not as an integral part of the new charter, but as a separate amendment thus not imperiling the municipal instrument.

Should Enforce Mile Limit.

Professor M. E. Jaffa suggested that the West Berkeley Improvement Club might pass resolutions demanding the enforcement of the mile-limit law. He did not believe that it was the duty of the North Berkeley club to try to purify the entire city. Jaffa thought that there was enough work to be done in eradicating liquor selling from East and North Berkeley.

Mile Limit Law Violated.

Victor Robertson said that he had heard it stated that liquor could be bought in the mile limit at any time.

G. H. Street was in favor of having Dr. Farrar's resolution passed. He believed that the question was an all-important one and the North Berkeley Improvement Club should put itself on record one way or another.

C. A. Sherman was of the opinion that the saloon question was one to be settled by public opinion and not by compulsion. The resolution was finally carried by the unanimous vote of the club.

William Wheeler said that a post-office box was necessary on the Wheeler tract, where there was only one delivery a day. He said that he was voicing the sentiments of all the residents of the tract in protesting against the inadequate postal facilities.

To Designate Boulevards.

In connection with the cutting up of the streets in North Berkeley by the heavy wagons of the Spring Construction Company, Stacey W. Gibbs suggested that the Board of Trustees designate certain streets in the residence section of the town that are well macadamized as boulevards and thus forbid their use to heavy teams much in the same way as Van Ness and Golden Gate avenues in San Francisco are utilized. Stacey's solution of the problem that has been agitating the north end for some time appealed to the club as the proper and the following resolutions to be sent to the charter revision committee was unanimously passed. The resolutions reads as follows:

"Resolved, That the attention of the Charter Revision Committee be called to the consideration of an amendment giving the Board of Trustees power to designate certain streets as boulevards on which heavy teaming and street car lines shall be prohibited."

Favor Bonds for Wharf.

The subject of the contemplated bond issue also came up for consideration last night. It appeared to be the opinion of the majority of the members present that the bond proposition be brought to an immediate vote. The club was especially in favor of bonds for a wharf in West Berkeley and for the erection of a new town hall. On motion of D. E. Newton, the following resolutions were passed:

"Resolved, That it be the sense of the North Berkeley Improvement Club that the Board of Town Trustees hasten the matter of issuing bonds, especially with reference to the wharf which is so greatly needed in the West End; also that steps be taken to secure water frontage for the purpose of encouraging manufactures to locate in our city."

August 18, 1905

Community Responsibility.

Rev. C. K. Jenness Exhorts His Congregation to Uphold Prohibatory Ordinance.

During the course of his sermon at the Trinity Methodist Episcopal Church last evening, Rev. C. K. Jenness gave a stirring appeal for temperance. He dwelt particularly upon community responsibility.

The sermon, which was upon "Making the Highways Safe," is in part as follows:

In our emphasis of the claims of the individual, we have lost that very valuable belief in social soladarity and social responsibility which we should have preserved as the best fruitage of the civilizations of antiquity. The Jews and the Greeks and the Romans taught a man that he existed for the benefit of the city in which he lived; his highest duty was accomplished when he could serve his city in arms, in eloquence, in learning, in reforms, in righteous administration. We teach a man that the city exists for his convenience, and as a consequence he does not make it the serious purpose of his life to serve his city. In ancient Jerusalem and in ancient Athens they considered the young people growing up as a public responsibily, and they thought that the best good of the city was attained when they made the highways beautiful for the inspiration of the young men, when they kept them clean for the health of the boys and finally when they wiped out every corrupting influence, so that the boys might grow in virtue and righteousness. We know in Athens they inflicted the death penalty upon a teacher whom they considered as corrupting to the young men. In our day it is a reproach to parents to say that the children grow up on the streets; in the days of old they thought the streets were the proper place for the children to grow up, and all the best products of antiquity went to make the streets a fit nursery for the youths.

It is because we in some small measure have this virtue of a community responsibility that we all interest ourselves in the fate of the anti-license ordinance here in Berkeley. They tell us that it only shuts the front door; that a man here in Berkeley can store his cellar full of any kind of liquor he likes, while maybe the day laborer in West Berkeley may not have the means to buy in quantity; that it deprives the poor man of his social meeting place, and that on the whole very nearly as much liquor is consumed in Berkeley as before the ordinance.

These may be the facts; nevertheless we have a community responsibility. The trustees whom we have elected represent us and our city; we have a standard of righteousness high enough to say that our city shall not be a partner in a degrading business; if the individual householder stores his cellar full of liquor the city is not responsible. It is a question of responsibility for evil, rather than the wiping out of the evil itself. We remember that our Master said: "It needs be that offence should come, but woe unto him by whom the offence cometh." It is because we would save our city from the condemnation of that "woe unto him" that we talk and think and agitate and nag our trustees. If it needs must be that the offense of drunkenness still is possible here in Berkeley, still we have done what we could to live up to our community responsibility, we have done what we could to make our highways safe, we have come up to the help of the Lord against the mightiest evil of our day.

Trinity Methodist Church at Fulton Street and Allston Way. Courtesy of the Berkeley Firefighters Association; photo from *Berkeley Reporter,* December 1906.

DID NOT FIND PROOF
THAT MILE LIMIT LAW
WAS BEING VIOLATED

Marshal Vollmer and Deputy Marshal Moran made a raid on the Acheson Hotel last night under the assumption that liquor was being held in the place in violation of the mile-limit law. The result of their raid was submitted to the District Attorney this morning, but he said they had no evidence that would secure a conviction on the charge hence no arrests were made.

Marshal Vollmer tells of the raid as follows:

"Shortly after ten o'clock Tuesday night Deputy Marshal Moran and I entered the Acheson Hotel by the Shattuck avenue entrance. We met no one in the main room of the hotel and at once took up our positions at the two entrances to the room in which we supposed liquor was being sold. At the south entrance to the room is a door opening into a hall accessible from either the University or Shattuck-avenue entrances to the main building. The other door opens into the main hotel room. I took my position at the door in the hallway while Moran stood guard at the door leading into the main room.

"I gave three raps on the door and an instant later William J. Acheson, proprietor of the place, opened the door at which Moran was standing. Moran stepped quickly into the room, but Acheson was much quicker and turned out the electric lights. Moran then flashed a pocket lantern on Acheson who was in the act of emptying two bottles. Moran ordered him to stop and at the same time seized him by the arm to prevent him from pouring out the liquor supposedly contained in the bottle. Acheson then turned one the lights. Moran called to me and I entered the place.

"When I entered there were three other men in the room who gave the names of John Johnson, 997 Howard street, San Francisco, John Brown, 1024 Twenty-fourth street, San Francisco, and Joe Gomez, a driver for the Berkeley French laundry. After securing the names of the men we made a thorough search of the place securing half a bottle of beer, another beer bottle half filled with whiskey and a gin bottle partly filled with that liquor. The bottles were sealed and held as evidence.

"The room entered by us is fitted out in a manner similar to a saloon. There is a bar, a large variety of glasses, and other paraphernalia necessary for the mixing and serving of liquors. Located as it is in the center of the main floor of the building a room within a room, it is safe from any raids that may be made upon it. There are no windows to the room and the two doors are so arranged that it is easy to walk from the inside room to the main room, should the side door be attacked, or in event of the other door being attacked, it would be possible to slip out the side door and escape to the rear of the building."

Deputy Marshal Moran went to Oakland this morning and stated the facts to the District Attorney, who said no warrant could be issued, as there was no evidence to prove that Acheson had "sold, given away or exposed for sale" liquor in violation of the mile limit law.

Acheson Makes Statement.

Acheson was interviewed by a Gazette reporter to-day and said: "I had just blown out the lights and was going to bed when Vollmer and Moran came in. When Moran flashed an electric pocket lamp in my face I thought at first I was being held up by a burglar. When I saw it was the officers I turned on the lights as I am perfectly willing for them to examine my premises at any time, day or night. While Vollmer talked with me, Moran went out back and broke down doors and did damage to my property. Had he asked to enter these rooms I would have unlocked them cheerfully. Moran broke open one room which contains vegetables and other eatables for the dining-room. Another room broken into by Moran was occupied by an old gentleman, who thought he was to be robbed when Moran came into his room and turned on the flashlight while he slept. As Moran had no warrant, I think the old man would have been justified in shooting had he been armed. The little room in which the officers say they supposed liquor was being sold contains a complete stock of cigars and some soft drinks. I am not violating the mile-limit law and do not sell liquor of any kind. I do not feel that the police are treating me right in presuming that I am as bad as a murderer, and without a warrant or proof, to break down doors and commit damage, especially when I am willing to let them in. In the little room referred to I have a large refrigerator where I keep meat and food for the dining-room. The fact that I am feeding from fifty to seventy people at each meal shows that it requires some food to supply the needs.

Marshal Vollmer regrets that he was unable to secure evidence enough to secures a warrant and proposes to ask the Town Trustees to pass an ordinance making it a violation of the law for a person to maintain a bar and other accessories that go with the sale of liquor and to provide that the possession of such things shall be sufficient proof to secure a conviction.

The Acheson Hotel at the northeast corner of University and Shattuck Avenues. It was torn down in 1925 to build retail stores. Courtesy of the Berkeley Firefighters Association.

19. Milk, the Problem

A problem, indeed. Dairy farms were scattered throughout Berkeley. A portion of the Ortman Dairy and Creamery sat on the site where the North Berkeley Branch of the Berkeley Public Library now resides. The Such Dairy was located in what is now Strawberry Canyon.

Berkeley's dairy farmers found their livelihood under assault by a new force, the Health Department. Science was making great strides into the possible link of tuberculosis in cows to the disease in humans. The Health Department wanted to inspect and regulate conditions at the dairies.

Dairy farmers questioned the reliability of the tests and worried their businesses would be endangered if their cows were confiscated. They insisted on inspecting their own cows. A great debate ensued.

Who would bear the financial losses for diseased cows? Did experts even agree that tuberculosis in cows could be transmitted to humans?

"Would'nt you prefer to get your milk from a Berkeley dairy that's removed from it's herd every cow found consumptive? The policy of doing just such things has increased our business over 600 per cent during the last year."

—Varsity Creamery Co., *Berkeley Reporter*, December 1906

Wagon of the Berkeley French Dairy. Courtesy of the Berkeley Historical Society.

Cows grazing on Such Dairy, located in Strawberry Canyon. Courtesy of the Berkeley Historical Society.

HEALTH OFFICER WILL FIGHT FOR PURE MILK AND CLEAN DAIRIES

The conflict between Health Officer Reinhart and the Berkeley Dairymen is growing in heat with intensity equal to the weather.

Dr. Reinhart says he proposes to keep up the fight until the people of the town have as pure milk as it is possible for them to secure. The dairymen say they are willing to submit to all of the requirements regarding cleanliness but will not submit to the tuberculin test. This is the main question but the Health Officer says some of the dairymen object to the other regulations.

The dairymen have applied to the courts for an injunction to restrain the Health Officer from testing their cows. They fear such a large percentage of their cows would be killed that they would be forced out of business.

Health Officer Reinhart says he proposes to see this matter through and will do his duty without fear or favor. he believed it is dangerous especially for little children to drink milk from diseased cows and will require dairymen to submit to the test or refuse to grant them a license.

In an interview this morning Dr. Reinhart said: "Here is the list of dairymen who have refused to comply with the rules and regulations of the Board of Health. I wish you would publish this list every day and let the people know who it is that are opposed to the law. These are the names:

"H. Ortman, C. N. Metcalf, J. H. Davidson, L. R. Harrington, R. D. Shuey, A. Elming, E. S. Fenton, L. Comenzing, F. O. Lane, R. L. Spencer, George Stutt, F. Alexander, W. P. Kennedy, W. T. Such, J. Sabbate, M. Cassady, J. Miller, J. Roberts, Alvera & Lopez, Floretz & Bettencourt and Morgan & Parker.

"Here are the rules of the Board of Health in regard to dairies and I wish every person in town who uses milk would read them and see if they want to use milk from dairies which refuse to obey such just regulations and rush into court for protection. If their cows are healthy why do they fear the tuberculin test? Do they want the people to use milk from diseased cows? Here are the rules of the board:"

1. Observe and enforce the utmost cleanliness about the cattle, their attendants, the stable, the dairy and all utensils.

2. Any person suffering from any disease, or who has been exposed to a contagious disease, must remain away from the cows and the milk.

3. It is preferrable to keep dairy cattle in a room or building by themselves and to have no cellar below and no storage loft above.

4. Stables should be well ventilated, lighted and drained; should have tight floors and walls and be plainly constructed.

5. Never use musty or dusty litter.

6. Allow no strong smelling material in the stable for any length of time. Store the manure outside the cow stable and remove it to a distance as often as practicable.

7. Whitewash the stable twice a year.

8. Use no dry, dusty feed just previous to milking; if fodder is dusty, sprinkle it before it is fed.

9. Clean and thoroughly air the stable before milking; in hot weather sprinkle the floor.

10. Promptly remove from the herd any animal suspected of being in bad health, and reject her milk. No animal should be added to the herd until it has been approved by the Board of Health.

11. Do not change the feed suddenly.

12. Feed only fresh palatable feed stuffs; in no case should decomposed or moldy material be used.

13. Provide water in abundance, easy of access, and always pure and fresh.

14. Salt should always be accessible.

15. Do not allow any strong flavored food, like cabbage and turnips, to be eaten, except immediately after milking.

16. Do not use the milk within twenty days before calving, nor for five days afterwards.

17. The milker should be clean in all respects. He should wash and dry his hand just before milking.

18. The milker should wear a clean outer garment, used only when milking, and kept in a clean place at other times.

19. Brush the udder and surrounding parts jujst before milking, and wipe with a clean, damp cloth or sponge. If the udder is washed it should be wiped with a cloth until no water drips.

20. If in milking a part of the milk is bloody or stringy, or unnatural in appearance, the whole mess should be rejected.

21. Milk with dry hands; never allow the hands to come in contact with the milk.

22. If any accident occurs by which a pail full or partly full of milk becomes dirty, do not try to remedy this by straining, but reject all this milk and rinse the pail.

23. Remove the milk of every cow at once from the stable to a clean, dry room, where the air is pure and sweet. Windows and doors of the milkroom must be provided with screens. Do not allow cans to remain in stables while they are being filled.

24. Strain the milk through a metal gauze and cotton cloth, or layer of cotton as soon as it is drawn.

25. Aerate and cool the milk as soon as strained. If an apparatus for airing and cooling at the same time is not at hand, the milk should be aired first. This much be done in pure air and it should then be cooled to a temperature as low as possible with the water available.

26. Never close a can containing warm milk which has not been aerated.

27. If cover is left off the can, a piece of cloth or mosquito netting should be used to keep out the insects.

28. If milk is stored, it should be held in tanks of fresh, cold water (re-

newed daily), in a clean, dry, cold room. Unless it is desired to remove cream, it should be stirred with a tin stirrer often enough to prevent forming a thick cream layer.

29. Keep the night milk under shelter so rain cannot get into the cans. In warm weather hold it in a tank of fresh cold water.

30. Never mix fresh warm milk with that which has been cooled.

32. Under no circumstances should anything be added to milk to prevent its souring. Cleanliness and cold are the only preventatives needed.

32. All milk should be in good condition when delivered.

33. In hot weather cover the cans, when moved in a wagon, with a clean wet blanket or canvas.

34. Milk utensils for farm use should be made of metal and have all joints smoothly soldered. Never allow them to become rusty or rough inside.

35. Clean all dairy utensils twice a day by first thoroughly rinsing them in warm water; then clean inside and out with a brush and hot water in which a cleaning material is dissolved; then rinse and lastly sterilize by boiling water or steam. Use pure water only. Never allow cold water to come in contact with any milk utensil after it has been scalded.

36. After cleaning, keep utensils inverted, in pure air, and sun if possible, until wanted for use.

37. Tuberculous animals shall not be retained for dairy purposes or allowed to remain in the dairy herd.

By stipulation the suit of H. Ortman and thirty other dairymen to restrain the town from enforcing its new dairy ordinance has been continued till July 17 by Judge Ogden. Attorney Walker, who represents the dairymen, stated that Town Attorney Johnson of Berkeley had arranged that the ordinance would not be enforced until the court had made a ruling on the validity of the measure.

It is alleged by the dairymen that the ordinance is inoperative in that the last Legislature vested the power to regulate dairies in the State Dairy Bureau.

Milk and Beer

Flow at the Corner of University and San Pablo Avenues.

The street at the intersection of University and San Pablo avenues was literally flooded last evening with a deluge of milk and beer. The liquids were spilled during a collision of wagons carrying the fluids.

A vehicle owned by the Enterprise Brewery was traveling on San Pablo avenue toward Oakland while a new Jersey Dairy wagon was heading for Peralta Park at an equally high rate of speed.

The trouble began when both wagons, which were traveling on the same side of the street met at University avenue.

Beer bottles, milk cans, drivers and horses were mixed in confusion as a result of the mishap. After the debris had been straightened out and the conglomerate flow of liquids had subsided sufficiently, it was found that the shaft of the beer wagon had been broken while but one wheel remained on the milk conveyance.

BERKELEY DAIRYMEN EXPLAIN OBJECTIONS TO DAIRY ORDINANCE

The dairymen of Berkeley are up in arms against the local Board of Health on account of its recent action in demanding that the town ordinance regulating the care of dairies and the testing of cows, be carried out to the letter of the law. They do not object to the enforcement of the sanitary regulations, and a most rigid inspection of cows, but will strenuously oppose the carrying out of the tuberculin test, which they declare is not just, in that it is not demanded by the State Dairy Bureau, and would inflict a great loss upon them.

The opposition of the dairy owners has taken the form of a temporary injunction preventing the board from enforcing the ordinances. The injunction proceedings were taken by the leading dairymen who have combined in the effort to protect their interests. W. T. Such, proprietor of the Berkeley Farm Creamery and who owns one of the largest and best equipped dairy ranches around here is strongly opposed to that section of the dairy regulations providing for the tuberculin test. In speaking of the recent action of the Board of Health, he said, to-day:

"There has been some misconception of the dairymen of Berkeley through their action in securing an injunction to prevent the Board of Health from destroying our cows, which can be readily understood when the dairymen have an opportunity to explain their side of the question.

"In the first place this tuberculin test, as I understatnd it, was vetoed by Governor Pardee; and, in the second place Berkeley is the only town in the State where the tuberculin test will be made should we be forced to comply with that section of the dairy regulations. I cannot understand why we should be forced to undergo a hardship that is not enforced in any other section of the State. Furthermore, the State Dairy Bureau in its regulations does not compel us to submit to the tuberculin test, when why should a local Board of Health presume to overreach the authority of the State institution and make such a demand

"We, the Berkeley dairymen, are willing that Dr. Reinhardt shall appoint a committee of five or ten men, all of whom may be physicians, to inspect our dairies. We are willing that this committee shall visit our respective dairies, examine them from end to end and pass upon the sanitary conditions. They may also examine our cows, and if they can discover any outward indications of sickness, we will allow them to take all the animals condemned under those circumstances, and kill them. What we want is proof that our cattle are diseased before they are killed. I, for one, do not believe in the tuberculin test. It is my opinion that the test does not prove a cow is infected. All we want is fair treatment in order that we may. continue in business.

"As for the health of my own cows I can say that they are in the best of condition and any person who can find an animal among them that does not appear to be in the best of health, is privileged to condemn it. I raised ninety per cent of them and know they are from the best stock. They are always open to the inspection of my customers and the general public, and I am certain the other dairymen of Berkeley are willing to make the same offer.

As far as I have been able to learn, authorities have disagreed on the question of whether bovine tuberculosis can be contracted by humans through milk. When eminent bacteriologists disagree on the question, who then, is going to decide And, if nothing definite is known concerning the question, why then should the dairymen be forced to suffer? A case cannot be conclusively shown where bovine tuberculosis has been carried to a human, and that is why we object to the enforcement of the tuberculin test.

"Should we lose in our fight and be forced to submit to this provision of the ordinance, it will result in many old established dairy firms going out of business. Four out of twenty cows in the University of California herd, were condemned and killed. The State can, no doubt, afford it, but can the individual firms? At that rate, and where tests may be made at any time a man would lose an ordinary herd in a very short time, and to make the business pay under those circumstances would necessitate selling milk at the rate of twenty cents a quart. To raise the cost of milk would force consumers to purchase outside milk, and as these regulations are not enforced in other communities, the people of Berkeley would still be purchasing contaminated milk and nothing would be gained by the enforcement of these measures. The dairymen alone would suffer.

"The dairymen here, as a whole, are honest, hard-working men. I don't believe there is a city on the Coast where the dairies in and around it are in better conditoin. They are kept in good shape, and the owners are square in their dealings."

J. H. Davidson, another prominent Berkeley dairyman whose dairy is located at Dwight way and San Pablo avenue, and who is among those who secured the injunction, expresses himself as opposed to certain points in the dairy regulations. He agrees with Such in that he is willing to have his dairy inspected at any time, favoring the rules of the Health Department relative to the sanitary conditions of dairies, but objecting to the tuberculin test.

TO FIGHT HEALTH BOARD

Apropos of the suit which the dairymen of Berkeley have begun against the board of health, Dr. George Reinhardt, Health Officer of Berkeley had the following to say:

"The Berkeley Board of Health has been enjoined from the enforcement of the town ordinances which require dairymen to supply consumers of milk in Berkeley with a product that is clean and from animals free from disease. The following dairymen have obtained a temporary injunction preventing the board from enforcing the milk ordinances: H. Ortman, C. N. Metcalf, J. H. Davidson, L. R. Harrington, R. D. Shuey, A. Elming, E. S. Fenton, L. Comenzing, F. O. Lane, R. L. Spencer, George Stutt, F. Alexander, W. P. Kennedy, W. T. Such, J. Sabbate, M. Cassady, J. Miller, J. Roberts, Alvera & Lopez, Floretz & Bettencourt and Morgan & Parker.

"In their petition to the court for a restraining order, they say that the enforcement of the town ordinances and rules of the Board of Health, are 'repugnant' to them, the dairymen. No attention is paid to a possible repugnancy on the part of the consumer for dairy products derived from diseased animals. Experience has shown that where careful attention has not been paid to the health of the herds, from 15 to 20 per cent are tuberculous. The use of tuberculin to determine the presence of tuberculsis in cows, a test that is absolute in its findings, has aroused the ire of dairymen. An animal may be seriously affected with tuberculosis and and not reveal that fact by outward appearance; consequently tuberculosis is a disease that can never be eradicated from a herd without the use of the tuberculin test. The matter resolves itself into the question, Does the public wish to consume milk from cows affected with a loathsome disease, a disease which may be contracted from the consumption of milk produced from a diseased animal?

"The thought of using milk produced from cows known to have diseased organs and tissues is repugnant and it is well within the province of a Board of Health to prevent the retention of such animals in dairies.

"On account of the high percentage of tuberculous animals around San Francisco bay, dairymen have come to regard it as a necessary evil and one that can not be eradicated. The belief that the eradication is impossible is not true. Experience with the disease has shown that it is quite possible to maintain healthy herds. The present conditions of affairs around the bay is due to the apathy on the part of the owners, and, secondly, to ignorance as to the nature of the disease and the means of its control.

Women on a dairy farm in the Berkeley hills. Courtesy of the Berkeley Historical Society.

DOCTOR REINHARDT
ANSWERS STATEMENTS
OF LOCAL DAIRYMEN

Health Officer Dr. George Reinhardt has replied to the Berkeley dairymen in the matter of enforcing the dairy regulations of Berkeley. Dr. Reinhardt declares that the tuberculin test is an absolute means of determining the presence of tuberculosis in cows, and avers that bovine tuberculosis can be carried to man. He further states that pure milk campaigns are being successfully conducted in Palo Alto and Pasadena. When seen to-day Dr. Reinhardt said:

"The dairymen have long known that the tuberculin test is an absolute means of determining the presence of tuberculosis in cows. It is quite natural then that they should object to its use because they know that nearly every herd has some diseased cows in it. They sell milk for the money there is to be made out of it and consequently are very desirous that you should use their product, even though they know it is taken from a tuberculous herd. What do they care for the public health as long as the public is willing to buy their disease-infected products?

"The communicability to man of bovine tuberculosis has now been determined beyond a doubt. Medical literature for the past few years has been teeming with the number of cases cited. There have been several fatal cases of meningitis, which is almost always tuberculosis in young children, here in Berkeley lately. Probably the dairies supplying families would be found to be the source of the infection. In some of these cases no other explanation is at all possible.

"Berkeley is not the first municipality in California to insist on having milk from cows free from tuberculosis. Palo Alto and Pasadena are successfully carrying out a pure milk campaign. Other cities are sure to follow where the seriousness of the situation is once understood by the people.

"For the protection of the health of a human being pure food is a necessity. There is no argument to justify the sale of milk from tuberculous cows, milk reeking with pus and the disease germs, which pus contains. Such a product should seem loathsome to every civilized person. The use of milk thus contaminated is harmful, especially to children. In bottle-fed babies the digestion may be seriously affected. There is often no other explanation for the present of fatal tuberculosis of the intestines and brains of babies than that the infection is carried by the milk from diseased cows. It is extremely desirable that the sources of our milk supply should be guarded from disease-contamination and kept normal and healthy. A departure from this is a menace to the consumer and an injury to the public at large."

To-morrow the rules of the Board of Health in regard to dairies will be published in full.

July 7, 1905

TALKS ON DISEASE IN MILK

In a lecture on tuberculosis before a summer school class in the agricultural college of the University of California, Dr. A. R. Ward, the veterinarian, pointed out the dangers of diseased milk. He said:

"Tuberculosis in cattle and its relation to public health has for the past decade occasioned a most bitter controversy between dairymen on the one hand, and public health officials on the other. The points of view of the two parties are so diametrically opposed that it is seldom possible to reach a compromise at all satisfactory to either party.

"Unfortunately the dairymen do not realize the extreme efforts that must be put forth to fight the disease, or they remain indifferent to the whole matter. The experience in Berkeley illustrates this point. A few years ago the herds were cleaned up, but to-day there is encountered an opposition to inspection which indicates that the disease is extensively prevalent again.

"In the absence of laws empowering the slaughter of condemned animals, and in the absence of funds available for the remuneration of owners, some localities have undertaken to meet the situation by merely excluding the milk from diseased cows from sale in their locality. The efforts of the Berkeley Board of Health furnish an example of such a case.

"Tuberculosis is a contagious disease, that is, one which is communicated from one animal to another by the close association of the animals, such as occurs in dairies. Since the disease is really transmitted by the germs of tuberculosis, already referred to, and by no other cause, a consideration of the ways by which diseases germs can escape from a diseased animal becomes a matter of great importance.

"Since the lungs are quite often affected, the germs from the diseased areas are discharged from the mouth with the saliva into the feeding troughs. Where cows do not take the same stanchion in the stable each day one single cow so affected may spread the disease extensively by distributing the germs where other cows will lick them up. Where cows are in the habit of taking the same stanchion each day, it is a well known fact that the disease is first communicated to individuals at either side of the animal so affected.

"But the contamination of the milk is a matter of great interest to milk consumers. When the udder is diseased as it is in about one per cent of tuberculous cows, the condition of the udder is necessarily loathsome, and the thought of consuming such milk is abhorrent, not to mention the danger from the germs of tuberculosis with which such milk teems. It is an unfortunate fact that tuberculosis in the udder is seldom recognized by the dairymen as such, but is mistaken for garget, a common and less alarming disease.

"The only way to eradicate tuberculosis from the herd is to remove from that herd the last cow with tuberculosis, to kill the last ...

July 27, 1905

Berkeley Farms, Such and Nelson proprietors. Located in Strawberry Canyon. Courtesy of the Berkeley Historical Society, catalog #1478.

BERKELEY DAIRYMEN GRANTED INJUNCTION BY JUDGE MELVIN

Despite the untiring efforts of Town Attorney Harry Johnson and Attorney Redmond C. Staats, to uphold the town ordinances regulating the conducting of dairies and the enforcement of the tuberculin test, the local dairymen last Saturday were granted a permanent injunction by Superior Judge Melvin, restraining the local Board of Health, Town Trustees, Health Officer, Marshal and Food Inspector from enforcing ordinances 56—A and 357—A.

The motion to secure the injunction restraining the enforcement of the ordinances regulating dairies, was filled about two months ago when Health Officer Reinhardt announced his intention of enforcing the ordinances requiring the tuberculin test of all cows in dairies supplying this city with milk. The plaintiffs in the action were H. Ortmann, C. N. Metcalf, J. H. Davidson, L. R. Harrington, R. D. Shuey, A. Elming, E. S. Fenton, L. Comenzing, F. O. Lane, R. L. Spencer, George Stutt, S. Alexander, M. P. Kennedy, W. T. Such, J. Sabbate, M. Cassidy, J. Miller, J. Roberts, Alveria & Lopez, Floretz & Bettencourt and Morgan & Parkhurst. They were represented by Attorneys H. G. Walker and W. W. Moreland. Town Attorney Johnson and Redmond C. Staats, represented the city.

Arguments in the suit were heard Saturday before Judge Melvin. Regarding the validity of Ordinance 56—A, which provides among other things that dairymen shall sign a written agreement to comply with all the provisions of the ordinance, was declared invalid on the ground that it was unconstitutional, in that it required the dairymen to sign away their rights. Judge Melvin stated that after signing the agreement a dairyman would have no legal recourse for injuries to his business that might result from the enforcement of the ordinance. Attorney Staats acknowledged that the clause was unconstitutional, but held that it might be dropped and yet not invalidate the rest of the ordinance. He cited Supreme Court decisions to the effect that such proceedings could be adopted without invalidating the other clauses in the ordinance, but Judge Melvin held to the contrary.

Ordinance 357—A, was declared invalid on the ground that it did not stipulate definitely what actually constituted an unsanitary dairy, thereby leaving it to the discretion of the Health Officer to determine whether the dairy was sanitary or not. Judge Melvin stated that the Trustees should have stipulated in the ordinance the conditions that would constitute an unsanitary dairy, thereby giving the Health Officer right to condemn all such places that violated any of the regulations set forth in the ordinance.

The right of the Trustees to provide that offenders against the ordinance should be imprisoned in the County Jail in default of paying the prescribed fine, was attacked by the dairymen, but no decision was given. They also attacked the office of the Health Officer and Food Inspector, claiming the Board of Trustees exceeded their authority in creating such offices. No decision on this point was given.

At the conclusion of the arguments and the granting of the motion of the plaintiffs, Attorney Staats requested Judge Melvin to give decisions on the various clauses under dispute in order to facilitate the drawing up of another ordinance should the Trustees decide to take such action. In asking that the court give an opinion in the matter Attorney Staats stated that, as the ordinances in question had been drawn up by a man who is considered one of the most able attorneys in the State, a decision on the disputed points would be of great aid. In reply to the request of Staats, Judge Melvin paid the attorneys representing Berkeley a high compliment by stating that in view of the apparent close study they had made of the case and their knowledge of the law points involved, he did not think an opinion from himself on the disputed clauses would be necessary.

September 25, 1905

Dairy Under Ban.

Health Officers Find Morgan & Parkhurst's Premises Filthy.

Health Officer Rowell, of this city, and Health Inspector Pierce of Oakland have commenced in conjunction a vigorous crusade for pure milk. Last evening they inspected Morgan and Parkhurst's dairies at Claremont and found the premises in such a filthy condition that they ordered the firm to stop delivering milk until they had cleaned the place.

It is the intention of the health officers to make a general tour of inspection and every dairy that is not up to the standard of cleanliness will be quarantined.

The Morgan & Parkhurst Dairy owns 108 cows. It was found that the bovines have been housed in poorly ventilated barns and that the sewage on the ranch is bad.

The quarantined milk ranch is situated on the Claremont road south of the Institute for the Deaf Dumb and Blind.

When seen by a Gazette reporter this morning, Dr. Rowell said: "The condemned dairy is simply reeking with filth and the place is over-flowing with sewage from old closets; the stables are poorly ventilated and the place in general is in bad condition. While everybody will be given a chance to clean up their premises, we propose to have pure milk."

December 10, 1900

Berkeley's Such Dairy milk delivery wagon on Russell Street. Circa 1897. Jack on seat. Courtesy of the Berkeley Historical Society.

20. Medicine

At the beginning of the twentieth century, medical doctors, naturopaths and herbalists touted cures or claims for anything that ailed their patients.

Celery soda water was advertised to cure headache, nausea and nervousness. Buckeye vapor treatments and other steams cleansed the mind and body. Distilled water proved a lucrative venture, capitalizing on people's desire for clean water. Berkeley boasted its own distilled water plant at the Pure Water Company.

In Berkeley, Friend James extracted teeth painlessly, for free and publicly while his dog Teddy performed tricks beside him. Here resided Dr. Wong, an acupuncturist and herbalist, and Dr. White Wolf, an Indian herbalist who advertised that he could locate disease without asking questions or examining his patients.

In March 1900 bubonic plague was suspected in the death of a man in San Francisco's Chinatown and the entire area was quarantined. Local cases of diphtheria were confirmed on the 1800 block of Addison Street and the 1800 block of Shattuck Avenue, resulting in fumigation of one residence and the quarantining of both.

The latest medical research on tobacco reported the habit-forming plant slowed nutrition and was a functional poison that disturbed the heart and blood.

One of the first ambulances in Berkeley, used to rush patients to Herrick's Hospital. Courtesy of Alta Bates-Herrick Hospitals.

Made a Mint of Money.

"Yes, Berkeley people are easy," said the doctor as he puffed again on a Havana filler. We came here to stay one week and stayed seven."

The foregoing little expression of appreciation for the kindness of Berkeley people was dropped by the manager of the travelling Medicine Company that has been showing here.

The company has had consigned here no less than 1200 packages of their specials and carry away only two hundred.

Immense crowds have witnessed their farcical attempts and have' purchased the drugs with pleasure.

The company has a $100 per week show and takes in an average of $40 per night. The little sack has grown and Berkeley people wonder why the local druggists don't have larger stores, and it is no wonder when from $1000 to $1500 worth of "cure-alls" are vended at the loss of local dealers.

"With a merry good quaff to the health of Berkeley the artists leave the community wiser and poorer.

November 21, 1900

THE OLD QUAKER DOCTORS.

Forden & Winckfield are permanently located at 1068 Broadway, Oakland, where they are fully prepared to treat Chronic Diseases of all kinds by Electricity, Magnetism, Osteopathy, Hot Air or Medicine as the nature of a case may require. They diagnose disease without asking questions.
Consultation free.   *

6-14-3m

PHYSICIANS AND SURGEONS

Hubert N. Rowell, M. D.—Hours 2:30 to 4:30 p. m., except Sundays. Office First National Bank Bldg. Residence 1820 Fairview st., Lorin. Telephone North 26.   7-21-r

J. Warren Stitt, M. D.—Hours 2 to 4 and 7 to 8 p. m. Office (formerly Dr. F. H. Payne's), SE. corner Shattuck and University avenues. Telephone Mason 291.   9-27-r

Thos. J. Gray, M. D.—Surgical and medical diseases of women, electrical and X-ray work. Office, 2124 Center st., hours 2 to 5 p. m.; residence, 2216 Dwight way, hours 7 to 9 a. m., 7 to 8 p. m. Telephone Berkeley 793.   7-3-r

J. E. Shafer, M. D.—Office, rooms 14, 15 and 16, Postoffice building. Hours 2 to 4 p. m., Sundays by appointment. Telephone Dana 2432. Residence 2534 Regent street. Telephone Berkeley 445.   5-2-r

July 18, 1905

A Growing Industry.

Pure Water Is What the People Want.

One of the most thriving and meritorious industries of Berkeley is the Distilled Water Plant of the Pure Water Co. They have recently made extensive improvements and purchased expensive machinery and are now enabled to meet the demands of their growing trade, and are established on a solid business foundation with every element of success in their favor.

This company started in the fall of '98 in a small way, as the prediction of almost everyone was "you cannot succeed in Berkeley with such an undertaking." They believed otherwise, knowing that the water supply of the city was of such a quality that a purer article was needed for drinking purposes and that the people were educated and progressive and would sustain by their patronage a truly meritorious business. Their business has increased so that it became necessary in December last to enlarge, therefore they purchased the finest still manufactured. It is of large capacity, with some very important features not embodied in any other still. The aeration of the water by hot air while the steam is fully expanded so that the air reaches every portion, and the draft and open flue for the gases and odors to escape is especially valuable here where the water carries so much organic matter. It is of copper, fire lined throughout with block tin, every portion of which is cleaned every day it is operated.

They have also put in a fine large steam boiler in which they use crude oil as a fuel, in that way getting a steady, even heat, so necessary in making good distilled water.

In all respects we find the company flourishing and with a constantly increasing business which is creditable to them as well as beneficial to the community, as there is no article so necessary for the health of a city as purewater. They also have a large number of customers in Oakland and Alameda.

February 17, 1900

Vapor Baths.

The "Buckeye" is the latest and best vapor bath made. You can take a Turkish, medicated or vapor bath at home for 5c. We are also wholesale and retail agents for Quaker Bath, $3.50; McCreery's. $5.50; Buckeye, $6.50. Ferry Drug Co., 8 Market street, San Francisco.   *

For Better Water.

The Pure Water Co., of 1930 Harte, have so thoroughly satisfied the public with their goods that there has been an increased demand for it this summer. New boilers, stills and bottling quarters have been provided. A handsome brass still, that is so constructed that it allows a frequent cleansing of the vat is a new improvement.

January 6, 1900

A reservoir of the Contra Costa Water Company. Courtesy of the Berkeley Historical Society.

Outbreak of the Bubonic Plague in San Francisco.

Special to Gazette.

San Francisco, March 7.—Chinatown is quarantined by the authorities. Fears of the bubonic plague are entertained owing to the peculiar death of a Chinaman yesterday. The symptoms indicated the plague and it was thought wise to lock up Chinatown this morning. The Chinese can neither get in nor out. The case is under investigation today. Several are of the opinion it is not the plague. But the city was wise to take precautionary measures. There is little excitement.

March 7, 1900

PLAGUE BACILLI IN THE TISSUES.

Report of Bacteriologist Hall for Board of Health.

His Opinion Is That the Chinaman in San Francisco Died of the True Bubonic Plague.

Boston, August 15.—Bacteriologist Hill, of the Board of Health, completed his examination of the cultures received from Johns Hopking University sent to Baltimore from the University of California. They were taken from the Chinaman supposed to have the bubonic plague. Hill developed the cultures, inoculated white rats which died at the end of three days. After the rats' death the baccilli were recovered from the tissues and the results obtained were typhical of bubonic plague. Hill has forwarded to the University of California his opinion the bacilli were those of bubonic plague.

August 15, 1900

Dies as a Result of X-Ray Experiments

San Francisco. Aug. 5.—Mrs. Elizabeth Ascheim, one of the most expert radiographers in the United States, died at her home in this city two days ago. Mrs. Ascheim has been a noted experimenter with the X-ray, and it is stated that her death was partly caused from too frequent exposure to the rays.

August 5, 1905

ANALYZE A PATENT MEDICINE

A widely advertised and freely used patent medicine which is known as "Liquozone" has been under investigation by the Board of Health of San Francisco.

Dr. Ragan, the Health Officer, in his report says that the Liquozone is made up of over ninety-eight per cent of water and that such substances as sulphuric acid, sulphurous acid, make up the remainder of the bulk, with traces of formaldehyde.

The across-the-bay Health Officer further described the article as "an advertised nostrum purporting to be an agent in which free oxygen and ozone are generated and which is recommended for all of the ills which human flesh is heir to." In a formal report he went on to state that he had procured samples from local drug stores which has been analyzed in the department laboratory, and added:

"The analysis from our laboratory is in harmony with the analysis made by the chemists of the laboratories in the various cities where this particular subject has been investigated. Liquozone contains no free oxygen or ozone, but is a mixture of acidulated water. Water consists 98.69 parts per 100, while the acids used are sulphuric acid and sulphurous acid in proportions of .9684 per cent of the former and .2016 per cent of the latter. It also contains traces of formaldehyde. Its use, therefore, as an internal medicament is prejudicial to the individual health, and its use to any extent in a community, in the same manner, is prejudicial to the public health.

"I therefore recommend that the same action be taken in respect to this deleterious drug as in the case of impure foods—viz: That the Police Department and this department act conjointly to have it removed from the shelves of all dealers handling this drug, and that the selling, exposing for sale or giving away of Liquozone in the city and county of San Francisco constitute an offense, the violation of which will be followed by ar-

rest of the offenders."

The board approved the findings of the Health Officer and ordered that his recommendations be carried out.

July 7, 1905

"Berkeley Hospital Association."

Organization to Establish a Hospital in This City.

The "Berkeley Hospital Association" has been organized to establish a hospital in Berkeley. The incorporators are six prominent physicians and five laymen of the town, who are some of our best known and strongest business people. The directors are Dr. F. H. Payne, Dr. H. N. Rowell, Dr. J. S. Eastman, Dr. F. R. Woolsey, Dr. G. B. Hoagland, Dr. E. A. Kelley, Madam E. M. Paget, Major Gale, Frank M. Wilson, A. W. Naylor, and Anson S. Blake. President Benjamin Ide Wheeler is Honorary President of this Association. These people are willing to give their services, their advice, and their ability to the furtherance of this project, but they desire the assistance of the people of Berkeley.

Berkeley has needed a hospital for many years, particularly for students of the University of California who become sick or injured while away from home and comparative strangers. The new hospital will be a place where they can have their own physician attend them, receive the best nursing, and have many home comforts. It will be of most benefit to those who are unable financially to have proper medical care, and good nursing, as well as furnishing a sanitarium for the care of those who desire a hospital where they may be under the care of physicians of their own selection, paying the usual hospital rates, thereby assisting to render the hospital self-supporting. It is in purpose, therefore, a self-supporting benevolent organization. It is hoped that churches, lodges, and societies will establish free beds, and that the town and University will lend helping hands.

First Alta Bates Sanitarium started in 1905. Courtesy of Alta Bates-Herrick Hospitals.

In fact, it is an organization for the people—for the whole town—and will be sustained by the people and those able to pay for beds. All will be asked to contribute. Those who give anything whatever, interest themselves in and become identified with the building up of the institution. Benefactors are those who give $1000 or upwards, patrons are those who give $250 to $1000, life members are those who give $5 annually Any benefactor, patron, life member, or annual member will be entitled to one vote at any meeting of the Association.

All receipts of whatever kind, over and above the necessary running expenses, will be used to build up and develop the institution. It is hoped that everybody will respond promptly so that a building already in prospect can be secured and the hospital soon opened.

July 31, 1900

Leroy Francis Herrick, 6'2"and 250 pounds, was a leader and an imposing figure. In 1904 he purchased the Victorian mansion of Joseph Hume on the corner of Dwight Way and Milvia Street. He converted it into the 20-bed Roosevelt Hospital, named for President Theodore Roosevelt, a hero of Herrick's. Courtesy of Alta Bates-Herrick Hospitals.

TOBACCO HEART.

The Way Smoking Acts Upon and Injures the System.

Are you "learning to smoke," boys? Learning by heart—"tobacco heart?" Read what a doctor says in the Medical Summary and then enjoy your smoke—if you can:

In smoking tobacco we take in carbonic oxide, several ammonias and a very poisonous oil containing nicotine. The ammonias and nicotine are the substances which by acting in numerous directions are so injurious to the system. The ammonias act on the blood, making it alkaline and fluid, thereby impairing its nutritive property.

The stomach is debilitated and dyspepsia induced. The innervation of the heart is disturbed, its action is weak, irregular and intermittent, and faintness and vertigo are the consequences.

Owing to the disturbances in the blood and heart the process of nutrition is slow and in the young seriously affected tissue is paralyzed and vision is impaired.

Tobacco is essentially a functional rather than an organic poison. It modifies the special energies and not the structure. Tobacco is eliminated by the kidneys and very rapidly; consequently the bad effects quickly disappear under proper treatment if, however, the habit is given up.

VACCINATION LAW IS TO BE TESTED BY ATTORNEY PHILLIPS

A decided sensation was sprung at the meeting of the Board of Education last evening by a communication from H. B. Phillips, a San Francisco attorney, residing at 1311 Grove street, in which he emphatically declared he would sue the town because his daughter was expelled from the Whittier school on account of not being vaccinated. Phillips said that the vaccination law was a dead one, the "doctor" and not the "governor" having vetoed the bill of the anti-vaccinationists, and that he had a right, if the board persisted in excluding his child from the benefits of the public schools, to sue the town to recover that portion of his taxes which he had paid towards the schools.

Does Not Mince Matters.

The letter, which was written in a straight from the shoulder style and which threatens to rekindle the old vaccination trouble, was as follows:

"Clerk C. S. Merrill—Dear Sir: Referring to enclosed communication from Mr. Miller of the Whittier School wherein he states it is the understanding that I appear before the board next Tuesday evening. I wish to say first that the appearance may be in the form of this communication instead of a personal appearance, or in legal term, submitted on brief.

Expulsion Would Work Hardship.

"There appears to be a movement on foot to expel my daughter from the Whittier school. She is in the upper grade there at the present time and will have completed her studies in the school at the time of the holiday vacation this year, and as she is now in the middle of this last term, I would like her to stay and complete the studies of the term. As she could not take a like line of study in a private school to patch out the uncompleted term, therefore an expulsion would work a hardship on her at the present time, overlooking any sense of humiliation she would feel at being expelled through no fault of her own.

A Breach of Trust.

"I have written to Mr. Miller, giving him my views in relation to this matter and have asked him to submit the letter to the board, therefore, it will not be necessary to repeat what I have said therein, but will add, that I think I have some rights in the matter. The State, county and town have taken a certain specified amount of my money, which may be considered in the nature of an express trust, in the form of my share of taxes apportioned to the support of the common schools, by which I am granted certain privileges, namely, that of sending my children to these public schools. Should my daughter be expelled, I hold it would constitute a breach of trust on the part of the State, county and town, and an action at law would lie for the return of the money and also for damages by reason of the expulsion. This would begin by protesting the payment of that portion of taxes set apart for the common schools, as a basis on which to erect a suit against the town.

"Another view would be to apply for an injunction restraining the authorities from expelling the pupil, on the ground that it would be a breach of trust to do so.

"Save Its Face."

"However, I do not wish to make this matter public if it can be avoided, and will make this offer, provided the board thinks in its wisdom that it must proceed in order to 'save its face.' Let her name be erased from the roll of the school and marked expelled thereon, then I will pay the town or the board, the sum of fifty ($50) dollars, or any other reasonable amount they may fix, to allow her to continue to receive instruction for the balance of the term, up to the Christmas vacation, in the Whittier school, and in the same classes and studies she is now taking, as a special student. ...

September 27, 1905

Diphtheria Appears.

John J. Haberlin Down With the Disease at 1819 Addison Street.

John J. Haberlin is ill with diphtheria at his home 1819 Addison street. His residence has been quarantined by Health Officer Rowell.

It is believed that Haberlin contracted the disease while working at his occupation of ship calker. It is possible that the deadly germs may have been contracted while Haberlin was at work in the hold of some vessel.

Haberlin, who is thirty years of age, has every chance to recover.

In discussing the case Health Officer Rowell said this morning: "There is no danger of the disease becoming epidemic. What with an abundance of water for sewer flushing purposes, the town is in a sanitary condition. There is no doubt in my mind but what the germs were contracted outside of this city."

December 8, 1900

Fumigated the House.

Health Officer Rowell fumigated the premises at 1800 Shattuck avenue, this morning—the residence of Mr. and Mrs. Albert J. Coons, whose son, Albert M. Coons, died Wednesday of diphtheria. Since Wednesday none but members of the family have been allowed to enter the house. The physicians believe that the source of contagion originated in the unsanitary conditions existing about the house.

March 2, 1900

DON'T GET THIN

Get fat; get nice and plump; there is safety in plumpness.

Summer has tried your food-works; winter is coming to try your breath-mill. Fall is the time to brace yourself.

But weather is tricky; look out! Look out for colds especially.

Scott's emulsion of cod-liver oil is the subtlest of helps. It is food; it is one of the easiest foods in the world; it is more than food; it helps you digest your food, and get more nutriment from it.

Don't get thin, there is safety in plumpness. Man woman and child.

21. Powder Mills

At the northwest base of what we know as Albany Hill was the nitroglycerin house of the Judson Dynamite and Powder Works. It was shortly after noon on August 16, 1905, and Will Edris was puttering around, alone, after his shift. He fixed machinery and just . . . well, puttered. He was a bachelor . . . BOOOOOMMMMMMMMMM!!!

A sudden and enormous explosion rocked Berkeley and the East Bay, shattering windows from Oakland to Point Richmond. Judson Dynamite and Powder Works' nitroglycerin house exploded, sending flames jetting into the sky with a force that rocked Berkeley. Forty-two hundred pounds of nitro mixture were torn to atoms and our putterer, William Edris, lay dead in the wreckage.

Flaming debris fell from the sky and lit the dry grass. The fires headed briskly for the dynamite house. Scores of men fought the fires. Yellow and black acrid smoke shot into the sky like a demonic spirit. Behind the clearing smoke, charcoal-covered men engaged in a Herculean battle. Police rushed to the scene to keep residents clear of danger. Wives, children and friends hurried to the site fearing they had lost loved ones.

The Judson Shepard Acid Works at Point Cordonices Lagoon after an 1891 explosion. This area is where Cordonices Creek was blocked by sand from emptying into the Bay and formed a lagoon. Louis Stein had said it was teeming with crawdads and crabs. It was destroyed by the building of roads and the freeway. The lagoon and acid works are now gone, but Fleming Point remains as the Albany Race Track. Courtesy of the Berkeley Firefighters Association.

In less than a week, Judson Dynamite and Powder Works was operating in its new quarters at Point Isabel. The plant was preparing to merge with the Vigorite Dynamite Company. The men returned to their jobs mixing nitro and powder. As they handled these volatile chemicals their thoughts likely returned to William Edris, the sole casualty of the previous week's disaster.

Despite the danger, men needed jobs and the powder mill trade attracted young men from Europe and China. The Chinese were particularly adept in the field but were hired as workers rather than foremen. In an explosion at the Giant Powder Works near Sobrante seven Chinese workers and one white foreman were killed. The name of the foreman was immediately known but it was several days before the identities of the Chinese men killed in the accident were available.

Explosions were an accepted part of life in the East Bay. Trees were planted on and around Albany Hill as explosion breaks, helping to protect the surrounding town. During the summer of 1905 there were similar accidents in Berkeley and Richmond. Regrettably, nine men died in these blasts.

The Acid Works in the aftermath of an explosion at the Powder Works to the north. Courtesy of the Berkeley Firefighters Association.

The first explosion at the Judson Dynamite and Powder Company at 12:45 p.m., August 16, 1905. This photo shows the explosion at the nitroglycerin house. The explosion was felt from Oakland to Point Richmond. Courtesy of the Berkeley Firefighters Association.

The second explosion at the Judson Dynamite and Powder Company at 2:30 p.m., August 16, 1905. This explosion at the dynamite house was started from cinders from the first explosion. Courtesy of the Berkeley Firefighters Association.

CHARRED REMAINS OF WM. EDRIS FOUND IN POWDER MILL RUINS

As a result of two explosions yesterday afternoon at the Judson Dynamite and Powder works, near the bay shore, two miles north of West Berkeley, William E. Edris, who resided on Fifth street, near Jones, in the West End, was killed, several Chinese laborers injured and a number of buildings demolished.

The charred remains of Edris were not found until this morning, as the great heat and danger made it impossible to search the ground about the wrecked buildings until to-day. Although the body was burned beyond recognition it has, through some mysterious manner escaped being torn to atoms by the terrible explosion.

Edris was foreman of the nitro-glycerine house, the first to go. The dynamite mixing-house, which exploded later, was also demolished. Minor damage was done about the works, while the shocks from the upheavals were felt for miles around San Francisco bay, many windows being shattered through Oakland, Berkleey and as far north as Point Richmond.

First Explosion.

Edris was in the glycerine-house when it blew up. Albert E. Olsen, who resides at 1529 Sixth street, was 200 feet distant examining tanks of soda, and he was struck by flying debris, being seriously cut on the head and the arm. A miraculous escape was that of Jim Ezro, driver of a dynamite car, which stood partly loaded on a track near the glycerine-house. The car and its contents were toppled over, but Ezro was not scratched, nor was old "Dan," the horse, a veteran of several explosions at the works.

The Chinamen who were hurt by debris were either in the dynamite mixing house or just outside. A heavy piece of lead was driven into the shoulder of one of them, but none of them were fatally hurt.

The nitro-glycerine house blew up at 12:50 o'clock yesterday afternoon, shortly after the material for the day's run had been worked up. It was stored mixing tubs ready to b

delivered at the mixing house for manufacture into dynamite.

Herman Felix, the helper in the glycerine-house, who also lives in West Berkeley, had cleaned up his work, leaving Foreman Edris alone in the place. For years it had been Edris' custom to remain there and potter about, examining the machinery and making repairs. With a sudden roar, a great volume of smoke shot upward, the boom and crash of explosion followed in an instant, a big jet of flame leaped into the air, and the glycerine house was gone, with 4200 pounds of the mixture.

Fire Is Scattered.

Burnish brands flew over the works, setting fire to the grass on the hillside, on shelves of which the various houses were built. Flaming debris set fire to the dynamite mixing-house. Men from all departments hastened to the scene to fight the spreading flames. There was danger of instant death every minute. Superintendent L. N. Nielsen set guards out to give ample warning, and it was the careful precautions then taken that averted a serious loss of life when the second explosion occurred.

The dynamite mixing-house exploded at 2:45 o'clock, almost exactly two hours after the first blow-up. In this house, which had been abandoned when the glycerine plant was destroyed, were 2000 pounds of dynamite and 2800 pounds of nitro-glycerine. On the hilltops in the dry grass were scores of men fire-fighting, and not a few more hardy spirits were in the open fields north of the houses. Again there was a cloud of smoke, a roar and a solid body of flame marking the destruction of the mixing-house. Newspaper men who were busy collecting details of the first explosion were shaken up by the concussion, but none of them, nor any employes of the works, were injured.

Fire continued to spread through the dry, grassy hillsides into the underbrush. Big gangs of men were sent out and after a hard battle got the

fire under control and saved further loss to the property.

Remove Explosives.

As soon as the glycerine-house had exploded a large quantity of dynamite stored in a packing-house near by was removed to a place of comparative safety. Four loaded cars of dynamite that stood on the Southern Pacific Company tracks close to the works were quickly hauled away, a switch engine crew from Oakland being hurried to the station. These were out of the way just after the second explosion had torn a great hole in the hill-side leaving only a blackened acid-burned waste of debris to mark the s——. The removal of these laden ——— great relief to the men at —, the dynamite there being in sufficient quantity to seriously endanger the lives of employes who were scattered all through the grounds.

Superintendent Nielsen, who resides in North Berkeley, took charge of the fire and rescue brigade as soon as the explosion's first shock had warned the works. In the first round-up several men were missed, but all were finally accounted for but Edris.

Physicians Arrive.

Dr. F. R. Woolsey from West Berkeley and Dr. Blake from Point Richmond were on the scene, summoned with all haste. They dressed the injuries of the men who were hurt and remained at the works until after the investigation proved that none had been hurt in the second blow-up. The fire-fighters were warned to keep as far away as possible from the dynamite mixing-house, which was slowly burning. In the debris about the houses were small tanks of glycerine. These burst with sharp reports, signals of the impending crash that should wreck the dynamite-house. Smoke, yellow and black from the acids, rose in dense columns for house afterward from the mess of wreckage, while through it were occasionally silhouetted the grimy forms of men beating back the running fire that was blackening the hill.

The mixing-plant proper and its auxiliary apparatus, tanks, oil tubes and the like face the north and were on the side of the knob-like hill that stands between the San Pablo road and the Southern Pacific Company's tracks. The plant is at the dividing line between Alameda and Contra Costa counties, the works being just across in Contra Costa.

Estimate of Loss.

The nitro-glycerine house, containing three mixing tubs, stood above the other house. To the east a little below was the dynamite-house. Beyond to the west is an abandoned black powder house, still farther west is the dynamite packing-house. There are small outbuildings connect. each these. To guard against spread of fire the grass around the buildings had been cleared and only bare ground surrounded them for some distance. But the debris carried over the hillside and lighting on the dynamite-house, set it afire. Great tanks of water on the top of the hill above the mixing houses were opened after the glycerine-house exploded, but on account of the extreme danger Superintendent Nielsen would not permit his men to get too near to direct the water to the dynamite-house. After that went up better work could be done in checking he spreak of fire. On the bay side of the hill stood large batteries of tanks containing nitric and sulphuric acid. These were emptied of their contents, while the grass fire was working over the crest of the hill towards the tanks. Manager Penniman estimated the loss to the works by the explosion at $7000. This includes the destruction of the houses, apparatus and loss of exploded material. It is a conservative figure.

Berkeley Officers Assist.

Immediately after the first explosion, a number of deputy constables from Berkeley rushed to the scene and assisted in keeping spectators from approaching the buildings. Among them were William H. Atchison, William H. Atchison Jr., and W. B. Pickett. When the second explosion occurred Pickett was laid out by the concussion but escaped injury. Atchison Sr., was lying on the ground when the explosion occurred and escaped being knocked down. With him was J. J. Lewis of Amador county, who was struck on the temple by a flying piece of lead which caused a serious gash of several inches.

E. Ingals of West Berkeley and Town Auditor Thomas Turner were also knocked down by the terrible force of the explosion. Both, however, received only minor bruises.

Turned, Ingals, R. Kruger and H. S. Scott, were the only outsiders near the mixing building when it was blown up.

Tells of Explosion.

Manager Peniman made the following statement:

"The explosion in the nitro-glycerine house did not occur until after the work of the day had been completed. The fluid had been mixed and all of the nitro-glycerine had been neutralized and subjected to the second test that is always made before it is run to the dynamite mixing-house. Foreman Edris remained in the building to clear up things for the day. The explosion, which cannot be explained, set fire to the dynamite mixing-house. The fire exploded a small quantity of dynamite, which causes the second big explosion. So far as we have been able to discover the nitro-glycerine house was in order when Felix left, shortly before the blow-up. The death of Edris is a sad loss. He was held in high esteem.

August 17, 1905

The gang from the Acid Works, also known as the Sulfur Works and Chemical Works, on Fleming Point, currently property of the Albany Race Track. The Chinese worked in "Nida Cake" and filled bottles with sulfuric and nitric acid. The man in front of the horse named Chubby is his driver, Mr. Stanton. The boss is Richard Trenoth (#5) with his baby George on his lap, who died early in life. Courtesy of the Berkeley Historical Society, catalog #1493.

ONLY ONE WAS KILLED

San Francisco, Aug. 18.—The terrific explosions of nitro-glycerine at the Judson Powder and Dynamite Works on Wednesday, near Point Isabel, were not as fatal as was at first supposed, a careful muster of the employes at the works revealing the fact that but one man was killed, William Edris.

The other two men reported killed Olaf Olson and Herman Felix, are alive, although badly wounded by flying debris.

Six Chinese, all members of the Ah family, were hurt, and one of them, Ah Lin, may die .

The fatalities would have undoubtedly have been more numerous had the explosion taken place ten minutes later, when all the employes had returned from their luncheons. As it was, few people were around the works at the time, and to this many escapes are attributed.

The loss sustained by the explosions is estimated at many thousands of dollars. As there was no insurance on the powder plant, it is thought that it will take between $30,000 and $40,000 to make good the loss. Many tons of dynamite and nitro-glycerine were exploded, but many tons more escaped.

The big magazine on the hill back of the works contained about twenty tons of dynamite, while 150 tons were packed in a train of cars on a railroad switch nearby. Both of these huge quantities of high explosive remain intact.

The second explosion, taking place at 2:47 p. m., was even more violent than the first and was due to flames caused by the first explosion reaching the big nitro-glycerine tanks, about 100 yards from the scene of the first explosion.

Edris was killed by the first explosion. He was literally blown to pieces.

August 18, 1905

JUDSON PLANT IS WRECKED

NOBLE STATION, August 16.—A terrible explosion occurred at seven minutes past one this afternoon at the Judson Dynamite and Powder Works, which completely wrecked the nitro-glycerine department and partially injured all the buildings at the plant. Three white men and two Chinese were injured, one of the latter having his leg torn from his body. Of the white men, Alex Olsen received the worst injuries, a chip of flying wood having struck him on the side of the head. Olsen was not rendered unconscious by the blow but walked about bleeding profusely. The other men were injured slightly chiefly from flying pieces of wood. H. Felix and W. R. Edris of West Berkeley were slightly injured.

That more men were not hurt was due to the fact that the employes on the afternoon shift had not yet begun working, but were approaching the building when the explosion occurred. The nitro-glycerine building was completely ruined, nothing being left but a small portion of the foundation stones. The roof and walls of the dynamite building that contained over fifty tons of the explosive were torn assunder by the shock but through some freak of fate, the dynamite was not exploded. The roof of the mixing plant was hurled off, and every structure on the grounds was badly injured. In the vicinity of the nitro-glycerine building large holes were torn in the ground.

Explosion Felt Here.

The shock of the explosion was distinctly felt in San Francisco, causing the larger buildings to tremble as if from an earthquake. In West Berkeley the reverbration caused considerable fright. Several panes of glass were shattered and dwellings were ̃dly shaken up. In East Berkeley ere was a short, quick shock. Many of the citizens climbed to the top of the National Bank Building, from

where a mass of vari-colored flames could be seen leaping upward. The sight was a beautⁱ̶f̶u̶l̶̶̶a̶n̶d̶̶̶t̶e̶m̶p̶t̶i̶n̶g̶ one. The windows̶̶i̶n̶̶t̶h̶e̶ building shivered and bent and it is almost remarkable that they were not cracked.

Second Explosion.

At 2:47 a second explosion occurred, ̶ ̶ ̶ ̶t of damage is not learned to press.

Deaths Reported.

p. m.—It is reported that two ̶e re killed in the first explosion, many spectators injured ...

MANUFACTURE OF DYNAMITE IS RESUMED

The Judson Dynamite and Powder Company has so far recovered from the effects of the big explosion of last Wednesday as to resume the manufacture of dynamite. The work is being carried on at Point Isabel, on the bay short, a mile from the site of the destroyed buildings. The company is preparing to amalgamate the dynamite plant with the Vigorite works.

Herman Felix and Olaf Olsen, employes of the nitro house, which was destroyed by the explosion, are back at their old jobs in the new works.

August 23, 1905

The Judson Shepard Acid Works by Fleming Point, which is now the Albany Race Track. Note the flat terrain. This is undoubtedly before the 1905 Powder Works explosion. Courtesy of the Berkeley Historical Society, catalog #1479.

WHITE MAN AND SEVEN CHINESE LOSE LIVES IN EXPLOSION THAT WRECKED MIXING HOUSE AT GIANT

[Special to the GAZETTE.]

SOBRANTE, July 13.—In an explosion which wrecked the mixing-house of the Giant Powder Works near this place at 7:30 o'clock this morning and rocked the country for miles around, William Dwyer, a white man and seven Chinese lost their lives, being blown to atoms by the powerful explosives. Fortunately, the flames of the mixing-house did not spread to the other buildings and no one was injured by the falling debris, most of the employes being at breakfast. The cause of the explosion will never be known.

There was no indication of danger when Dwyer and the squad of seven Chinamen went to work early this morning. Everything appeared to be all right in the mixing house and preparations were begun for the day's work. The tanks and apparatus were put in readiness for the mixing to begin.

Suddenly, without a hint of warning to the men, there was a terrific explosion and a huge column of yellow colored smoke shot high in the air, bearing within its embrace the fragments of human bodies. Men were thrown off their feet and dishes knocked off the shelves in the houses of the powder company, while many were rendered temporarily deaf by the concussion.

When the thick vapor had subsided, the men put out the incipient blaze that had started in the ruins of the mixing house and begun searching for the scattered remains of Dwyer and the Chinese. Had it been in the middle of the day, the loss of life would have undoubtedly been far greater.

Frightened women and children, with the fear that their husbands and fathers might have been killed in the explosion that shook their homes tugging at their hearts, hurried to the scene.

Dwyer was about 50 years old and was unmarried. He had been employed in the mixing house for some time.

The names of the Chinamen were unobtainable.

STAUFFER CHEMICAL WORKS, STEGE, July 13.—A severe shock was felt here this morning about 7:30 o'clock, dishes being knocked off shelves and the houses rocked with great force. It was feared that the Pinole works had blown up.

POINT RICHMOND, July 13.—The shock this morning caused by the explosion at Giant was one of the severest felt here in the history of the town. It was thought that the entire works had blown up at first and the families of men employed there were greatly frightened.

The shock in this city was severely felt, especially in the northwestern part of town. Houses were shaken severely, but no damage done. There seemed to be two explosions, the first at 7:30 o'clock and another one a second later. Dwyer, the dead man, is not known here.

July 13, 1905

TRICKS OF SOBANTE EXPLOSION

Men interested in the manufacture of explosives and in the industries akin thereto are still busy discussing the fearful explosion that wiped out eight lives at Sobrante on the Richmond shore on Thursday morning last, and the features that are most prominent in these discussions are not those relating to the loss of life, but to the vagaries of the exploding force. Why was it that the force of the explosion was almost entirely westward, and why was it that the force that was projected westward traveled along the earth with sufficient force to rip a tremendous hole in the surface of the ground, yet did not even jar the workers in a building less than ten feet distant from one edge of that hole?

At Sobrante nothing but the coarse-grained powder or dynamite was manufacured, and the demand was not for skilled labor. The heads of departments and the gang foremen there were white men, but Mongolians did well enough on the rough mechanical work. Where the finer grades of powder and the smokeless varieties are manufactured, however, skilled labor is demanded, and men come to such places and join in the work from all grades of life. Most of them are well-educated cool-headed citizens, attracted to the work in part by its risks and in larger part by the high average of compensation to be had. For powder companies must compensate their men to a degree for the fact that insurance companies will have nothing to do with them. Naturally fire insurance companies do not accept powder mills as risks, and just as naturally life insurance companies absolutely refuse to consider powder-mill employes as customers. So the men are paid well, principally because they risk their lives during every instant they are in or about the mills.

Not many of them dissipate, except during vacation periods. Then, occasionally, if a man is of nervous temperament, a protracted spree serves to bring forgetfulness, and, once sobered up, he is, to his own mind, refreshed and rejuvenated for the work. But drunkards are as bitterly avoided as matches about a powder works, and every visitor is searched for matches before he is permitted to enter a powder-mill house.

The mills themselves are built in flimsy fashion, that the loss may be as small as possible when they are blown into small bits. and there ...

CAUSE IS STILL A MYSTERY

In the blackened and blood-stained ruins of the mixing-house of the Giant Powder Company, near Sobrante, that was blown up yesterday morning, men are sill engaged in searching for the remains of Ah Quong, Ah Toi, Mah Won and Bock Cooe, four of the Chinese crew of seven that were instantly killed by the explosion. The mangled and hardly recognizable remains of William Dwyer, the old and trusted foreman of the place, and the scattered remains of three Chinamen, Wong Wey, Ching Sing and Chin Fook, have been recovered. The cause of the fatal explosion remains as unexplainable as ever.

Dwyer Never Had Accident Before.

Because of the hazardous nature of the work in the mixing-house that building and the storehouses in connection with it were erected at the most isolated point of the works' plant. Dwyer, who had charge of the manufacture of the high explosive, was one of the oldest employes of the company, thoroughly familiar with every detail of the operations in the "Chili mill," as the place was technically known. He had been handling the dangerous stuff for many years and had never before had an accident of any kind. Superintendent Frank Roller and Assistant Superintendent Louis Leveall could offer no explanation for the explosion. They made a thorough investigation, but were blocked by the absence of any remaining evidence that might give a clew to the cause of the trouble. Leveall said last night:

Cause Is Unknown.

"The explosion was one of those unscrutable occurrences that leaves nothing to tell the story. Dwyer, a most competent man, had been too long in the business to overlook a point. ...

July 14, 1905

Powder Works Explosion.

Three Men Killed by the Eruption— Cause Not Known.

The gelatine mixing house of the Giant Powder Company, near San Pablo, was the scene of an explosion yesterday, and John Hasselmier, foreman of the mixing works, and two Chinese laborers were killed.

As usual no one, who could possibly give any explanation or cause of the explosion, is alive. Hasselmier and the Chinese were the only persons employed by the company for a long time and was accredited with being very careful and painstaking and thoroughly familiar with the handling of highly explosive mixtures with which he has been working for years.

The Chinese, like Hasselmier, had been engaged in the manufacture of explosives for several years, and neither Superintendent Frank Rolker nor his assistants, George Phillips and Louis Leavitt, can offer any theory as to the cause of the accident. Hasselmier was a married man, his wife and two children residing near Siege station. The destroyed mixing house was located on a bluff overlooking San Pablo Bay and in the locality set apart for the manufacture of explosives. It was set near a bluff, so that the force of the explosion was considerably broken, though the report was heard for miles around, and though the shock was very distinct none of the other buildings were injured. The value of the destroyed building is placed at $4000 and will be replaced without loss of time. In fact within two hours after the explosion workmen were engaged in the work of clearing away the debris preparatory to the erection of another building.

Prior to locating at Giant the works were at Fleming's Point and while there a number of explosions occurred, but yesterday's was the first explosion since the works have been located at Giant.

November 14, 1900

22. Fire

Oil lamps were a common light source in 1900 and were the frequent cause of many home and business fires. Fires were common on Berkeley's dry hillsides. Hydrants didn't always function and although the city had purchased the most modern fire truck, the prized possession was demolished by a Key Route train on the truck's maiden voyage.

A powder used to extinguish fires was sold at the Driggs-Butterfield Company. Charles E. Chapin, a mechanical draftsman from Berkeley, invented an apparatus that protected a firefighter's head and provided tanked air. His invention revolutionized fire fighting.

Women garnered their share of heroism in this arena. The *Gazette* admired the pluck and presence of a handsome young lady, Miss Lola Edwards, the bookkeeper at Samson's Market. Upon reporting to work she accidentally toppled an oil lamp to the floor. The flames quickly spread, yet Miss Edwards remained composed, using her stylish cape to contain the fire.

Mrs. S. N. Shaplin demonstrated rare courage in saving the home of her invalid neighbor from a fire that was spreading to the roof of the house. Risking her own safety, Mrs. Shaplin hoisted a ladder against the neighbor's house. Remarkably, when the ladder fell short, she somehow propelled herself to the roof. With her bare hands, Mrs. Shaplin pried off the burning shingles and saved her neighbor.

"The North Berkeley Improvement Club has on many occasions voiced a strong protest against the practice of crowding buildings in the insurance sections, on the ground of appearance, but more especially in the dreaded increase in the community fire hazard, which must be of general concern. Imagine the result of a conflagration, originated in one of these crowded groups of houses, during the prevalence of a high north wind. The entire district, perhaps the entire town would be seriously menaced."

—Victor J. Robertson, *Berkeley Reporter*, December 1906

"The fire department has also been greatly improved, it now being practically on a paid basis, volunteers having been dispensed with without prejudice to the capable work they have done."

—Mayor Thomas Rickard, *Berkeley Reporter*, December 1906

Firemen of the Columbia (Marston) Volunteer Station in Berkeley. Circa late 1800s. Courtesy Berkeley Firefighters Association.

BRAVE WOMAN CLIMBS OVER ROOF AND SAVES HOUSE FROM FLAMES

Attired in a white spring dress and weak from a recent illness, Mrs. S. N. Shaplin of 1924 Louisa street, climbed a ten-foot ladder and by the aid of cleats nailed to the side of the building reached the roof of C. R. Whitman's residence and extinguished a fire that had started beneath the shingles. Although she had left a sick bed but a few hours earlier Mrs. Shaplin did not hesitate in her work to save the home of her friend and neighbor. Mrs. Whitman, who was seated on the porch of her home when the fire was discovered, is suffering from a severe attack of heart failure brought on by the excitement.

Shortly before 5 o'clock yesterday afternoon Mrs. Ray Peterson, who resides across the street from the homes of Mrs. Shaplin and the Whitmans, observed smoke coming from the roof of the Whitman house, which adjoins that occupied by Mrs. Shaplin. Knowing that Mrs. Whitman was a sufferer from heart trouble, Mrs. Peterson feared to inform her that the house was afire. Finally, however, she called Mrs. Shaplin to one side and told her of the fire. Mrs. Shaplin immediately rushed to a nearby house and secured a ladder, at the same time calling to Mrs. Peterson to get a garden hose. After securing the ladder the woman placed it against the rear of the Whitman house and climbed to the top rung, to discover that it was a few feet short of the roof. A cleat was within her reach and seizing it with both hands the courageous woman drew herself up to a level with the roof. She then swung to one side and gained a footing. After reaching the roof Mrs. Shaplin remembered her white dress, which was of flimsy goods, and fearing it might become ignited, she removed her waist and skirt and threw them to the ground.

This accomplished the woman crawled along the roof to the front of the house from where she directed the attaching of the garden hose. When the hose was finally attached by Mrs. Peterson it was thrown to Mrs. Shaplin.

Dragging the hose with one hand the woman again worked her way over the roof until she reached the spot from which the flames were then issuing. Tearing away shingles with her hands the woman soon made a small opening into which she turned the stream of water. After fifteen minutes she had the fire extinguished.

Shortly after Mrs. Shaplin had reached the roof Alan G. Clarke, who was passing the place, turned in the alarm, and by the time the fire department arrived, a few minutes later, the fire was out. A ladder was placed against the front of the house and the brave woman reached the ground in safety. She refused to allow the fireman to assist her down the ladder, declaring that she was able to make the descent unaided. How she reached the roof with the short ladder is the wonder of the entire neighborhood. Every one acquainted with the affair are high in their praise of the woman's bravery and presence of mind.

Mrs. Whitman is still seriously ill as a result of the shock, and has been under the almost constant care of a physician since yesterday afternoon.

July 6, 1905

She Has a Good Head.

A Serious Conflagration Prevented By a Young Lady's Presence of Mind.

What might have been a serious disaster from fire was averted last evening by the pluck and presence of mind of a handsome young lady. Miss Lola Edwards, bookkeeper at Samson's market, went to her office shortly after 8 o'clock, to get some papers which she required. She lighted an oil stove, and a minute later, by some mischance, she upset it. The oil spilled out onto the floor, and a sheet of flame burst forth. Instead of becoming panic-stricken, as would naturally be expected of a young lady under such circumstances, Miss Edwards quickly smothered the flame with her cape and threw the burning stove into the street, to finish the conflagration in the roadway. The total damage consisted in shocked nerves and a ruined cape, on neither of which there was any insurance.

A large crowd assembled at the sight of the burning oil on the highway, and Miss Edwards received many compliments for the bravery, coolness and good head-work which probably prevented heavy damage and which may have saved her life.

February 26, 1900

INCIPIENT FIRE PUT OUT BY BRAVE YOUTH

Presence of mind was never better exemplified than was shown by one of the Marston Fire Company members on Saturday last. The facts of the case are these.

Sherman Boyd had a trunk to deliver on Ellsworth street. While driving up to said street, the happy idea struck his massive brain that a pleasant smoke would add to his happiness, Accordingly the trusty corncob was filled and lighted, and our hero gently guided his celebrated steed up Allston way. Arriving at the house, the namesake of old Tecumseh first pulled off his coat, after carefully placing his still lighted pipe in the pocket. Then shouldering the trunk, the brave boy wended his way upstairs, and, after depositing the trunk and collecting the "four bits," he hastened to return to the depot. Not like Alexander, "sighing for more worlds to conquer," but wishing for more trunks to carry.

As he reached the wagon a fearful sight met his eyes. The coat was ablaze in the neighborhood of the pocket. What did this heroic youth do? Did he rush to the nearest fire alarm box and call out the fire department? Did he shout "Fire, fire," and create a panic and throw all the women into convulsions? No, the worthy son of a worthier sire simply sat down on the coat and the fire was smothered. Damages 15 cents; no insurance.

BY HIS NOBLE SIRE.

SERIOUS FIRE IS AVERTED

Had it not been for the timely return home of F. Prickrell and family to their house at 1904 Channing way last evening and the quick work of Frank McAllister, local mail distributor in the postoffice, they would have lost their personal belongings and furniture. Upon the discovery of the flames, a still alarm was sent in and the Marston's responded. The damage will amount to $100.

The Prickrells moved in Saturday night and yesterday afternoon built a fire in the grate to dry off the house, which had just come from the builder's hands. Shortly before 7 o'clock they put the fire out and went up town to get their supper.

Upon returning home at 8 o'clock, they found the house full of smoke which came from around the grate. Becoming alarmed, they asked Frank McAllister, their neighbor, to turn in an alarm. After notifying the Marston hose company, McAllister secured a fire extinguisher and proceeded to fight the flames alone, in spite of the suffocating smoke.

So efficient was his work that the worst of the fire was out when the hose company arrived. The fire-laddies quickly discovered that the fire was due to the faulty construction of the chimney, it being built around the floor joists in a most dangerous manner. It was necessary to hack the chimney to pieces before the last of the fire was out.

Berkeley Fire Department responds to a fire. Courtesy of the Berkeley Firefighters Association.

Saved From Death.

Henry Mansfield Carried From His Burning House.

But for the assistance of W. C. Reveal, Henry Mansfield would have lost his life Saturday night in a fire which destroyed his home. Reveal broke open the door and dragged Mansfield from his bed in a semi-conscious condition. The bed was on fire.

Mansfield, who is 72 years old, returned to his home at 2126 Parker street Saturday night at about 10 o'clock from Oakland. After he had retired he upset his lamp and set fire to his house. Mrs. Maddux who lives next door saw the flames and got Reveal's assistance. Mansfield was nearly suffocated when carried out.

The fire companies responded to the alarm and put out the fire, although the Mansfield house was practically destroyed. The George Primer place and the Maddux house were badly scorched but were saved through the efforts of the firemen.

Mansfield's loss amounted to $2,000. He not only owned the house which was destroyed, but the two adjoining ones. The fire caused considerable excitement and there was an unusually large number of people out for that time of night. Following were the companies who responded: Peralta, Alert, Marston and Lorin.

September 24, 1900

FIRE CAR IS SMASHED ON KEY ROUTE

A serious accident occurred Monday afternoon on the Key Route pier at Emeryville.

The new fire car, which has been built and equipped at a great expense, and which was provided with a heavy motor and all the modren appliances for the fighting of railroad fires, was being run along the track preparatory to a trial to demonstrate its usefulness as a fire extinguishing machine.

But the trial was destined never to take place, for just as the final preparations were being made, the Key Route ferry train from Berkeley, which was being switched, came swiftly down upon the same track, and before it could be stopped a collision occurred which completely demolished the fire car and rendered it useless.

Luckily the Key Route train was empty and no one was hurt.

July 20, 1905

HOUSE BURNED TO GROUND FOR WANT OF WATER

The residence of J. George at 2432 Seventh street was burned to the ground this morning at 11:35. The fire department answered the call immediately but there was no water available to extinguish the fire and all that it was possible to do was to keep the conflagration from spreading. A few articles of furniture were saved. There was no insurance.

August 1905

A new fire truck—a Knox Chemical Hose Wagon. Courtesy of the Berkeley Firefighters Association (and thanks to Mike Flynn, Berkeley Fire Department, for the information).

The morning after a fire at the southeast corner of Center Street and Shattuck Avenue, April 6, 1906. Courtesy of the Berkeley Firefighters Association.

Fire in Hays Canyon.

A fire burned over thousands of acres in Hays Canyon and destroyed the oaks of the hillsides of Oakland park yesterday morning. It 'was started on the Hays Canyon road near William J. Dingee's former home, "Fernwood," probably by campers. The fire ate its way over the ridges and down the canyons until at noon the hills beyond Oakland Park were a mass of flames. Within an hour the dry grass of Inspiration Point was ablaze and the fire enveloped the underbrush and old oak trees within a few hundred yards of the park bandstand.

North Berkeley grasslands and landscape in the early 1900s. Courtesy of the Berkeley Firefighters Association. Photo from Berkeley Chamber of Commerce election pamphlet, 1908.

Gigantic Grass Fire

Fanned by the heavy north wind, a fire swept the hills north of Berkeley this afternoon, consuming many acres of grass and brush. The smoke was so dispersed that it alarmed the residents not living in that portion of the town, who believed that a conflagration of homes was in progress.

While nearly every year some careless hunter sets fire to the dry grass, the blaze today was fiercer than has been seen for some time.

The ranchers on the hills, fearing that their fences and barns would be destroyed, formed themselves into a firemens' brigade. With wet sacks and a system of backfiring they succeeded in saving much valuable property.

The flames crept along with great rapidity until the gum tree groves were reached. Under the eucalyptis was a layer of dried leaves which burned like tinder and emitted a heavy black smoke.

Lively Grass Fire.

A grass fire in University avenue near Magee street caused considerable excitement yesterday morning. About a block was burned over and the Kavanaugh and Pringle homes threatened by the flames. The fences caught on fire but were soon extinguished. The Marston Hose Company was called out but reached the fire too late to render any assistance.

July 2, 1900

INVENTS DEVICE FOR FIREMEN

Life-saving and fire-fighting prom ise to be revolutionized by the intro duction of a respiratory apparatus in vented by Charles E. Chapin, a me chanical draughtsman of Berkeley With this device, Chapin claims the firemen will be able to enter a smoke filled building and breathe with ease and comfort in blinding smoke and choking gas which before would have brought suffocation in five minutes. The supply of air comes from cylinders strapped on his back.

The idea of the apparatus is simple and it seems a wonder that it was not thought of many years ago. Light, weighing but twenty-three pounds, it does not impede the fireman. A can vas oil-silk-lined hood covers his head. On his back is strapped the air cylin der, divided into three chambers. A rubber tube conducts the fresh air to the headpiece, the fireman breathes this with easy regularity and the ex hale passes out through a valve before the mouth.

Around the head of a strap to pre vent the inrush of smoke or fumes. The cylinders carry air enough to last the man an hour and allow him to regulate the pressure at will. It is fixed, however, so that no frightened impulse will allow the fireman to waste his air in a short time. He can get no more than will just satisfy his lung capacity. The contrivance can be plac ed on the back in twenty seconds and there seems to be no possible way by which it can get out of order and leave its bearer helpless. The small chamber in the middle is a sort of safe ty device, allowing the fireman to call on this supply only after the other chambers are exhausted.

Tests have been made in San Fran cisco by V. E. Stein, who has shown the apparatus to Chief Sullivan of San Francisco. In a room filled with sul phur fumes, where a man would quick ly succumb, Stein entered with this sav ing device and for a full hour worked with all he energy of a life-saver in a

Old Berkeley City Hall burns, September 1904. Courtesy of the Berkeley Firefighters Association.

burning building. At the end of that time he came out, his lungs and throat as free from fumes as though he had been exercising in the open air.

Stein is a San Franciscan and he is confident that the apparatus will even tually be adopted by all the principal fire departments of the world. He has shows it to the Fire Commissioners and they have promised to give it a practical demonstration as soon as Chief Sullivan returns from nis vaca tion.

January 26, 1900

An early pumper truck in Berkeley. Courtesy of the Berkeley Firefighters Association.

The men of Station #9 during a moment of leisure at Jake's Cigar Store. Courtesy of the Berkeley Firefighters Association.

23. Commerce

Retail advertisements in the early 1900s add vibrant detail
to our perceptions of life a hundred years ago.

Supplies from manufacturing centers on the East Coast initially
arrived in Berkeley by boat. By the 1870s the Transcontinental
Railway had reached Berkeley, making goods from heavy machinery to
fabric readily available to the growing town and increasing the area's
ability to export. By 1890 California was also rising as an agricultural
giant.

Throughout these advertisements Berkeley's new urban growth and
sophistication is evident. In spite of this change the city remained
close to its agricultural beginnings. Though farming was integral to
the economy and daily life, industrial innovations and thoughts were
changing the town.

Most of the stores, restaurants and businesses were small scale. The
most commonly advertised businesses were related to food, but shoe
ads were ubiquitous.

Factory workers at lunch hour in Berkeley. Circa 1900. Courtesy of both the Berkeley Firefighters Association
and the Berkeley Historical Society, catalog #1491.

But it should be noted that the larger industries that were growing and arriving, mostly in West Berkeley, did not advertise in the newspaper. Their impact, though huge (especially environmentally), was not revealed in this newspaper.

After the major economic depression in the 1890s prosperity was flowing into Berkeley.

⸺

"'A change has come o'er the spirit of our dream,' or rather it would be more correct to say that during the last five or ten years we have been shaking off that sleepy feeling and are just awaking to find that business is knocking at our door.

"The whole system has undergone a process of evolution or revolution; the infusion of newer ideas into our mercantile world, together with modern business methods, greater variety of goods and at prices no higher than those charged elsewhere, have all combined to shake us up, quicken the public pulse and we are now doing our trading at home."

—H. A. Sully, *Berkeley Reporter*, December 1906

BILLBOARD ORDINANCE

Is to Be Enforced After Two Weeks Grace Given by the Trustees.

Marshal Lloyd Brings the Proprietors of a Publicly Declared Nuisance to Time.

Despite the fact that an injunction was flaunted before them, the Town Board of Trustees voted last evening to sustain their recently passed ordinance which prohibits the maintenance or erection of billboards in Berkeley more than four feet high.

Yesterday Marshall Lloyd went to San Francisco and informed Siebe and Green, proprietors of the local billboards which have been legislated against, that the obnoxious signs must be rebuilt to conform to the ordinance. His action resulted in the appearance of representatives of the company before the Trustees last evening. One of these, Walter Foster, who was formerly a crack bicycle rider, acted as spokesman.

He said that Marshal Lloyd had called at his office and informed them of the ordinance which had been passed by the Trustees. "By asking us to place the boards at a height of four feet, you practically legislate us out of business," said Mr. Foster. "We are perfectly willing to remove all objectionable boards." He then expressed a fear that the Marshal would tear down the signs.

Trustee Frame, boiling with indignation, said that the billboards were a flagrant outrage that should not be tolerated in any respectable community.

In telling his side of the affair, Marshal Lloyd stated that he had gone to see the proprietors of the boards before making a complaint. "I have no intention of pulling down the boards said the marshal." The billboard owners said they were willing to do whatever was right in the premises. I told them that there was an ordinance in effect and that I would enforce it."

Trustee Turner then moved that Siebe and Green be given ten days in which to remove the boards.

Trustee Staats, who is now looked upon as a legal light by the members of the board since he passed the examination to the bar, informed the board that the only correct way to proceed in the matter was to arrest the owners of the nuisance. "These people have thousands of dollars invested all over the State," said the Lorin Trustee, "and the best thing to do is to compromise. If we are not reasonable with these people they may take advantage of us while the matter is dragging along in the courts. They may put up 20-foot fences while the matter is being settled and we will be helpless. Of course I would like to see the billboards abolished."

Mr. Foster then broke in and said "We do not want to be antagonistic, but we will not put back the fences from the property line one inch. We propose to stand on our rights and we have decisions to the effect that you cannot compel us to recede from the property line. There are many San Francisco firms who wish to use our billboards to sell their goods, the making of which gives employment to thousands of people. The putting up of fences, the making of the tons of

**paper used in the advertising all
give employment to countless workmen. . . .**

July 24,1900

---

*"...the confinement and isolation of such
places as Berkeley are necessary to the
greatness of the United States. There are in
this new country so many business men,
bankers, lawyers, manufacturers, farmers,
real estate men, stock brokers, millionaires, that our humble dealers in literature,
science, and fine arts would be distracted,
their ears deafened, their intelligences
obliterated, if they had to dwell in the
midst of that noisy organization, so different from their own ideal. The clink of gold
on the counter is not an accompaniment
adapted to the harmony of thought in
human minds."*

—Robert Duponey, *Berkeley
Reporter*, December 1906

Fonzo's Cafe located at 2067 Center Street. A. F. Fonzo resided at the same address. Courtesy of the Berkeley Historical Society.

CLEVELAND WHEEL

Standard of the world—the wheel that brings success to the dealer and satisfaction to the buyer. One price to all—that one right.

The College Cyclery

Difficult Repairing Solicited   Cor. Center and Shattuck.

Bicycle Sanitarium, Berkeley. Courtesy of California Prudential Realty, photo #g4-2.

Sheet Metal Works. Courtesy of the Berkeley Firefighters Association.

French Laundry on Shattuck Avenue near Blake Street. Courtesy of the Berkeley Architectural Heritage Association.

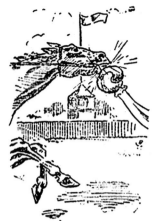

A rugged laundry. Courtesy of the Berkeley Historical Society.

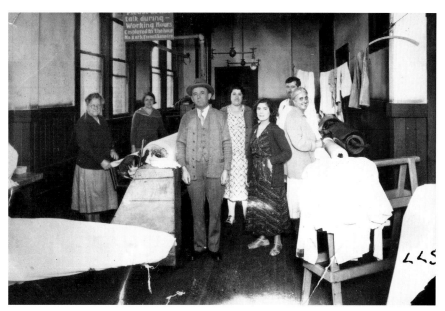

North Berkeley French Laundry at 1520 Shattuck Avenue. P. Momas appears to be the proprietor. Note the sign which forbids talking while working. Courtesy of the Berkeley Historical Society, catalog #1485.

WAGONS CUT UP STREETS

A large meeting of the North Berkeley Improvement Club was held last night at the local firehouse. Victor Robertson acted as chairman, while Professor M. E. Jaffa was temporary secretary. Robertson reported that the conference committee was investigating the water supply and the proposition of printing a booklet advertising Berkeley. Dr. J. T. Farrar of the water committee made a report; also A. L. Ott of the fire committee.

Fire Chemicals.

Ott brought to the attention of the club the need of at least three chemical engines in Berkeley, one in West Berkeley, one at the central station, and the other in the second ward. There was not sufficient pressure in the hydrants nor sufficient hose in the department to make a satisfactory fight against any fire that might occur in the thickly populated sections of the town. Ott was of the opinion that if a conflagration were to get a good start in the neighborhood of Telegraph and Bancroft way, where the residences are thickest, blocks and blocks would be destroyed before the fire could be put out. The chemicals were excellent fire extinguishers inasmuch as no damage could be caused by a surfeit of water. Robertson thought that if a dollar tax rate existed in Berkeley, the fire department would be efficiently supplied.

Are Ruining Streets.

Robertson stated that the large teams from the quarries were ruining the macadam especially on Cedar street, where deep ruts had been cut into the road making it resemble an unimproved country road. A. L. Ott called to the attention of the street committee a nuisance for which the telephone company was responsible. Wires are stretched from one telephone pole at a height of four feet from the ground to the top of the next pole as a brace to the latter. On a dark night the wire was invisible and

many people had had the unpleasant experience of running into them.

Transportation Committee.

C. A. Sherman in behalf of the transportation committee reported that nothing could be done toward having the trains removed from Berryman station where they stop for a long time between every run. It seems that there is only a single track between North Berkeley and East Berkeley and of necessity the Southern Pacific locals are forced to wait at Berryman until the arrival of the next train. Some of the members of the club objected to the continual ringing of the train bells which was the cause of much annoyance. It was pointed out, however, that the railroad company was but complying with the law which requires the ringing of a bell at every street crossing. Objection was also made to the excessive rate of speed between the two stations. The law states that the speed in the city limits be ten miles at maximum, but according to A. L. Ott the rate was at least twenty miles.

Will Have More Carriers.

C. A. Sherman reported that the postoffice had attended to all the requests of the North Berkeley Improvement Club. He was assured that as soon as the college term began extra carriers would be added to the force and a much better service installed. A special service for points east of Colfax had also been arranged for, so that now the mail leaves in the morning instead of in the afternoon as formerly. Sherman had nothing but praise for the promptness and courtesy of the Postoffice Department.

"HOME" PHONES WANTED

At the regular meeting of the East Side Improvement club Tuesday night the club went on record as favoring the esttablishment here of a Home Telephone system and a communica-

tion was forwarded to that telephone company inviting it to construct a system here. It was also the sense of the meeting that present telephone system has for the past few months and is still rendering poor service. Among the members who condemned the present telephone service were G. B. Ocheltre, Oscar Barber, W. C. Glenn and W. T. Gillihan. Each addressed the meeting at considerable length reciting numerous specific instances of poor telephone service, and declaring that the company now here has recently shown no apparent desire to accommodate its patrons. Following the general discussion of the question, Secretary W. T. Gillihan was instructed to communicate at once with the Home Telephone company, and the following communication was prepared:

"To the Home Telephone Company of Alameda County.

"Gentlemen: In pursuance of a resolution passed by the Berkeley East Side Improvement Club, we respectfully invite your company to consider the construction of a competing and modern telephone system in Berkeley, pledging in such event our hearty support and co-operation to the end that the necessary franchise be obtained. (Signed) W. T. GILLIHAN, Secretary."

The club also took up the question of the small boy and his coaster, which was unanimously declared to be a public nuisance and a menace to life and limb of pedestrians as well as the youngsters who operate the coasters. Numerous instances were cited where youngsters had been injured, together with many persons who have been struck by the coasters. The members of the club were unanimously of the opinion that some action should be taken to put a stop to the practice. After considerable discussion it was decided to carry the matter over to the next meeting, when it is probable that resolutions will be adopted asking the Town Trustees to pass an ordinance prohibiting the use of coasters on the sidewalks.

Harness, contracting, antiques, paints and a number of other businesses at 2113 Shattuck Avenue. Circa 1891. Courtesy of the Berkeley Historical Society, catalog #1492.

Southwest corner of San Pablo Avenue at Addison Street. Circa 1895. Courtesy of the Berkeley Historical Society.

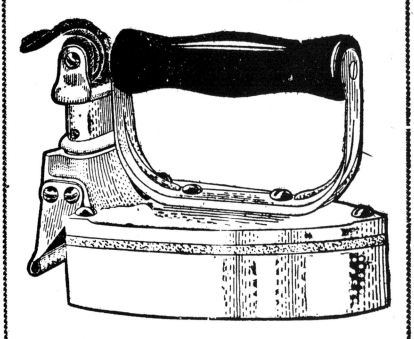

Students' Express Company staff and van. Courtesy of Berkeley Firefighters Association.

The Barker Building at the northwest corner of Shattuck Avenue and Dwight Way. Mr. Barker was one of the most influential citizens of Berkeley. Arriving in 1886, he was instrumental in getting the Central Pacific Railroad to extend its line to Adeline Street and then Shattuck Avenue. Before this, there were no real roads into this section of town. Mud in the winter was mindboggling. A local joke suggested the wagon rider carry a buoy to mark the spot his wagon sunk. Courtesy of the Berkeley Firefighters Association; photo from *Berkeley Reporter*, December 1906.

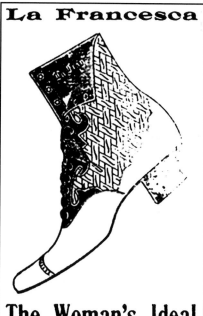

Mr. Mauch's shoe repair store in South Berkeley at 3015 Adeline Street. Circa 1914. Courtesy of the Berkeley Historical Society, catalog #1488.

Villa des Roses Restaurant at Fourth Street and University Avenue, run by the Vegnes family from France. Circa 1898. Courtesy of the Berkeley Historical Society.

The Golden Sheaf Bakery in Berkeley. Courtesy of the Berkeley Historical Society.

Homemade bread wagon of the Golden Sheaf Bakery. The bakery was located on Shattuck Avenue between University Avenue and Addison Street in Berkeley. Courtesy of the Berkeley Historical Society, catalog #1481.

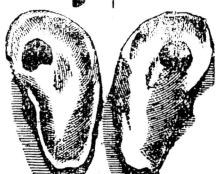

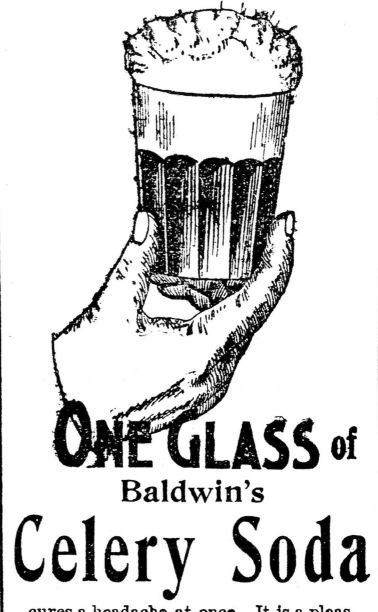

ONE GLASS of
Baldwin's
Celery Soda

cures a headache at once. It is a pleasant, sparkling, effervescent drink that acts immediately. It cleans and purifies the stomach, gently quiets the nerves and relieves all pain. It cures sick and nervous headaches, seasickness and mental fatigue. 10c, 25c, 50c, $1.00

"... along the waterfront there has been going on another class of improvements which are the main factors in the making of a great city. There have been established iron foundries, machine shops, acid works, knitting factories, furniture factories, chemical and printing ink factories, oil refineries, etc., with large additions to the many industries already established, the soap factory, candy factory, coffee, spice and planing mills."

—F. A. Leach, *Berkeley Reporter,* December 1906

Hoffman's Ashby Coal Yard, South Berkeley. Courtesy of the Berkeley Historical Society, catalog #1487.

"... all classes of help employed by our local manufacturing plants are inclined to make their homes near their place of employment, and prefer to remain here, even when offered higher wages at other places. The price of land makes it possible for them to own their own places and many cozy homes have been built in that district by the working men. This keeps the men interested in the locality—they feel that they are near home in case they are wanted quickly at any time and it is surely a great advantage both to employer and employee."

—L. H. Lewars, *Berkeley Reporter,* December 1906

D & D Grocery at the southwest corner of Shattuck and University Avenues. Circa 1890. Courtesy of the Berkeley Historical Society.

Big Money From Little Money.

When a man has a little spare money he wants to put it where it will bring the best returns, or he ought to. He can put it in a savings bank and save it, but that is all. If he takes a few ten-cent pieces and invests in dollar shares of oil stock, the dimes do the developing, and that done they are worth dollars to him. Money invested in oil stock of a safe company for development purposes is better than working the sands of Nome. When a dime comes back a dollar it is like finding ninety cents already coined. Stock in the Great Northern Oil Co. is going to do this sort of thing for the holders. It is now selling at only 10 cents for dollar shares.

Inspecting Oil Wells.

A party of Oakland people left W. E. Barnard's office at 6 o'clock this morning for Contra Costa county, to visit oil wells near Lafayette. The trip was made by way of the Fish road. The wells near San Pablo were also visited and the party returned to Oakland on the 4:30 train.

November 9, 1900

Old Industry Revived.

The Eureka Oil Works on Third street has again commenced operations after being shut down for two years. The large shipment of linseed will be worked up at once by a force of workmen. Daniel Cotton is superintendent of the works and A. J. Williams owner. The industry was hindered for some time by litigation, but now all the differences appear to have been settled.

March 30, 1900

Looked for Oil.

Strangers Claim They Found It In West Berkeley.

No little excitement was occasioned in West Berkeley yesterday by the rumor that oil had been discovered in the vicinity of Third, Rose and Second streets. Two men who did the prospecting, exhibited portions of the soil in that locality which they claimed was highly saturated with the precious liquid.

One of the prospectors is said to be Emile Ceresa of San Francisco. He and his companion worked quite a while about the premises, finally telling the results of their labor to Mr. James Paine of Third and Rose streets.

Whether oil really exists in the locality described is a matter of conjecture, but the actions of the visitors, who seemed to be acting in good faith, occasioned considerable comment.

Berkeley workers. Courtesy of the Berkeley Firefighters Association.

"...those philosophers, mathematicians, physicians, historians, literators, would be spoiled of their moral, intellectual, and social influence, which is so essential as counterbalancing and correcting the impetuous rush of the nation towards a splendid future of material wealth."

—Robert Duponey, *Berkeley Reporter*, December 1906

Oil Stock

GREAT NORTHERN OIL CO.

40,000 Shares of Treasury Stock

————FOR SALE AT————

10 Cents Per Share.

Land is in GLENN COUNTY, the finest field yet Discovered on the Coast. 440 Acres, with a perpetual Lease. Organized by Oakland and Berkeley men, under California Laws.

B. F. ARNOLD, Pres.,
2145 Center St., Berkeley.

GEO. A. GRAY, Sec.,
1070 Broadway, Oakland

THINK IT OVER

Isn't it the easiest way to to make money? Just investing a little—say $200, and get 2000 shares of Great Northern. It will make you money faster than bonds. —Try a few thousand.

Great Northern Oil Company
2145 Center Street,
BERKELEY

1070 Broadway,
OAKLAND

Oil at Orinda.

Considerable interest is being taken in prospecting for oil in Contra Costa county. The well which was sunk on the Miner place near De Laveaga station on the California and Nevada railroad reached a depth of some 1400 feet with promising prospects when the drill was lost and it was found impracticable to proceed further. The result has been that a new well has been started near the old one which is now down about 700 feet.

It is stated that two derricks have been put up in the vicinity of Lafayette and a thorough test is to be made in this locality in which a number of Oaklanders are interested.

There are said to be indications of oil and bitumen on the Moraga ranch, although as yet no effort has been made to determine whether oil or bitumen exist there in paying quantities. The nearness of these sections to Oakland would be a great advantage, should there be satisfactory developments. In connection with these projects there has been some discussion of the proposition of building a pipe line into Oakland, should oil be found in sufficient quantities to warrant such an outlay.

Inspecting Oil Wells.

A party of Oakland people left W. E. Barnard's office at 6 o'clock this morning for Contra Costa county, to visit oil wells near Lafayette. The trip was made by way of the Fish road. The wells near San Pablo were also visited and the party returned to Oakland on the 4:30 train.

Capital Market delivery man Jerry McCullough. The market was located at 2110 Vine Street. Courtesy of the Berkeley Historical Society, catalog #1480.

South Berkeley Coal Yard. Courtesy of the Berkeley Historical Society, catalog #1505.

Durgin-Gompertz Furniture and Carpets was at the site of the old J. C. Penney Store on Shattuck Avenue in downtown Berkeley. Courtesy of the Berkeley Historical Society, catalog #1508.

Berkeley Grocery Company at 2478 Telegraph Avenue, between Dwight Way and Haste Street. Henry Jacobs, proprietor. Courtesy of the Berkeley Historical Society, catalog #1482.

Steam train on Shattuck Avenue in downtown Berkeley. Courtesy of the Berkeley Firefighters Association.

University and Shattuck Avenues, northwest corner. Circa 1887. Fischel Hotel, University Bazaar and the Liberty Market. Current site of McDonald's Restaurant. Courtesy of the Berkeley Historical Society, catalog #1489.

Bancroft Way and Telegraph Avenue around 1906 as the electric train is turning onto Bancroft Way. Courtesy of the Berkeley Firefighters Association; photo from *Berkeley Reporter*, December 1906.

Looking east from University Avenue below San Pablo Avenue. Circa 1906. Courtesy of the Berkeley Firefighters Association; photo from *Berkeley Reporter*, December 1906.

"The invaders of our University town are still of a peaceful sort; retired navy and army officers, or business men who have their home here and their offices in San Francisco. But will the welcome of Berkeley be always limited to such harmless newcomers? Is it not to be feared that [what] Berkeley will have some day is speculators, and smoky manufacturers, and big enterprises, and sky-scrapers, and political grafts, and all the rest? Will not the industrial world infringe on this still unviolated sanctuary? There is already a terrible clamor of the real estate business around Berkeley. Some professors, I hear, are tempted by that awful racket and begin to go out of their 'Tour d'Ivoire.' It would be a great pity, indeed, if some day Berkeley happened to be submerged in the waves of an industrial money making population."

—Robert Duponey, *Berkeley Reporter*, December 1906

24. Leisure

Judging from the advertisements and photographs in the *Gazette*, outdoor activities ranked high among leisure activities of our Berkeley predecessors.

People gathered, donning their Sunday best, to enjoy the Bay Area's natural beauty. Large picnics were held at Shellmound Park in Emeryville, Tilden Park or Orinda. Often, picnickers would listen to an outdoor concert. A day at the beach in Berkeley (a crescent-shaped beach beginning at Delaware Street and ending at Gilman Street—now the freeway), was an all-day outing.

Berkeleyans dined out and took in vaudeville shows. They went to dances, circuses, animal shows and athletic events. They fished for trout, salmon and bass in the area's lakes and rivers.

Berkeley's Ida Hanscom spent her 1905 summer vacation climbing Mt. Rainier and Mt. Hood. Residents enjoyed bowling at J. Weills on Center Street or for fifty cents, theatergoers could attend a production of "Pretty Peggy: The Pathetic Story of Peg Woffington" at the Liberty Playhouse.

"There are few places that can boast of such artistic homes, and consequently such ideal places for entertainment as Berkeley. As is natural for a college town there are many sets. Some purely social, others interested in music, art and literature, but all co-mingling and forming an atmosphere which is delightful."

—Miss Lucile Wollenberg, *Berkeley Reporter*, December 1906

The Donogh and Durgin families of Berkeley on a picnic. Courtesy of the Berkeley Architectural Heritage Association.

Mrs. Moisan and her baby, Charles Sonny, enjoy a day at the beach of Berkeley which ran from the mouth of Strawberry Creek (near University Avenue) to Fleming Point (now the Albany Race Track). Note Cordonices Lagoon in the background, formed by the natural buildup of sand which blocked the flow of Virginia and Cordonices Creeks to the Bay. They formed a lagoon and the water slowly reached the Bay northeast of Fleming Point. The Lagoon was destroyed by road building and the freeway. Courtesy of the Berkeley Historical Society, catalog #1490.

LOCAL
FISHING
IS GOOD

The fishing season this year bids
fair to break all records both for the
quantity and quility of the fish that are
being taken daily by the anglers. During the last week reports from the
northern part of the State have lured
many away from the cares of the city,
while those who have intended to make
but short stays have decided to stick
while the sport continues to be good.

The upper Sacramento River is a
mecca for anglers at the present time.
The trout are running there as they
have not run in years and every day
splendid catches are reported. The
weather there is about right for trout
and bids fair to hold out for some time
to come.

Fishing along the Truckee River is
the best in years. Many anglers made
the trip there last week and they all
reported the sport to be the finest they
ever experienced in that section of the
country. The supply this season seems
inexhaustible, having held out so far
without the slightest signs of letting
up.

The best catches of trout are being
made above Boca. At the present time
workmen are engaged in cleaning an
ice dam below this place and as this
makes the water muddy the trout are
all heading for the clear parts of the
river several miles north of the dam.
The best flies there are the Cahill,
blue upright and shane.

Salmon are beginning to run along
the McCloud River and fly fishing will
be slack there for a while. When the
salmon spawn the rainbow trout follow them and eat the spawn. Consequently they will not take flies except
in the early morning and late in the
evening and even then it is hard to
land them.

The sport at the Big Meadows continues good. The trout are taking
grasshoppers and also hair lug flies.
Big Springs, Hamilton Branch and
Spring Branch are attracting many
fishermen and the trout are running
well at these places.

August 1, 1905

Berkeley Mayor J. W. Richards on a Yosemite fishing trip. Courtesy of the Berkeley Architectural Heritage
Association, photo #10.

Striped Bass Confiscated.

Sacramento, Aug. 9.—County Game
Warden George Neale yesterday
morning confiscated a ton of striped
bass shipped from Black Diamond
on the Sacramento river to this city.
The fish were seized by the game war
den because they were under the
minimum size required by law. The
seizure was made early in the morning and the fish were distributed by
the game warden to the orphan asy-
lums and county jail. The shippers
will be arrested.

August 9, 1905

ADRIFT IN THE DESERT

After wandering aimlessly about in the desert for three long days without a drop to drink or a morsel to eat, W. A. Ryder, the city electrician of Berkeley, was at last picked up in a complete state state of exhaustion. He returned to Berkeley yesterday weighing eighteen pounds less than when he started on the trip and visibly showing the effects of the sufferings he had undergone.

Ryder left town about three weeks ago to take a tramp through the Grand Canyon of the Colorado. He provided himself with food and water sufficient to carry him on the trip. Then he secured a burro, and packed his supplies on the animal. Everything went well until the desert in Arizona was reached, when, after being out three days, the burro bucked off the five-gallon keg of water, their sole supply, and smashed in a stave. Ryder managed to get some of the water into the empty canteen before it all leaked out.

On the advice of a Williams citizen, he left the trail and attempted a cut off toward El Tovar.

The next day the water gave out, and the burro becoming exhausted, Ryder left everything and continued to walk blindly over the desert. He went through all the horrors of the thirsty, his tongue swelling until it filled his mouth and his lips cracking open in half a dozen places. Unable to sleep from pain, he staggered on night and day, finally reaching the pine forest that borders the canyon. At one time he was within two miles of El Tovar, but the forest hid the hotel. He later discovered that when he left his burro he was but fourteen miles from the same place.

Ryder dropped exhausted on the road along the canyon between El Tovar and Bright Angel. A young woman tourist passed him on horseback, but as he was unable to speak she thought him drunk and galloped away when he attempted to rise. Stage Driver Curry, who runs the line between the two hotels, picked him up and took him to El Tovar, the end of the railroad line from Williams to the canyon. Here he was taken care of and resuscitated.

Ryder is a student at the University of California. He is a son of M. L. Ryder, a Southern Pacific official and a former Town Trustee of Berkeley, and resides at 2619 Shattuck avenue.

July 11, 1905

HILLS ARE CLIMBED BY SIERRA CLUB

The Sierra Club, eighty strong, took possession of the Berkeley hills Saturday night, climbing "Little Grizzly" from the University of California Greek Theater, which was the rendez-vous. The occasion was the fall out-door reunion of the outing members, and the party made a jolly climb to the appointed hill and there partook of the supper, which had been brought by individuals. Songs, musical selections and speeches by Professor Joseph N. Le Conte, William E. Colby, Professor William E. Bade and other Sierra Club leaders constituted the jinks for the evening's entertainment.

WEATHER FORECAST

[Special to THE GAZETTE.]

SAN FRANCISCO, September 25, 8:12 a. m.—For San Francisco and vicinity: Fair tonight, Tuesday fair.

A. G. McADIE, Forecaster.

September 25, 1905

MISS HANSCOM CLIMBS LOFTY MOUNTAINS

Miss Ida Hanscom, daughter of M. L. Hanscom of this city has just returned from a vacation trip with the Sierra Club in the northern part of the State. Miss Hanscom was one of the few women accompanying the party, who had the hardihood to climb to the summit of Mt. Rainier and Mt. Hood. Miss Hanscom also visited the Columbia river and Puget Sound.

August 15, 1905

UNIVERSITY Y. M. C. A. TO CLIMB MT. TAMALPAIS

The annual trip to Mount Tamalpais under the auspices of the Y. M. C. A. will be made Saturday. This is the customery date, and as it is Admission day, a large number of freshmen as well as other class men always attend.

A list for signatures has been placed in the reading-room of Stiles hall, and already it contains a score of names.

All University men are invited. The round trip costs seventy cents.

MOONLIGHT TRAMP TO TAMALPAIS

The social committee of the town Y. M. C. A. is arranging a moonlight tramp to Mt. Tamalpais for Friday evening next. The party will leave Berkeley on the 10:25 train and be up the mountain in time to see the sun rise. After breakfast on the mountain, a trip will be taken to Redwood Canyon, returning in the evening. A party of fourteen has already been formed and others are considering the matter. The party is not limited to Y. M. C. A. members, any young man will be welcomed.

September 7, 1905

THE FARRARS ARE GOING ON CAMPING TRIP

Dr. J. J. Farrar, accompanied by his sons, Wendell and J. Teal Farrar, and Robert Heans, will leave to-night for a two weeks' vacation in Trinity county mountains. All are enthusiastic sportsmen, particularly the doctor and it is expected that they will secure plenty of game.

From here, the party will proceed by rail to Sherwood, where they will take the stage to Round Valley Indian Reservation. There they will be met by Indians, with pack horses and saddle horses, Dr. Farrar having arranged for these in advance, and will strike out for the mountains Tuesday night. It is the intention of Dr. Farrar to take the trails leading far back in the mountains, where deer and bear are plenty and the snow is never off the ground in spots.

August 17, 1905

HEAVY BUCK IS SHOT BY TEEL FARRAR

Dr. J. T. Farrar and his son, J. Teel Farrar returned last Saturday night from a successful hunting and fishing trip in the vicinity of the South Fork mountains in Trinity county. During the fourteen days Dr. Farrar and his son were away, they each killed two deer, young Farrar bringing down a buck which tipped the scales at 160 pounds. Trout fishing the Farrars report was excellent.

PICNIC AT ORINDA IS ENJOYED

One of the most enjoyable Fourth of July outings was held at Orinda Park by a number of prominent Berkeley people. A large bus drawn by four horses was secured to carry the party, which left Berkeley at 9 o'clock in the morning. The route taken was the road out San Pablo avenue, thence along San Pablo creek on the picturesque road leading through Oak Grove and Bryant's. When the Orinda Park canyon was reached, the jolly party disembarked and made a cool spot in the creek their camping place. A camp fire was built, where hot tea and coffee was made and then an elaborate luncheon, including a freezer of ice-cream, which had been brought along by one of the ladies as a surprise, was enjoyed.

Late in the afternoon the crowd returned home, amid singing and cheers, taking the scenic tunnel road on the way home and driving back to Berkeley via the Fish ranch and Claremont.

The party included Mr. and Mrs. James Rose, Mr. and Mrs. Frank Heywood, Mr. and Mrs. George James, Captain and Mrs. John R. Oakley, Mr. and Mrs. Burton Rose, Mrs. Samuel Heywood, Miss Gertrude Heywood, Miss Ethel Rose, Miss Ruth Heywood, Messrs. Charles Heywood, Nelson Frater, Baby Amy Oakley and Baby Charles Rose.

July 6, 1905

DISPLAY WILL BE GREATEST IN THE WEST

The special train of twenty-one cars, bearing the small army of pyrotechnists, electricians, stage mechanics, performers, dancing girls and the immense amount of scenic paraphernalia of Pain's stupendous spectacle "Last Days of Pompeii," reached Oakland from Portland on Wednesday evening. From the hour of its arrival until the doors are thrown open next Monday evening, nearly two hundred skilled workmen will be busy on the big scenic city that is to represent the ill-fated old Roman town of Pompeii, which is to nightly meet its doom in the fiery holacust of Mt. Vesuvius. Fully five acres of ground on San Pablo avenue, between Thirty-seventh and Thirty-ninth streets will be covered with this mimic city. The entire area of ground will be encircled by a canvas side wall fourteen feet high, within which will also be comfortable seats for 10,000 people.

September 15, 1905

POMPEII WILL FALL TONIGHT

Tonight the greatest outdoor attraction in the world will begin its limited week's engagement at Thirty-ninth and San Pablo avenue. "Last Days of Pompeii" has been heralded for the past four weeks until every man, woman and child is interested and anxious to witness this marvellous midsummer night's spectacle and judge for themselves as to whether the press reports have been exaggerated and the people of the Eastern cities right in their praise of this great show. It has been called the most spectacular and gorgeous amusement enterprise that has ever been conceived, but the citizens of Berkeley always demand that they be shown before they will commit themselves.

All day yesterday there were thousands of people gathered around the big five-acre lot at Thirty-ninth and San Pablo, watching the hundreds of skilled workmen, electricians and pyrotechnists erecting this gigantic enterprise.

The tiers upon tiers of seats so arranged as to afford each of the 10,000 a perfect view of the entire stage, which is 400 feet wide and 300 feet deep set with acres of massive scenery so cleverly painted that even in the daylight, it seemed that they were gazing upon a real instead of a painted city, caused all manner of favorable comment. Many watched for hours the skilled pyrotechnists constructing the beautiful set pieces which are to be shown tonight. "Niagara Falls by Moonlight," 50x200 feet and "The Last Rose of Summer," 60x20 feet are but a few of the special features that will be shown. After tonight the people of all of the surrounding country will be ready to add their praises to this tremendous attraction and vote it the most beautiful spectacular exhibition ever seen.

September 18, 1905

1789   1905

Fall of the Bastille

Alameda County Grand Celebration
Sunday, July 16th, 1905, at
California Park, West Berkeley

DAY AND NIGHT FESTIVAL

IN THE AFTERNOON—Grand Concert; Dancing; Literary
Exercises; Oration an English, by Hon. F. K. Mott, Mayor of
Oakland; Games, Races, &c.; Oration in French, by Prof. Rob-
ert Derponey.
IN THE EVENING—Grand Banquet; Concert; Ball; Illuminations

Admission to Park.....25c

Vaudeville Show

And Dancing at Sisterna Hall, West Berkeley.

Tonight at Sisterna Hall, West
Berkeley, Adam's Vaudeville Company will give a performance consisting of features worth witnessing
to be followed by a dance.

Stanley and little Alma Wurthrich in a sketch and wire act, Guion
the juggler; Morrell, monologist
and banjoist; little Alma Wurthrich
character singing and toe dancing;
the shadowscope and descriptive
singing with pictures.

Great Vaudeville Performance

At the Berkeley Opera House Thursday and Friday Evenings.

The vaudeville stage now pre-
dominates over everything else in
the theatrical line. The theatre going public who have heretofore
sought the precincts of the house
announcing its attraction of a drama
or a farce comedy, with its three or
four acts and a plot, are now seeking the vaudeville house and its
variety of features.

Famous actors, operatic stars and
other leading lights of the profession have of late been allured to the
vaudeville stage by the enormous
salaries offered.

The Orpheum of San Francisco is
an instance where it is utterly impossible to purchase a seat unless it
is ordered several days ahead of
time. Such is the demand of the
theatre going public for the vaudeville class of entertainment.

The Orpheum has not procured a
better list of talent than that which
has been selected for Berkeley patrons next Thursday and Friday
evenings. Artists who were specially engaged from the East, for
those seeking amusement at the San
Francisco theatres during the Native Sons' celebration are among the
performers to appear.

Note the list of numbers on the
progam:

A juggler and equibrilist.
A ventriloquist.
A phenominal soprano.
A humorist and impersonator.
A slack wire walker.
Descriptive singing illustrated by
stereopticon views.

Berkeley's Part

In the Native Sons' Parade.

The residents of this town turned out enmasse yesterday to be present at the parade of the Native Sons' of the Golden West.

Berkeley's part in the procession was a conspicuous feature of that event. The Volunteer firemen, University Cadets and Veterans reserves all contributed to make the day a remarkable one.

The firemen were marshalled by Chief James Kenny, and showed up strong. Six companies of the department, viz: Marston, Beacon, Peralta, Alert, Lorin and Posen were all largely represented, the members wearing the regulation red shirts, black pants and firemen's caps. Marston Hose Cart No. 2, gaily decorated with red, white and blue and poppies, was in the lead. The department turned out 120 strong.

Cherokee Tribe of Red Men No. 101 had a large float representing an Indian camp. The wigwam of deer skins was plentifully decorated with strings of wampum, while the campfire blazed beneath foliage of young scrub oak. The big chiefs to the number of a dozen or more were arrayed in frontier costumes, feathers in hair, and faces slashed with red paint.

The Veteran Reserves, Company A, with several local members, Captain C. K. King, commanding, with the reserve band at their head, with the reserve band at their head, turned out. Not a man in the ranks was less than 55 years of age. The reserve band in the unavoidable absence of the regular leader was directed by Chief Musician Leonard Clark, a former Berkeley boy. They were tastefully uniformed in blue jackets and white pants.

The University Cadets, Companies A, B, C and D, headed by Captain Waite, presented an excellent appearance. They marched in true military style and were greatly complimented for their creditable appearance.

TO REPEAT
SCOTS DAY
PROGRAMME

So successful was the Scottish day celebration on July 15 in the Greek Theater at the University of California that on the evening of September 8 the entire program, with several additions, will be repeated. It is expected that the performance, given at night in the great semi-circular theater, will be a most unique production and will attract even a larger crowd than the previous affair.

The celebration is reproduced at the request of hundreds of people who were unable to witness the first one. Dr. Crawford will have charge of the affair. The hornpipers and reel dancers will be present and other features introduced.

CELTIC UNION TO HOLD
PICNIC AT SHELL MOUND

The United Irish societies composing the Celtic Union will hold their fifth annual picnic and games this year at Shell Mound Park, near Berkeley, on Admission day, Saturday, September 9th. The executive committee and officers of the Celtic Union which compose the picnic committee, outlined a program of athletic events and Irish dances, with prizes that should bring out the best talent in San Francisco and vicinity. A souvenir program will be printed, which is in charge of a special committee particularly qualified for this work. The general committee will meet every Thursday evening.

Berkeley Socialist Band. Courtesy of the Berkeley Historical Society.

An early photograph of U.C. Berkeley's Greek Theatre. Courtesy of the Berkeley Firefighters Association.

SCOTTISH DAY AT THE GREEK THEATRE
UNIVERSITY OF CALIFORNIA, BERKELEY
FRIDAY, SEPTEMBER 8, AT 8 P.M.

Characteristic Tableaux, Highland Reels, Songs, Old Time Psalmody, &c., &c. Fine Scenic Effects,

REPEATED BY REQUEST - - - **ADMISSION 25 CENTS**

Proceeds to go to the University Library for purchase of Scottish Literature.

A wagon full of picnickers from the Native Sons. Courtesy of the Berkeley Historical Society.

A wagon loads up downtown in front of the Shattuck Hotel for a picnic at Currans Ranch. Courtesy of the Berkeley Historical Society.

A mother suns herself on Berkeley's beach. The natural crescent-shaped beach was a favorite for locals and San Franciscans alike. Old-timers reported the tradition of swimming from the outlet of Strawberry Creek at the Bay to Fleming Point. Courtesy of the Berkeley Historical Society, catalog #1510.

Campers Were Visited.

Many visitors drove over the hills yesterday to visit the various camps in Wild Cat Canyon, Orinda Park and Bear Valley. A majority of the visitors were business men who went over to see their families.

The valleys over the hills are more popular this year than ever before as camping places.

Coming To Shell Mound.

Edward H. Goetze of San Francisco, who is in the East, writes to a friend in this city of the enthusiasm prevailing among crack shots he has met concerning the coming international shooting festival, which will be held at Shell Mound Park in 1901. He has visited New York, Brooklyn, Chicago, Indianapolis, Richmond, Va., Washington, D. C., Baltimore, Philadelphia and many other places. Everywhere he spoke of the great shooting festival and was received with the greatest enthusiasm. He has been assured that large contingents of the most noted rifle shots will visit San Francisco and participate in the great festival. Fully two hundred of the best shots of New York have signified their intention of making the journey, and they are gaining accesions to their number. They will travel in a special train. From Boston and Philadelphia large numbers will also cross the continent to attend the festival.

WELL KNOWN MUSICIANS AT CONCERT

Edwin S. Belknapp, who is connected with the school of dramatic art in New York City, and M. Loomis, the noted New York composer, were visitor to the half-hour of music, which was given in the Greek Theater yesterday afternoon. he program was rendered by Mrs. Milton E. Blanchard and was an exceptionally good one, the vast theater being filled in spite of the threatening aspect of the weather.

Berkeley folks prepare for an outing. Courtesy of the Berkeley Firefighters Association.

25. Sports

In 1905, the first U.C.-Stanford Thanksgiving football game was being planned. The U.C. football players were eating the University out of house and home preparing for their games.

Boxing was news whether it was Battling Nelson politely decking someone in a bar in Truckee or the famous champion Jack Johnson leaving a courtroom after responding to a statutory offense, insulating himself from his detractors with his confident personality and style.

If you were going to choose a competitive sport in 1900, it probably wouldn't have been track and field. You would have done well to choose crew as if your life depended on it. There was some evidence in the *Berkeley Gazette* that it did!

Joe Larrine vs. Charlie Tate Event takes place at Sisterna Hall. Courtesy of the Berkeley Firefighters Association.

Sisterna Hall, a popular meeting and event hall in Berkeley, built in 1883, was located at Sixth Street and University Avenue. Courtesy of the Berkeley Historical Society.

COLLEGE
FOOTBALL
TO START

The football players are commencing to gird on their armor and practice will soon be in full swing on countless gridirons. The arrival of the Eastern coaches at Berkeley to-morrow will be an event. In a short time they will have their men lined up so that they may judge the material upon which they will have to work to develop a winning team.

Seven of the Berkeley men who played in the early stages of the intercollegiate game last year are back in college. Five other men who played at one time or another in the big game are also back in college.

Stanford has only three of last year's eleven enrolled this season. This will not count against the Cardinal as much as might be supposed owing to the system employed successfully by Coach Lanagan last year. In every game played he changed the team's line-up repeatedly, thus giving every man on the squad valuable practice. He seemed indifferent whether he won the preliminary games or not. When substitutes were put in they worked as smoothly as any part of the great machine.

Berkeley, on the other hand, had its team selected early in the season and the only chance a substitute had for practice was when some one was injured.

Manager "Pete" Smith, upon which team the college relies for the bulk of their practice, will have a strong eleven this year. McFadden, the former Stanford tackle, will probably captain the team. Kavanaugh and Smock will be absentees, although the latter may be here late in the season.

For quarterback, there are two men available—Monohan, a Southern man, now at Stanford, and Goshen. Shouchuk, the Eskimo who played center for the Carlisle Indians, will coach the Lowell High School team and Manager Smith will try to secure him for his team.

Ables, Keegan and Larry O'Toole will be available for the guard positions. Martin, who has played tackle for two years, will be in his old place. Long and Eiseman, last year's ends will be in the line-up again. Bishop, the fullback, and Lemon, the halfback, will also be in the line-up.

Kearns, the University of California halfback, will play with the team if he does not return to college. Four men from the Mare Island Navy Yard, including a fullback, two halfbacks and an end will be with the team.

As the high schools of this city are opening later than usual this year, the season will be late. The Alameda High School has already opened and the team will have two weeks' start of the other eleven. McFadden will coach the team. Ten of last year's team are back at school. Twenty-one players turned out for light practice on Monday and much enthusiasm was shown.

March 9, 1905

WOULD HOLD
BIG GAME ON
THANKSGIVING

STANFORD UNIVERSITY, August 82.—According to the statements of Manager R. W. Barrett, it is almost sure the intercollegiate football game will be played on Thanksgiving day, beginning with next year. The athletic authorities of both Stanford and the University of California are reported as being strongly in favor of the idea, and it has been decided to bring the plan up for ratification before the intercollegiate committee at its annual meeting in January of next year. Several advantages of the Thanksgiving game are advanced by those who are encouraging the change. Aside from the financial aspect the most important feature in favor of the proposition is that it will do away entirely with the possibility of post-season games, which are considered very inadvisable. It is also pointed out that the regular season need not begin so early if the big game should be moved forward to Thanksgiving day.

August 29, 1905

FOOTBALL PROSPECTS PROMISING

Notwithstanding the fact that but two days of the college term has passed Trainer Christie has already a fair conception of the material for football work. Of course, the freshmen are an entirely unknown quantity and will remain so until their registration on Monday. But, as regards the other three classes the outlook is most promising. In fact, Christie has found a decided improvement in the appearance and general condition of the veterans of last season who are back in college.

The majority of the big C men have returned, but unfortunately three of the best players that have represented California on the gridiron will not be here. These are Ben Stroud, captain of last year's team, "Heine" Heitmuller, tackle, and George Kerr, guard. Of those who are still in the game there are Haffy and Taylor at center, Stern, Gray, Foster Richardson and Stowe in the line. At end are Elliot and Kittrelle, and Henry. For the back field positions there are Snedigar, Kern and Sperry.

Besides these there are very many who came out regularly for practice last year but did not make the team. With the experience derived from the season's training there are some who will make the big C veterans work hard to retain their positions on the team.

Besides all this material there are the freshmen, concerning whom nothing definite can be determined at this early date.

Trainer Christie asks all men now in college who intend to come out for football practice to respond at the first call. He wishes to be able to make a fair estimate of the material at hand and also desires to show to the coaches a good example of California spirit and determination. Those who intend to try out for the team should call at the gymnasium Saturday at 9 a. m. to get suits.

Although no final decision has been made, it is probable that all the playing games and otherwise, will be done exclusively on California field. The first practice of the year will be held there on Monday afternoon at 4 o'clock. The men are to be at the gymnasium promptly at 3:30 p. m., where they will meet the coaches. J. W. Knibbs, Jr., and Dr. F. B. Griffin and Trainer Christie.

August 19, 1905

SQUAD OF SIXTY IN PRACTICE

Never before has football started as early and never before has the first practice of the year been carried on with greater vim than was manifest last night under the direction of Coach Knibbs and Assistant Coach Griffin. It was a start that augurs well for the building up of a team that will have all of the speed, sureness and strength that the old Dartmouth system can give.

At 4 o'clock sharp the coach met all of the men on the basket-ball ground near Hearst hall, and for a half-hour outlined in a clear-cut fashion the work for the season. The meeting was open to none but football men, but from the expressions of the men as these trotted out to the old practice field it was easy to see that every man out on the squad means business this time. All men were out either last year or before, and all realize what it means to put in a hard three months on the gridiron.

For over an hour and a half the big squad of sixty men practiced punting, falling on the ball, and passing. Particular notice has been given from the start by the coach in the proper snapping back of the ball. Boothe, De Armond, Whitman and Geary, were all given some fast practice work for the quarter back position. In the meantime the assistant coach was busily employed in attending to the light work of the rest of the squad.

The men who were given suits yesterday were, F. Abbott, J. E. Allen, R. G. Arlett, G. F. Ashley, P. E. Bowles, F. T. Barker, F. W. Bush, A. Coogan, C. Coil, G. R. Carter, L. J. Duprey, E. Dyer, D. C. Dutton, C. F. De Armond, R. Elliot, K. C. Gillis, L. D. Graham; W. Gabriel, J. W. Geary, W. R. Henderson, C. Henry, C. Haffey, S. Hammond, P. Herriot, Hooten, R. Jordan, W. N. Luce, D. H. Morse, F. D. Merrill, J. G. Newman, J. F. S. Northcroft, H. H. Mathieson, C. G. Osgood, C. Ollason, Parker, S. M. Richardson, J. G.

Schaffer, E. Stern, Smith, A. Seabury, St. John, G. L. Small, Shuey, H. W. Taylor, W. K. Tuller, F. M. Twitchell, T. L. Weddle, T. D. Watson, T. T. Waterman, J. C. Whitman. In addition to these men the following big C men had already obtained their suits and were on the field with the others: P. Gray, Jim Force, H. B. Foster, W. E. Sperry, R. W. Kittrelle, D. P. Boothe, W. Henry, and C. R. Zach-

Quite a number of men who were unable to turn out for the first practice will come out to-day and will swell the number of men on the field close to seventy. The freshmen were not given suits, but will be given them to-day or to-morrow and will appear on the day after for practice. It is expected that there will be a large number of the 1909 men out on the first day of practice.

The coach said: "I am pleased with the showing made to-night and will continue the same form of light practice for several days yet. There will be the regular punting, falling on the ball, etc., much the same as to-night. Later on we will conduct secret practice but it is now, of course, too early to tell when that will be. Although the men were a trifle awkward, as they naturally would be after a year of no football, they showed a great willingness and took to the new work well.

"We need men and every fellow in the University who has the ability should come out and work. Many men often think they have no powers and are afraid to come out. Oftentimes good material is lost in this way. We want every member of ...

August 22, 1905

RULES IN FOOTBALL CHANGED

The changes in the football rules for 1905, of which there are quite a number, for the most part bear upon more strict interpretation rather than anything that will affect the detail of the play itself.

Under rule 6, relating to a scrimmage, a distinction has been made between act of the snapper-back and act of any other players of the side in possession of the ball. If the snapper-back make a motion as if to snap the ball, whether he withholds it or not, the ball is regarded as in play and the scrimmage begins. If any other player of the side in possession of the ball make an attempt by a false start to draw the opponent offside and the ball is then snapped it shall be brought back and not be regarded as in play or the scrimmage commenced.

August 1905

They Lived to High.

Football Team Was Victim of Overeating.

Prof. Jaffa has put new light upon the football situation in his recent experiments on the kind and quality of food used by the football players. The bulletin shows the comparative value of certain foods and the test is made between teams of different parts of the country. An idea of the extravagance attendant upon the feeding of the teams is given by the author, who shows that fresh meat was served each meal and nothing that was left at one meal could be used again. Speaking of the expense as compared with any household he says:

"This dietary, compared with that of an ordinary well-to-do household, was very expensive. The average daily cost per man, 97 cents, greatly exceeds the amount paid by the majority of housekeepers. An average of a number of even more than ordinarily expensive dietaries would give a cost not over one-third of this amount. The cost of meat alone was 35 cents per man each day. Another large item of expense is the ale, which costs nearly 20 cents per day. The excessive cost of the diet, then, may be said to be due in considerable measure to the cost of the beverage, and of the large amounts of animal food purchased, and the great waste."

YOUTHFUL FOOTBALLERS DESIRE TO GET GAMES

The Pacific Football team would like to hear from any team in Berkeley under twelve years of age who will meet them on their own grounds or on the Pacific's gridiron. The team is composed of S. Rizzano, left end; F. Bertheaud, left tackle; C. Bennett or J. Smith, left guard; E. Sumnes, center; W. Hunrick, right guard; B. Johnson, right tacke; N. Claire or A. Lloyd, right end; E. Bradford, quarter back; A. Jones (captain), right half; A. Rizzano, left half; A. Johnson, full back; substitutes, M. Amnes, W. Connolly and C. Morehouse. Challengers should address Manager E. Bradford, 1734 Grove street, or telephone Mason 958.

Berkeley High Football Team. Courtesy of the Berkeley Architectural Heritage Association, photo #315.

BASEBALL RULES ARE ARRANGED

Cincinnati, Sept. 26.—President August Herrman and Secretary John E. Bruce were re-elected yesterday by the National Baseball Commission which then proceeded to the formulation of rules for the series of games for the world's championship between the National and American Leagues. No schedule of the world's championship games will be announced until the season is finished. For the same reason the umpires will not be made known at present.

After re-affirming the rules adopted for the games by the two leagues last fall the commission adopted a number of supplementary rules, among which are those requiring that all players eligible to take part in the games must have been under contract not later than August 31; the posting of a forfeit of $10,000 by the owners of the participating clubs for a faithful carrying out of the rules and provisions of the series and the fixing of the salaries of the umpires at $400 each for the series. It also was decided that the world's championship pennant should be raised in the presence of the National Commission on a date to be agreed on, this to be after the opening of the championship season of 1906.

In the matter of field rules it was decided that no spectators should be allowed nearer than 235 feet from the home base in right and left fields, or 275 feet in center field at these games, nor within less than 25 feet of the foul lines in any portion of the field.

September 26, 1905

The Berkeley Merchants Baseball Team. Standing third from left appears to be Marshal Vollmer of the Police Department. The men seated third and fourth from the left are both labeled as "Judge Waste." Courtesy of the Berkeley Historical Society.

Two baseball players after a game in early Berkeley.
Courtesy of the Berkeley Firefighters Association.

SAN FRANCISCO, September 15.—A bomb was exploded here yesterday in sporting circles when "Billy" Nolan, manager for "Battling" Nelson, mode an affidavit to the effect that he had been approached on several occasions by Harry Corbett the well known sporting man, who demanded that he contribute to the fund for the purpose of accomplishing the defeat of the Ralston anti-prize fight bill.

In his affidavit Nolan furthermore states that Corbett is now holding $1300 of his money in hopes that he (Nolan) will give up $1000 towards defraying the expense of boodling legislators in order to accomplish the defeat of Senator Ralston's bill at the last session of the legislature.

In case District Attorney Seymour of Sacramento sees fit to have the grand jury indict the leaders of the anti-Ralston forces, the affidavit of Nolan will naturally be the most important piece of initiative evidence. Senator Ralston is now debating the advisability of personally laying the matter before the grand jury of Sacramento county. He is convinced that money was used to defeat his bill. The affidavit of Nolan he considers a vindication and corroboration of his theory of boodling and bribery.

In an interview yesterday Senator Ralston, who fathered the measure, said, in part:

"There is no question in my mind but that money was used to influence the votes of several members of the Assembly against the anti-prize fight bill, as it was the common talk on the floor of the Lower House before and after the defeat of the bill. My reason for this belief is that a week prior to the defeat of the bill several of the members who were interested in its passage in the Assembly stated that they were assured of enough votes to put the bill through.

"While the anti-prize fight bill met with defeat at the last session of the Legislature, it is my firm belief that the people of the State of California will insist on their representatives passing such a bill at the next session of the Legislature. The expose now being made as an aftermath of this last fight at Colma will undoubtedly lead to this change of sentiment."

September 15, 1905

NEGRO FIGHTER IS FINED $200

[By Direct Leased Wire to the Gazette]

NEW YORK, April 1.—Jack Johnson, the black heavyweight champion prizefighter, was fined $200 here today on the charge of attempting a statutory offense upon the complaint of Amy Douglas, a mulatto woman.

The big negro appeared in the courtroom with confidence that bordered on affrontery and paid the fine with a great assumption of gusto, taking the bills from a large roll of currency.

There was a marked difference in the attitude of the people in the street and courtroom toward the negro as compared to his reception upon his arrival here, but he apparently was oblivious to it.

As he left the courtroom to enter an automobile he was taunted by two negro girls concerned in the charge, but as the car started he called back: "I certainly got off cheap; that was just cigarette money."

The car then whirled away amid the jeers and hoots of the street crowd.

April 1, 1909

LIVES OF ATHLETES ARE LONG

Berkeley High School Track Team. Circa 1897. Courtesy of the Berkeley Historical Society, catalog #1497.

According to Dr. William G. Anderson, in his article on "Making a Yale Athlete" in Everybody's Magazine for July, college athletics tend to prolong rather than to shorten life. "The hostile criticism," says Dr. Anderson, "that athletes 'die young' has been so often made without definite refutation that it passes for truth among those who mistake rumor for fact. An investigation of the health and longevity of college athletes must be exhaustive to furnish trustworthy data. Realizing the importance of such statistics, Professor Franklin B. Dexter, the librarien of Yale, has recently completed the task of collecting the records of 761 athletes who competed in intercollegiate events and won their 'Y's' on the eleven, the nine, the crew, and the track team between 1855 and 1904. This material was gathered for a prominent life insurance company, and later given to the director of the gymnasium. The main deductions are as follows:

"Of these 761 athletes, 51 have died since graduation. The causes were: Consumption 12, pneumonia 4, drowning 6, heart disease 2, suicide 2, war and accident 3, died from unknown causes, or disappeared 10, from various diseases (fevers, appendicitis, cancer, diphtheria, paresis, dissipation, etc.) 12.

"Of these 51 men, 18 rowed, 16 played football, 11 were track athletes, and 6 played baseball. The ages of those who have died show these extremes and averages:

Sport.	Extremes of age.	Average ages at death.
Crew	20 to 68 years.	47.7 years
Football	22 to 37 years.	30.3 years
Baseball	20 to 39 years.	28.3 years
Track	21 to 33 years.	25.4 years

"Turning to the 710 living athletes, those who have passed 40 may be thus grouped:

113 are between 40 and 49 years of age.

86 are betmeen 50 and 59 years of age.

22 are between 60 and 69 years of age.

"Of the Yale athletes in their latter years, 14 are between 60 and 65 years, 1 is 65, 3 are 66, 1 is 67, 2 are 68, and 1 is 69. In brief, barring violent deaths, only 40 of these 761 Yale athletes, in a period of nearly fifty years, have been lost from the ranks of the living.

"I have been assured by a life insurance expert that college athletes, barring the track men, show a better average expectation of life than their non-athletic classmates, and much better than the general average of insured lives."

July 13, 1905

26. International

At the turn of the century, Ireland's Ulster Orangemen called for an end to the sectarianism dividing Protestants and Catholics. In the Boxer Rebellion, China fought against foreign missionaries and the industries that always followed their arrival. A Berkeley soldier wrote home to his mother from the front lines about the battle for his life and his struggle to do his duty.

Though the news in some cases is identical one hundred years later, some of the *Gazette's* reporting styles are much more personal than those of today.

TO STOP RELIGIOUS STRIFE.

Would Bury Sectarianism Which Divides the People.

Belfast, July 15.—An independent section of Ulster Orangemen headed by Commoner Sloan, has issued a striking manifesto to the country calling for the burial of sectarianism, which now is dividing Protestants and Catholics, and invoking the co-operation of all secular forces for the promotion of the national welfare.

The manifesto expresses distrust of English parties, which, it says, will continue in the future as in the past to play off Catholics and Protestants against each other to the prejudice of the country's higher claims. The country, too, has been neglected in the strife of party and creed, the manifesto continues, and there now is room for a patriotic party having the policy to rid Ireland of the domination of impracticable creeds and organized tyrannies and to secure the desired redress.

Berkeley soldier Claude Venther. Courtesy of the Berkeley Firefighters Association.

Berkeley Boy Tells of Fighting in China.

The following letter, dated Fort Taku, China, July 1, 1900, has been received by Mrs. Farrar of Virginia street from her son J. T. Farrar, who is with the U. S. S. Newark, now stationed at China:

MY DEAR MOTHER:—I suppose you hear all the news in the papers about our hard fighting against the Boxers and the Imperial troops. On the twelfth of June we were attacked by a few thousand Boxers. That fight lasted a long two hours. Our men were not cut up so badly as the other nations. We slaughtered the enemy.

We were all on one train, Americans, English, Germans, Russians, Japs, Austrians and Italians, about 3000 in all. The railroad was all torn up between Peking and Tien-tsin and we were building the road as we went.

We were constantly having a little "rub" after the twelfth until the eighteenth, when we were met by the Imperial army. We fought them half a day and at dark they retreated. At that time I was so sick I could hardly walk but I turned out and grit my teeth and kept at it. Our loss that day was one man killed and two men and Captain McCalla wounded. He did not report his wound until next day, and the same day I could not walk, so the two wounded men and I were sent back on the "armored train," the last train to get back as they tore up the track we laid. The British lost heavily on that day.

On the twenty-second of June my best friend, Harry A. Broman, was killed by a shrapnel. It knocked his brains out and hit him in the body in three places. He told me while we were ashore, "Joe I'm not coming back." I tried to cheer him but I could not.

My best suit of blue is ripped to pieces by shrapnel. It tore through my knapsack and spoiled my clothes. Captain McCalla was wounded three times and is now on board.

We expect to start for San Francisco in a few months. The rumor has it that we start the last of September. I am able to be around a little now and feel much better. J. TEEL FARRAR.

August 7, 1900

BERKELEYANS IN CHINA.

The trouble in China has caused particular local interest to center around the Berkeleyans who are there.

A. Roy Lyon recently sent the following interesting letter to his parents, Mr. and Mrs. A. J. Lyon. He is a first-class apprentice on the U. S. S. Yorktown, which was stationed at China at the commencement of the Boxer uprising.

When the Yorktown was at Mare Island Mr. Lyon distinguished himself by diving from the high yard arm of the vessel to save the life of a drowning comrade.

His letter is in part as follows:

"I guess China's days are all numbered now. It will take all she has to pay for what she has done this time. All hands will want a piece of China now. Guess old Uncle will want a good coaling station. We need one in China badly. Coal costs $36, Mexican, a ton in Chee Foo and is very poor at that.

"I think we will lay in Chee Foo a month or so. You see we belong to Admiral Kempff's fleet and it is quite probable that we will remain in China instead of going back to the Philippines. We hope to see a little of Japan before returning and the chances are we will. I will look for Earle Swan if we go around Tokio.

"We left Shanghai on the 13th of June for Chee Foo and arrived there on the 15th. We lay there until the 18th, when we received the news of the trouble in Taku. Then we went to Taku and arrived there early on the 19th; lay there all day and then pulled out for Chee Foo again.

"There were at least fifty of the finest battleships and cruisers of all nations lying in Taku. It was the prettiest sight I have ever seen. It was a pity that the large ships could not get within firing range of the forts. They never would have known what struck them."

July 25, 1900

Members of Berkeley's Volunteer Fire Department were quick to volunteer to serve the nation's military needs. In this photo (taken about 1898) these six young volunteer firemen had signed up, received their uniforms and were having a last photograph before departing into the military. The third man from the left is fireman Frank McCourt. He would become the first Berkeley soldier killed in the Spanish-American War. An article written in the Berkeley Daily Gazette *sheds light on his sacrifice. Courtesy of the Berkeley Firefighters Association.*

McCourt Died Fighting.

A Letter From Luzon Tells of His Heroic Conduct.

Details of the sad death of Joseph McCourt, the well-known Berkeley boy who was killed in the Philippines, are contained in the following letter from Sergeant Chester T. Smythe:

Quingua, Luzon, P. I.,
July 25, 1900.

EDITOR BERKELEY GAZETTE: Dear Sir—Among the bundles of papers sent to me by friends in California I was much delighted to find some late issues of the BERKELEY GAZETTE. In looking over them I saw a notice, in the issue of June 12, 1900, of the death of Joseph McCourt. It simply said that he was killed near San Miguel de Mayumo, adding: "At that time Captain Charles D. Roberts was captured, together with two privates, and a comrade of Mr. McCourt's. Private John A. Green was also killed." As this is

but part of the story and as Joe was a Berkeley boy, having many friends in Berkeley, I trust you will kindly publish an account of his heroic death.

On the night of May 28, 1900, the town of San Miguel de Mayumo, containing a population of 21,000 and garrisoned by Companies "K," "L" and "I" of the 35th Regiment of Infantry, was fired upon from all sides.

The troops turned out and a fusilade of shots was exchanged in the darkness, after which the attacking party of "Insurrectos" withdrew. This was the first intimation the military authorities had that any considerable body of Insurgents had congregated in that vicinity.

The next day Captain Roberts with six men, all mounted, went scouting in the direction of Cabul. After exploring the country for some miles in all directions they reached the vicinity of the barrio of Santa Lucia, a place seven miles from San Miguel, about noon time. The men being hungry a halt was

made, and they proceeded to cook their dinner of bacon, hard tack and coffee under the shade of a large mango tree, their horses being staked about twenty-five yards distant.

The men had just commenced to eat when a volley was poured in upon them. The shot fell like rain, it being almost impossible to tell where they came from.

Quartermaster Sergeant Galen was the first to fall dead. At the first volley McCourt received a shot in the chest. An attempt was made by the men to reach their horses, but the fire was too hot to allow of it.

Private Green fell mortally wounded and Kinger, reaching his horse, had one foot already in the stirrup when he received a shot in the knee. He fell, and his horse starting to run, he was dragged some distance. This left but five men to contend with an unknown number of the enemy, who seemed to be increasing every moment.

Captain Roberts exhausted all the ammunition of his revolver and then secured the kit and gun of one of the dead soldiers. The bravery of Piper Frindlater has been commented upon, but no mention, in print, has ever been made of the heroic co_duct of Private Joseph McCourt. Although this was the first time that he had ever been under fire, he did not seem to know what fear was. Riddled with bullets as he was, (five shots were found in his body), he fought like a hero. He seemed to be a special target for the enemies' bullets for they fell around him like rain. Never once did he dream of asking for quarter but fought until he finally fell, shot through the heart.

Not until all the men were either dead or wounded, with the exception of one other beside himself, and all the ammunition was exhausted did Captain Roberts surrender. The Insurrectos, contrary to former custom treated the prisoners with great consideration. Kinger, being too badly wounded to travel, was placed on a cariboo and escorted, in the night, to a short distance from the American out-post near San Miguel. Of the final release of Captain Roberts and his companions, everyone has heard.

Four or five days before Joe's death, he and some of his comrades were discussing the probability of an attack and of what their conduct would be in such an event.

Poor Joe, who as I have stated, had never been under fire, said he didn't know what he would do in such a case, but he guessed he would run! This only shows that a man can never tell what he will do until the moment for action comes. No braver soldier ever fought than Joe McCourt.

CHESTER T. SMYTHE,
Serg. Co. H., 35th Infant., U. S. V. I.

September 5, 1900

Major Rice and the California Heavy Artillery and Hospital Corps. Courtesy of the Berkeley Firefighters Association.

WARNING AGAINST JAPANESE

Walter MacArthur of San Francisco, in a stirring address, informed the members of the Chinese, Japanese and Corean League of Alameda County last night of the dangers of unlimited immigration of Asiatics. The speakers gave the members of the league much good advice and urged them on in their campaign to secure more stringent exclusion laws.

"It is a question," said MacArthur, "whether or not all the territory of the United States west of the Rocky mountains shall be saved to the American people, or whether it shall be abandoned to the people of Asia." Continuing. he said that when the people of the United States had been told the condition as they exist they "will arise and demand that this country remain, and absolutely so, in the possession of the American people."

MacArthur then outlined the inroads the Oriental laborers are making in the labor market, and said they were gradually crowding more and more into the industrial and business world, and that their encroachment was being felt, and seriously so, by the people of the West. He concluded his address with an eloquent period, in which he said: "I feel that the people of the West will be worthy of their noble heritage, and that they will settle this grave problem, peaceably or otherwise, as necessity commands, but it will be settled right."

President T. F. Marshall in opening the meeting created considerable enthusiasm with a brief address in which he said the league had been gaining members rapidly; that the membership now numbered over 400, and that within a short time there would be at least 1000 members enrolled. Efforts, he said, had been made to secure money with which to pay the expenses of the league, and controbutions had been coming in rapidly, and he believed no trouble would be encountered in securing sufficient funds to carry on the work.

Chinese Prisoners Slaughtered.

Germans Revenge the Killing of a Patrol.

Berlin, Nov. 1.—Papers here have published a letter from a German soldier in China in which he says: "We captured, Sunday, seventy-four Chinese who had killed a German patrol. They were sentenced to death and in order to save cartridges were ordered to be stabbed with bayonets. It is impossible to describe the fearful slaughter. We forgot we had once been men."

November 1, 1900

President Marshall appointed J. R. Kelley, G. T. Stone, H. C. Matthews, E. E. Travis and J. O'Byrne, members of the organization committee. A. E. Maliden was elected financial secretary.

JAPAN WILL IGNORE CHINA.

Latter Country Will Have no Voice in Peace Conference.

Pekin, July 13.—The Chinese government recently notified the Russian, Japanese and also the other legations that China would refuse to recognize any arrangements made at the approaching peace conference in the United States, regarding Chinese interests, unless China was consulted in the matter.

The Japanese replied politely, plainly intimating that the notification received from China would in nowise affect the plan of action adopted by Japan.

No reply has yet been received from Russia.

FACES DEATH
IN AN AIRSHIP
FOR 13 HOURS

Count Zeppelin and Four Passengers Battle
With Windstorm Which Disables
Great Airship's Motor.

[By Direct Leased Wire to the Gazette]
DINGOLFINGF, April 1.—After a battle of thirteen hours with adverse winds, with one motor out of commission, Count Zeppelin landed his great airship near here late this afternoon.

The accident to the rear motor caused the ship's helplessness and made necessary the evolutions which caused great apprenension to those who witnessed the struggle with the wind.

The forward motor worked well, but it did not produce sufficient power to drive the ship against the air currents, which at this time reached great velocity. On his way here the count dropped the following note to the cavalrymen who were following the route of the ship:

"Beloved Comrades: Many thanks. Please continue to follow me until the wind dies down."

Count Zeppelin's masterful management of the crippled airship in the face of the windstorm is proclaimed one of the most wonderful feats of aerial navigation the world has seen, and his voyage of today has added new glory to the career of the veteran admiral of the air.

Loses Control of Craft.

BERLIN, April 1.—The great Zeppelin airship with Count Zeppelin and four passengers aboard, was driven by a terrific storm from Friedrichsaffen to the environs of Munich today and was sighted this evening after having been missing more than ten hours.

Though Munich was the count's destination he evidently could not control the great craft in the storm and made no attempt to descend.

Zeppelin steered the ship about and started to return toward Friedrichsaffen a distance of 11 miles, but could make little or no headway against the wind.

When last seen the ship was driven rapidly in a northwesterly direction from Munich. The city authorities are following it in automobiles and several squadrons of cavalry are also ordered to follow it closely.

Fear for Party.

BERLIN, April 1.—Grave fears are entertained today for the safety of Count Zeppelin, the famous aeronaut and a party of fourteen friends, who made an ascent this morning at sunrise at Friederichsaffen and attempted a flight to Munich, in the new monster Zeppelin airship.

The great dirigible balloon was caught in a fierce gale that sprang up soon after the ascent.

The idea of reaching Munich evidently was quickly abandoned. The ship was driven out of its course.

When last seen the air monster was drifting in the wind and apparently was unmanageable.

After ten hours had passed without any further report of the vessel, the fear that the count and his guests had met with some serious accident became general. Great uneasiness is felt by their friends and relatives.

April 1, 1909

27. Trivia

These lively stories and anecdotes peppered the pages of the *Gazette* in the early 1900s.

Legend has it that Chinese magical bracelets were made of jade. A Chinese emperor was said to communicate with the living from the land of the dead through his jade bracelet.

Can you believe that a physician saved a patient's life by causing an explosion in the man's belly? And how do you explain the unique gait of the Native American woodsman or an eight-foot-tall Indian skeleton found near Baltimore?

How does a skillful Burmese make a fire? How did the Chinese name their children? How about the Chinese villagers who believed they had water buffalo in their stomachs?

His Seidlitz Powder Cartridge.

How a man's life was saved by a common seidlitz powder is described by a German physician, Dr. Franck, who was called to treat a man who had swallowed a large piece of tough meat which stuck in his gullet. As it was impossible to dislodge the meat by natural means and as the patient's condition was critical, the doctor tried the efficacy of the gas which is generated when the constituents of a seidlitz powder are mixed. He directed the man to swallow the two halves of one of the powders separately, and the resulting pneumatic pressure, aided by the man, who shut his mouth and closed the nasal passages, was sufficient to drive the piece of meat out of the gullet into the stomach.

THE BREAD WAS AN EXTRA.

An English Cafe Charge That Surprised an American.

"One of the strangest things about the management of English restaurants," remarked a gentleman who has recently returned from a visit to London to the writer, "is the custom of charging diners for every slice of bread which they eat. For instance, a day or two before my departure from the British capital I, as a mark of esteem, invited several English friends to dine with me at one of the most celebrated of the fashionable west end restaurants. Well, the repast was served in a private room, and everything went off splendidly until the coffee and cigar stage was reached and I asked that my bill be brought to me. There, to my utter astonishment, the head waiter, in the hearing of the assembled company, approached me and in a loud voice asked, 'And how many breads 'ave you 'ad, sir?'

"This question I could not answer, as I had not been engaged in counting the number of slices consumed, but one of my guests, who had evidently kept track of the bread, noticing my embarrassment, said in my behalf, 'Four plates.'

"'Ah,' muttered the waiter, 'that's 1 shillin hextra.' And after adding the amount to my bill he handed it to me for inspection.

"Of course I paid for the bread, but I have been wondering ever since I did so why the American custom of not charging for 'the staff of life' is not introduced over there."—Washington Star.

A Village of Lunatics.

Laos, in Cochin China, is, according to Dr. Lefevre, a village of out and out fools or lunatics. A common form of mania with them is to believe they have a buffalo in the stomach. Hopeless cases of this delusion, or "pipop," as they are called, are thrown into the water and if they save themselves are accounted free from the possession.

How the Burmese Make Fire.

One day a Burmese messenger brought me a note. While he was waiting for the reply, I observed an object something like a boy's popgun suspended around his waist. On asking what it was he showed me that it was an implement for producing fire. It was a rude example of a scientific instrument employed by lecturers at home to illustrate the production of heat by suddenly compressed air. A piston fitted into the tube; the former was hollowed at the lower end and smeared with wax to receive a piece of cotton or tinder, which when pressed into it adhered. The tube was closed at one end. Placing the piston at the top of the tube, with a smart blow he struck it down and immediately withdrew it with the tinder on fire, the sudden compression of the air having ignited it. I was so much struck with the scientific ingenuity of this rude implement that I procured it from the Burman and sent it to the Asiatic society of Bengal, with a short description of its uses.—"Recollections of My Life," by Surgeon General Sir John Fayer.

FIND ANIMAL REFERRED TO IN THE BIBLE

Naturalists have discovered in American Fork Canyon, near Salt Lake City, a single specimen of the coney, an animal spoken of in the Bible and supposed to be extinct! For several months miners in the canyon had noticed the animal because of its peculiar habits. It makes its appearance on a rock at intervals of almost exactly one hour and utters twenty or thirty sharp barks ending with a low, weird and uncanny sound. Then it disappears for an hour.

The animal is about fifteen inches long with a snout like a hog. Its eyes are bright and snappy; it has no tail and its hair is gray brown. The miners protect the animal and will not permit it to be molested. Utah naturalists have seen it with glasses and declare it is a coney.

Naming the Chinese Baby.

In China girls are called instead of Mary Ann or Marguerite "Spring Peach," "Cloudy Moon," "Celestial Happiness" or what may not be considered so nice, "Come-along-a-little-brother" or "Add-a-younger-brother" or "Lead-everlasting-younger-brothers." The latter means that a son would have been more welcome than a little "go away child," as they call the girls. They belong to the family of the husbands to be and do not count in the family of their birth, so that when a Chinaman is asked, "How many children have you?" he makes no count of the girls, although he may have ten. The boys only he counts, and his reply will indicate only the number of boys.

He gives his sons such names as "Ancestral Piety," "Ancestral Knowledge," "Practical Industry," "Able to Sing Out," "Second God of Learning," "Excite the Clouds," "Beginning of Joy," "All Virtue Complete." The little slaves who begin life as household drudges before they graduate lower answer to such names as "As You Please," "Sparrows' Crumbs," "Joy to Serve," "Your Happiness," "Not For Me."—Kansas City Journal.

"HERE IS THE TRAIL."

Signs Used by Indian Tribes and White Hunters.

First among the trail signs that are used by Indians and white hunters and most likely to be of use to the traveler, says a writer in Country Life In America, are ax blazes on tree trunks. These may vary greatly with locality, but there is one everywhere in use with scarcely any variation. This is simply the white spot nicked off by knife or ax and meaning, "Here is the trail."

The Ojibways and other woodland tribes use twigs for a great many signs. The hanging broken twig, like the simple blaze, means, "This is the trail." The twig clean broken off and laid on the ground across the line of march means, "Break from your straight course and go in the line of the butt end," and when an especial warning is meant the butt is pointed toward the one following the trail and raised somewhat in a forked twig. If the butt of the twig were raised and pointing to the left it would mean, "Look out, camp," or "Ourselves or the enemy or the game we have killed is out that way."

The old buffalo hunters had an established signal that is yet used by mountain guides. It is as follows:

Two shots in rapid succession, an interval of five seconds by the watch, then one shot, means, "Where are you?" The answer, given at once and exactly the same, means: "Here I am. What do you want?" The reply to this may be one shot, which means, "All right; I only wanted to know where you were." But if the reply repeats the first it means: "I am in serious trouble. Come as fast as you can."

THE INDIAN'S GAIT.

It Gives Him Perfect Balance, With Great Economy of Force.

A woodsman walks with a rolling motion, his hips swaying an inch or more to the stepping side, and his pace is correspondingly long. This hip action may be noticed to an exaggerated degree in the stride of a professional pedestrian, but the latter walks with a heel and toe step, whereas an Indian's or sailor's step is more nearly flat footed. In the latter case the center of gravity is covered by the whole foot. The poise is as secure as that of a ropewalker. The toes are pointed straight forward or even a trifle inward, so that the inside of the heel, the outside of the ball of the foot and the smaller toes all do their share of work and assist in balancing. Walking in the woods in this manner one is not so likely either to trip over projecting roots, stones and other traps as he would be if the feet formed hooks by pointing outward. The advantage is obvious in snowshoeing. If the Indian were turned to stone while in the act of stepping the statue would probably stand balanced on one foot. This gait gives the limbs great control over his movements. He is always poised. If a stick cracks under him it is because of his weight and not by reason of the impact. He goes silently on and with great economy of force. His steady balance enables him to put his moving foot down as gently as you would lay an egg on the table.—Field and Stream.

Gigantic Skeletons Found.

Baltimore, July 7.—A number of gigantic skeletons of prehistoric Indians, nearly eight feet tall, are reported to have been discovered along the banks of the Choptank river, in this state, by employes of the Maryland Academy of Sciences and are now at the academy's building, where they are being articulated and restored.

The Useful Donkey.

In Syria, says a traveler, I saw a donkey put to an extraordinary use. One evening just before the dinner hour in our tent the Arab cook rushed hurriedly out of the door of the kitchen tent with a glass carafe in his hand. He went up to the row of donkeys, horses and packages tethered close by. Seizing the tail of the smallest of the donkeys, he hastily thrust it into the carafe, gave it two or three vigorous turns inside the bottle and then as quickly removed the unconcerned tail. Thus he had cleansed the water bottle for our dinner. It is in Syria also that the strange fashion exists of shaving the donkeys' coats in different ways, much as a lady of fashion shaves her French poodle. A choice breed of donkeys, known as "Bagdad mules," is much cherished in the neighborhood of Damascus. Their long, hairy coat, usually of pure white or pale gray, admits of fantastic clipping.

HOW ZULU WOMEN SEW.

They Use Skewers For Needles and Giraffe Sinews For Thread.

The skill of the Zulus of South Africa in sewing fur is a household word in South Africa, and some of the other tribes compete with them. The needle employed is widely different from that used by the ordinary needlewomen. In the first place, it has no eye; in the second, it is like a skewer, pointed at one end and thick at the other.

The thread is not of cotton, but is made of the sinews of various animals, the best being made from the sinews in the neck of a giraffe. It is stiff, inelastic, with a great tendency to "kink" and tangle itself up with anything near it. Before being used it is steeped in hot water until it is quite soft and is then beaten between two smooth stones, which causes it to separate into filaments, which can thus be obtained of any length and thickness. Thus the seamstress has a considerable amount of labor before she commences with the real work in hand.

Finally she squats on the ground (for no native stands to work or do anything else who can possibly help it) and, taking her needle, bores two holes in the edges of the rug or garment on which she is working. The thread is then pushed through with the butt of the needle, drawn tight, and two more holes are made with a like result, the skewer progressing very slowly, but fast enough for a country where time is of no value whatever.

The skin upon which the seamstress is working is damped with water before she commences, and as the damp thread and hide dry out they bring the work very closely together.

SOME QUEER DREAMS.

VISIONS THAT RESULTED IN THE CAPTURE OF CRIMINALS.

Marvelous Manifestations That Baffle the Ingenuity of Man to Explain and Which Prove Anew That Truth Is Stranger Than Fiction.

A very remarkable instance of the tracing of a criminal by means of a dream occurred in St. Louis. A woman named Mary Thornton was detained in custody for a month, charged with the murder of her husband. A week or so after her arrest she requested to see one of the prison officials and told him she had dreamed that an individual named George Ray had murdered her spouse, giving the official at the same time full details of the tragedy as witnessed in her vision. The man Ray was not suspected at the time, but the prison authorities were so much impressed by the woman's obvious earnestness that a search was at once made for him.

After some delay he was traced and charged with the crime, the details of the same as seen in the dream being rehearsed to him. Overcome with astonishment, he then and there confessed that he had committed the crime. Curiously enough, the woman had only met the murderer once and believed him to be on the very best of terms with her husband.

Almost as remarkable was the case of a woman named Drew, who dreamed one night that her husband, a retired sailor, had been murdered by a peddler at a Gravesend tavern, where the said husband was in the habit of putting up when visiting the town in question. The first news that awaited her on rising in the morning was that her spouse had been assassinated at the very tavern she had seen in her extraordinary vision, whereupon she burst into hysterical tears and cried out that her dream had come true.

She calmed down somewhat after a few hours and then handed the police officials an exact description of the peddler of the vision, giving a minute account of his dress, which included a blue coat of a very peculiar pattern. Marvelous as the fact may appear, a man wearing such a coat and following the occupation of a peddler was discovered two days later at an inn some six miles from Gravesend, and, on being taxed with the crime, he at once admitted that he was guilty and that robbery had been the motive of the outrage. He was hanged soon afterward, his doom having been brought about by the flimsy evidence of a woman's dream.

Women as dreamers seem more successful than men, but a rather peculiar instance of a crime being traced by a vision and in which the dreamer was a member of the male sex comes from Rennes, in France. A worthy merchant, having quitted his office one Saturday evening, proceeded home to dinner and after enjoying a substantial meal lay down on the couch and fell into a light doze. A very vivid dream then came to him wherein he saw two men of the burglar type engaged in rifling the safe in his office, and so much impressed was he by the vision that he resolved, upon awakening, to at once go to the office and see that everything was under lock and key.

His amazement may be imagined when, on arriving there, he discovered the door forced and a burglary in progress. To summon a couple of gendarmes was the work of an instant, and five minutes later the thieves, who proved to be notorious housebreakers, were on their way to the police depot, where the prosecutor told his extraordinary story. In view of the fact that the safe contained valuables to the extent of some thousands of pounds, the dream in question proved a very fortunate one for the dreamer.

How to explain these marvelous manifestations, which prove once more that truth is stranger than fiction, is a task beyond the ingenuity of man to compass. Perchance the theory of telepathy may have something to do with the mysterious business, but even that theory would appear rather inadequate in such cases as the aforementioned.

A skillful forger who moved in the highest circles of society was once detected by the agency of a dream. The affair occurred in Boston and caused the greatest excitement of the time.

The forger, a young man of eight or nine and twenty, had become acquainted with a rich publisher, at whose house he became a constant guest. One day the publisher's bankers discovered that some one was forging their client's signature to various large checks, and two detectives were at once instructed to look out for the culprit.

Their efforts proved useless, but one evening the publisher's youngest daughter, a little girl of 11, dreamed that she saw a man whom she described as "like Mr. Blank," the visitor to whom reference has been made, sitting in a room in Maine street copying her father's signature. The child's dream was communicated to the police, who, though inclined to ridicule the same at the outset, eventually promised to have the gentleman in question watched, with the result that his lodgings were raided and a complete plant for the making of bank notes found there. It then transpired that he was a man who was wanted for manifold forgeries throughout the Union, and he was sent to prison for a very long term.

The child's dream was all the more extraordinary in view of the fact that she was too young to understand the leading incidents of the business and attributed the copying of her father's signature in the dream to the gentleman wanting to write slowly, like papa. Strange, very strange, but none the less true, and proving once more that, as Hamlet remarked, "There are more things in heaven and earth, Horatio, than are dreamed of in your philosophy."—Philadelphia Times.

28. Looking Forward in 1900

Having left Berkeley in 1888, one former resident called his home a struggling village. He recalled how residents had reluctantly consented to a sewer line being installed on Dwight Way. They believed Berkeley would never be large enough to justify the expense. When this prior resident returned to Berkeley in 1900, he was taken aback at what he saw. As he debarked from the train, he recognized only one building. He was amazed at the blocks of new buildings and stylish homes.

The spirit of progress was alive and growing. Businessmen in Berkeley were engaged in a venture to purchase three or four flying wagons, as the automobile was then called. The auto would carry up to ten passengers and for a dime would take passengers anywhere in town. Their plans were delayed only by the backlog of orders at the automobile manufacturing plants.

The car, a symbol of increasing status and freedom, wasn't always warmly received. Americans were hotly engaged in a love-hate relationship with their new icon. Some were disturbed that drivers, fueled by power and speed, drove their vehicles recklessly through the towns with little regard for human and animal safety.

All over the country the romance was on a rocky road. Reports from the East Coast depicted some residents waiting for automobiles to pass through their towns so that they could stone them. In the Bay Area, Marin county residents were irate that drivers brazenly disregarded the law and drove over their mountains. South of Oakland, some were so opposed to the car that they refused to sell gasoline to car owners!

Two automobiles rigged up for a spirited ride in Berkeley.
Courtesy of the Berkeley Firefighters Association.

EDITORIAL COLUMN

(Friend Wm. Richardson, Editor.)

AUTO-MANIA.

Some time ago the Gazette called attention to the growth and spread of that dread disease auto-mania.

We showed how the average sane man when he placed his hand on the power lever of the automobile frequently became a maniac who would endanger his own life and the lives of others.

There has been quite a little complaint in Berkeley on account of the reckless driving of automobiles. The local drivers show much caution but the drivers who come over from Oakland and San Francisco seem to have no regard for human life. There have been a number of narrow escapes of little children on Telegraph avenue. This is a broad street and the insane autoists come flying up the street at a mile-a-minute clip.

The town should pass an ordinance bringing these crazy individuals to time.

The secretary of the state organization of automobilists has written to the county and city authorities all over the State and ask them to strictly enforce the laws against fast driving on the public highways.

The automen have found out that public sentiment has reached such a pitch of indignation that all autoists are suffering for the sins of the few.

We are glad to see that the automobile men have taken such a wise stand.

The auto in the hands of a safe and sane driver is a thing of comfort and pleasure. Let the reckless and insane driver be punished and it will be for the good of automobiling and the general public.

August 31, 1905

AUTOMOBILE INSANITY.

Take a sane man and give him an automobile and in the majority of cases he becomes a reckless demon who will not only endanger his own life but the lives of others.

There are some staid people who can become the owners of automobiles and drive them at a moderate rate of speed and have due regard for life. The auto-owners in Berkeley are, we are pleased to say, sensible and careful. There are many sane drivers but there are many insane ones and these are the class under discussion.

Every day the dispatches contains accounts of deaths and accidents by the reckless use of autos. Prominent men, millionaires and business men, are being killed off. These accidents are all due to reckless driving. When a machine is driven with care and at moderate speed there is no danger.

But the autoist grasps the lever, he feels the thrill of power as the machine darts forward, he goes faster and faster, he fairly flies along in a desire to beat a record, he has lost his reason, he is a maniac.

Suppose an inmate of Napa should get in an auto and proceed to lower the record between San Francisco and Los Angeles. What of it? Nothing. That would be the correct thing for the legally adjudged insane man to do. But what of the man outside the insane asylum? What of the man supposed to be sane who does these things?

It is certainly a strange thing that men will sacrifice their lives in an attempt to lower a record or merely go fast.

Would it not be well for the officers to bring a few of these mad autoists before the lunacy commission and have them committed to the State institutions until they recover from their wild hallucinations?

There is another phase of the question and that is the danger to the lives of others. The mad autoist drives his car along at reckless speed without regard to others.

In some places in the east the country people have become so incensed that they line up along the roads when autoists are expected and pelt them with stones.

In Marin county the people are aroused over the outrageous action of the automobile men in trying to run over mountaineous roads in violation of the county ordinance. In Napa county there is a fight on between the people and the auto owners. The people on the roads south of Oakland in this county are so angry at the auto-men that they will not sell them gasoline for their machines.

All over California and for that matter all of the country there is a popular uprising against the mad autoist.

The man who recently lowered the record between San Francisco and Los Angeles to some twenty-one hours should be a subject of one of two of our great state institutions. If the lunacy commission find him sane, the criminal courts should attend to his case. This man with extraordinary recklessness ran through San Jose and other cities at a rate of speed that endangered human life.

Think of this maniac or criminal rushing over the Santa Barbara mountains at a high rate of speed utterly regardless of the lives or comfort of

July 31, 1905

Interesting Innovation.

Movement on Foot to Provide Berkeley With an Automobile Service.

That the spirit of progress is in the air in Berkeley is a fact easily discernable even to the casual observer. Improvements of many kinds are in contemplation, and many of them have lately been put into operation in different features of life in this beautiful town.

One of the former variety is a proposition, which has long been under consideration, for the equipment and operation of an automobile service for the Berkeley public, and there appears to be every probability that Berkeley will be one of the first places on the Pacific coast to be supplied with this up-to-date mode of passenger traffic.

A mining man who is a resident of Berkeley, and who, for obvious reasons, desires that his name be withheld for the present, is the prime mover in this enterprise. Associated with him are several other capitalists, and the intention is to start the service with at least three or four automobiles, each with a carrying capacity of eight or ten people, beside the driver, and to increase the equipment as the patronage may warrant.

The rapidly-moving vehicles are intended to cover any desired route within the town limits, and it is the expectation to make the maximum fare ten cents. On the shorter trips only five cents will be charged, and at these very low rates it is thought that the flying wagons will be kept very busy by an appreciative public. It is hoped to be able to inaugurate this new movement during the coming spring, and the only thing which can delay the matter is the rush of orders under which all the automobile manufacturers of the country are now struggling. The parties interested have definitely decided to move in the matter and the money is all ready to put the undertaking on its feet in excellent shape.

January 18, 1900

Hello, North Five!

General Changes in Telephone System Tomorrow.

Very important changes are made in the telephone system of Berkeley and elsewhere, to take effect tomorrow, the 25th. There seems to be some reason for the change, as will be noted by the following announcement of the company:

"Owing to the close proximity of Oakland, Alameda and Berkeley, and the subscribers in each of the changes having had similar prefixes, to prevent confusion in the future it has been decided to give each exchange a different set of prefixes. This necessitated changing the prefixes as follows:

"Berkeley: Main to North; Red to Dana; Black to Mason; Vine to Stuart; Grant to Derby.

"Alameda: Main to South; Red to Grand; Black to Paru; Oak to Eagle; Park to Union." There are also a few changes in East Oakland on individual and party lines.

Now you will get your "hello" all mixed up for the next year to come—also your temper. There is, as stated before, some reason for this change, but it is rather insignificant in comparison with the trouble and expense these changes will cause the patrons. Everything will be wrong; all printed matter, signs, advertising, etc., worth thousands of dollars to patrons in Berkeley and Alameda. It is likely the phone at this office is used more than any other of the 718 in Berkeley and there has been no "confusion" on "prefixes" here—a hundred times less than these changes will occasion for months to come. The "close proximity" of these cities existed when the system was being organized; that was the time for the prefixer to get in his work. The changes will probably effect two thousand or more phones, and it will not help the service, unless it be at central. However, the greatest need there is a

"switch" that will take the place of "Line busy—call again!"

Taken all around the change is going to be a nuisance, but we all propose to keep up the "hello" just the same if we do have "hello" of a time at it.

Hello—GAZETTE, North 5?

Yes—hello—what is it?

"News item—Mrs. Jo P. Q. Siskiyou is visiting for a week with Mrs. Al Z. Plunderwasti at 4009 Muchakinek street; goodby North 5."

"Call again."

February 24, 1900

To Revive An Old Industry.

San Francisco parties have purchased the old Stewart tannery, in West Berkeley, and are preparing to start brisk work in the way of tanning hides and finishing leather at this one-time busy but long deserted old plant. This will make another good industry for the West end, and it is one of several which have recently started up. On the whole, prospects seem bright for West Berkeley's future as a manufacturing district.

January 26, 1900

BERKELEY'S GROWTH.

Startling Changes for the Better Observed by a Former Resident.

Magic Transformation Wrought by the Spirit of Modern Enterprise Within a Dozen Years.

"...here facing the Golden Gate, which opens to us the opulence of Oriental commerce, with the serene beauty of the grand Berkeley hills looking down upon us, with the best of educational advantages, with art, music, and the drama throwing their subtle spell and their uplifting influences about us, Berkeley's growth in material things is assured.

"Is it too much to hope that with all these advantages and blessings this favored community will so manage its municipal affairs that its example will afford lessons in civic righteousness to all our land?"

—S. N. Wyckoff, *Berkeley Reporter,* December 1906

C. H. McLenathen, a former well-known and popular Berkeley real estate dealer who left here in 1888 for New Mexico, has returned hither with his family for permanent residence, satisfied that nowhere else in all the broad land can be found a city possessing so many great advantages to the homeseeker.

Mr. McLenathen was simply amazed at the changes for the better which had been effected for physical Berkeley during the past twelve years. He says that when he alighted at the Berkeley station the only edifice which at first glance he recognized as a familiar of the olden days was the Odd Fellows' building, and he could hardly believe his eyes as he gazed upon the large and substantial new business blocks which have been erected during the past few years. Later, he was no less surprised, on looking over the residence portions of the town, to see the immense number of new homes and the admirable character of the residences recently erected.

"When I left here, in 1888," said Mr. McLenathen during a pleasant chat with a GAZETTE reporter, "Berkeley was a straggling country village, and I think there were very few of the citizens of the place at that time who would even have hoped for such conditions as we see here to-day.

"The mossbacks were more in evidence than they are now, and it was a well-nigh impossible thing to work up the public sentiment in favor of improvements. I well remember what a time we had before we could get a vote which should authorize the laying of the Dwight way sewer. It took several elections to settle the matter, and the so-called crazy scheme was met by fierce indignation from the "conservative" men, some of whom declared that there would never be in all Berkeley enough people to warrant the expense of laying that one sewer—that a sewer system in Berkeley was not needed, and that it never would be a necessity, and all that silurian rot.

"I am delighted to find that a more enterprising spirit obtains at the present day—and that it has for some years past, as the public improvements of the town so emphatically attest. The money paid out by Berkeley in street improvements

January 17, 1900

Sewer trenching on Sacramento Street in the early 1900s. Berkeley Wileges family horse teams. Courtesy of the Berkeley Historical Society, catalog #1495.

Watch Factory Reminiscence.

One of the few survivors of those who came from the East to work for the Cornell Watch Company in the old watch factory building which was recently burned at West Berkeley is G. L. Parker, who is now visiting here. His reminiscences form an interesting story of the early days in Berkeley.

It was in 1874 that the factory was moved from San Francisco to Berkeley, the machinery and ninety skilled workmen having been brought from Chicago. Millionaire William Ralston erected the building at West Berkeley at an enormous cost, as lumber was very high. The company prospered until 1876, when Ralston committed suicide. A man named A. L. Troller then leased the building for a year and affairs again looked well for West Berkeley. Troller, at the expiration of his year's lease, could not obtain a renewal The Wentworth Shoe Company then took the building for the years 1877 and 1878.

Mr. Parker has kept himself informed of the whereabouts of the workmen who came out with him. There are many pioneers in Berkeley who well remember the men, many of whom built homes in West Berkeley. Frank Stiles lived for many years in North Berkeley, having occupied the position of Superintendent of the Standard Soap Works after the Cornell failure. He is now farming in Middletown, Lake county. Daniel Crotty resides in East Oakland. Wm. Day occupies a responsible position with the Union Iron Works. Fred Lake went back to Rockford, Illinois, as did William Wilkes. John John K. Bigelow lives on Stevenson street, San Francisco. Charles Soper lives at Ann Arbor, Michigan.

Mr. Parker concluded by saying to the GAZETTE reporter, "Where the GAZETTE building now stands, there was, in 1876, an apple orchard, so you see things have changed greatly since then."

March 29, 1900

By the early 1900s the town founders were passing away. *Berkeley Gazette* articles duly noted the deaths of pioneer men and women, stating, for example, in the case of William B. Story, that his life was crowded more full of experiences than falls to the lot of most men.

The building of the Cornell Watch Company on Gilman Street between Sixth and Seventh Streets. Originally in San Francisco, it relocated to Berkeley during the economic depression of the 1870s. It later became the California Watch Company and then the Wentworth Shoe Factory. Its final use was as an incredible residence of a Dr. Rohan de Baronides. On October 22, 1899, this structure burned down. Courtesy of the Berkeley Historical Society.

"The long ago of Berkeley is not long ago as father time reckons, but customs, conditions, and casts make it seem eons apart. Only a period of twenty-five or thirty years, but what a difference between the sociability of that early day and the society of today. Society had no formal boundary lines in those days. The people were too few to form factions and cliques and the intermittent events were of general community interest.

"Then the houses were mere dots in large open commons and paths led every where. Those were times of neighborhood comradeship with a pleasant afternoon cup of tea and a little harmless gossip. Everybody knew everybody else, and were interested in the same things. Pink teas were unheard of and a clean dress was sufficient sartorial elegance. With the coming of more people to Berkeley and the gradual growth of the town came a change."

—Miss Lucile Wollenberg, *Berkeley Reporter*, December 1906

FAMOUS PIONEER IS DEAD

Alameda, Sept. 12.—William B. Storey, who was known to all the old-timers as the crack shot express messenger of the fighting days of the gold rush, died Saturday night at Stirling, Butte county, at the home of his daughter, Mrs. C. L. Nash, at whose house he was visiting at the time. Death was due to exhaustion following injuries sustained a while ago, when one of Storey's feet was badly injured by a log rolling across it and crushing it.

The deceased was 75 years old and his life was crowded more full of experiences than falls to the lot of most men.

Mr. Storey was a native of England and came to California in 1853, crossing the Isthmus of Panama. Immediately upon arrival he entered the employ of Wells, Fargo & Co. as shotgun express messenger between Stockton and Columbia. Later on he became a member of the clerical staff of the company in San Francisco, following this by being made manager of the company's interests at that place. He held various other positions of trust with the express company, being retired on a pension only three years ago.

The deceased is survived by a wife and three children, Chester Storey, Mrs. C. L Nash and W. B. Storey Jr., the latter being chief engineer of construction of the Santa Fe at Topeka. Mrs. Storey is so ill at the present time that it was deemed hazardous to inform her of her husband's demise.

Mr. Storey was a Knight Templar and a member of the Oak Grove Lodge, Free and Accepted Masons. The funeral will take place Tuesday morning at 10 o'clock under the auspices of the Masonic lodge.

September 12, 1905

Death of a Pioneer, Mrs. Sarah S. Rowntree.

After a brief illness from pneumonia, Mrs Sarah S. Rowntree passed away this morning at two o'clock, at her home, 1519 Oxford.

The deceased was a pioneer, having come to Berkeley with her husband, William A. Rowntree, in 1873. During that year they built the house in which Mrs. Rowntree's death occurred. She came to California in the spring of 1851. Mr. Rowntree was a superintendent of mines and his wife accompanied him to the scene of his work which lay a portion of the time in Mexico and again in Mariposa county. She also saw much frontier life. It was while she was on "The Fresno," in Kings river country, that the memorable killing of Indian Agent Savage took place.

Mrs. Rowntree, who was a widow, leaves the following children: Mrs. C. C. Hail, Mrs. W. A. Perry, Mrs. A. M. Locke and W. A. Rowntree.

March 16, 1900

Death of Francis L. Such.

W. T. Such of the Berkeley Farm Creamery was called to San Francisco yesterday by the death of his father, Francis L. Such. He was 71 years of age and a native of England, and leaves a wife, and W. T. Such of Berkeley, and a daughter, Mrs. W. E. Turrell, of Tacoma.

Mr. Such was interested in the pioneer days of Berkeley, being one of the organizers of the first water company of the town, which was succeeded by the Alameda Water Company.

The funeral services will be held tomorrow at 2 p. m. at Masonic Temple, San Francisco. Interment private.

March 2, 1900

HORRIBLE REMEDIES

THOSE USED BY DOCTORS IN THE SIXTEENTH CENTURY.

Patients Cast Into Wells to Cure Convulsions—A Ladder Used In Setting a Dislocated Shoulder—Dead Bodies Made Into Medicine.

A fragment of a curious volume has fallen into the hands of a local physician which graphically describes the methods of surgery of several centuries ago. When it is considered that anæsthetics were unknown in those ancient days, the modus operandi of the surgeon of the sixteenth century must appear startlingly cruel in the light of the present day.

The work is that of Ambrose Parey, who in 1579, being then the much famous "chirurgion" of his day, published a bulky volume which became such an established authority and held its place for so long a time that 70 years afterward it was translated into English and published in London.

In his first book he considers the general phenomenon of the body in health and disease, and in the chapter relating to temperaments and humors he writes, "An humor is called by physicians what thing soever is liquid and flowing in the body of living creatures inclosed with blood." Proceeding to the "manifold divisions of humors," he separates them into four parts, distinct in color, taste, effects and qualities—namely, blood, phlegm, choler and melancholy. Exact in his subdivisions, he says: "All men ought to think that such humors are wont to move at set hours of the day as by a certain peculiar motion or tide. Therefore, the blood flows from the ninth hour of the night to the third hour of the day; choler to the ninth of the day. Then melancholy the blood flows from the ninth hour of the night is under the dominion of phlegm."

Equally curious is the following on spirits, which he divides into "animall," "vitall" and "naturall."

"The animal spirit hath taken his seat in the brain. It is called animal because it is the life, but the chief and prime instrument thereof. Wherefore it hath a most subtle and aery substance. This animal spirit is made and harbored in the windings and foldings of the veins and arteries of the brain, brought thither sometimes of the pure air or sweet vapor drawn in by the nose in breathing. The vital spirit is next to it in dignity and excellency, which hath its chief mansion in the left ventricle of the heart. The natural spirit, if such there be any, hath its station in the liver and veins."

Describing "certain juggling and deceitful ways of healing of cures by such means as fear, surprise and even by music for spider bite, the music causing the patient to dance so lustily that he shakes all the poison out of his system," he sums up some of those heroic remedies thus: "I would not cast the patient headlong out of a window, but would rather cast them sodainly, and thinking of no such thing, into a great cistern filled with cold water, with their heads foremost. Neither would I take them out until they had drunk a good quantity of water, that by that sodain fall and strong fear the matter causing the frenzy might be carried from above downward from the noble parts to the ignoble."

A medicine upon which he dilates at great length is "mummie," referred to as the usual remedy for contusions, and he describes it as follows:

"Mummie is a liquor flowing from the aromatick embalmens of dead bodies, which becomes dry and hard" and being ground into medicine was "administered either in whole or portion to such as have fallen from high places, the first and last medicine of almost all our practitioners at this day in such a case."

He also gives some grewsome facts connected with the preparation of "mummie" when he says: "Certain of our French apothecaries, men wondrous audacious and covetous to steal by night the bodies of such as were hanged and embalming them with salt and drugs they dried them in an oven so as to sell them thus adulterated instead of true mummie, whereupon we are thus compelled, both foolishly and cruelly, to devour the mangled and putrid particles of the carcasses of the basest people of Egypt, or of such as are hanged, as though there were no other way to help or recover one bruised with a fall from a high place.

"I have not thought it fit in this place," he says, "to omit the industry of Nicholas Picart, the Duke of Guise, his surgeon, who, being called to a certain countryman to set his shoulder, being out of joint, and finding none in the place besides the patient and his wife, who might assist him in this work, he put the patient, bound after the forementioned manner, to a ladder, then immediately he tyed a staffe at the lower end of the ligature, which was fastened about the patient's arm above his elbow, then put it so tyed under one of the steps of the ladder as low as he could and got astride thereupon and sate thereon with his whole weight and at the same instant made his wife pluck the stool from under his feet, which, being done, the bone presently came into its place."

March 25, 1900

"The streets were few, foot paths ran in all directions and led across the fields to everybody's door, and those were the days of neighborly comradeship and gay sociability. The town was for the most part as nature and a few ranchmen had made it. Here and there fields of hay and grain ripened in the July sunshine, and all else was flourishing tar-weed."

—Unknown writer, *Berkeley Reporter*, December 1906

Guarded Lincoln's Dead Body.

An Old Soldier Who Witnessed the Death of the Martyr President.

William Gallagher, whose home is in Los Angeles, and who has for some time past been employed as a brass molder in a foundry in San Francisco, is visiting Berkeley friends.

Mr. Gallagher, who is an old soldier was connected with one of the most exciting scenes known to the history of our nation. At the time of Lincoln's assassination, on the night of April 14, 1865, his regiment, the Tenth Pennsylvania, was stationed at Washington. As is so generally known, the awful tragedy occurred at Ford's Theater, while the great Laura Keene was playing a benefit performance, President and Mrs. Lincoln, accompanied by several people of high station, occupying the President's box.

At the time of the shooting by John Wilkes Booth, of infamous memory, Gallagher was on provost duty within a block or two of the theater, to which he rushed as soon as he heard of the tragedy, a few moments later, and helped to carry the stricken Chief Magistrate to a house opposite the theater, where he died at an early hour of the following day. Gallagher was one of the first men detailed to guard the dead body of the murdered President.

Mr. Gallagher is a member of Heintzleman Post, No. 33, G. A. R, of San Diego, and is well known and popular among the Grand Army men of the State. He served four years during the Civil War, and is as full of army reminiscence as an egg is of meat.

PIONEER CROSSES DIVIDE

George White Webb, a prominent pioneer of this state and a well known resident of this city for the past twenty-one years, died last evening at the family home, 2131 Bancroft way, after suffering for many months. The deceased was a native of Weymouth, Mass., and leaves a wife and four children.

In the death of George W. Webb, California has lost one of her best known and most respected pioneers. Webb received his early education in Massachusetts and then went to Maryland. There the talk was all of the California gold fields and the young man decided to try his fortunes in the great West, whose possibilities were as yet undreamed of. He took passage in the sailing vessel Nebo, and had a stormy voyage around the Horn.

Arriving in San Francisco in November, 1850, Webb immediately became identified with the early history of the metropolis, choosing to cast his fortunes with the city rather than the gold fields. He was appointed a member of the famous Vigilance Committee. His brother C. C. Webb joined him some years later and the two went to Siskiyou county where they engaged in ranching. In 1884, Webb came to Berkeley and has since made his home here, taking a deep interest in the affairs of the town.

He leaves a wife, Angeline S. H. Webb; two sons, George Standish and Christopher Webb, and two daughters, Margaret Webb and Mrs. Willard P. Inglish of Vacaville, whose husband died at the Webb home but a week ago.

Acknowledgments

In any endeavor one relies on the previous works of others and the help of many people. This book would not have been possible without such help.

To Steve Brett for his computer help, technical assistance, friendship and generous use of his office for scanning at all hours of the day and evening; to Michael Flynn of Station Four of the Berkeley Fire Department and Berkeley Firefighters Association whom I always interrupted from sharpening a chain saw or some scheduled fire station maintenance, but who always made time to generously share his knowledge and Berkeley history materials with a smile; to Chris Treadway of the *Berkeley Voice* who sat with me and went over these newspaper articles and saw their value to our sense of sharing history and offered to run some of these articles in our Berkeley newspaper, the *Berkeley Voice*; to Burl Willes, Ken Cardwell (and his special help in editorial comments), Linda Rosen, John Stansfield and Carl Wilson of the Berkeley Historical Society for their generous assistance, friendship and their donation of the newspapers that sparked this entire project; to Anthony Bruce, Director of the Berkeley Architectural Heritage Association for his ever-present willingness to help and his love of Berkeley; to Sauda Burch for her editing of the text and her awareness of so many topics and viewpoints while preserving my voice in the text; to Sayre Van Young who really was the best copyeditor west of the Mississippi as Burl Willes said; to John Strohmeier of Berkeley Hills Books who was so generous with his time and expertise, it seemed like we were old friends; to Berkeley's Mayor Shirley Dean who took time to read the manuscript and write a statement about it; to Michael Holland of the Berkeley Police Department for his enthusiastic help and his readiness to promptly help again and again with the Department's history files; to Liz Stevens, manager of Prudential California Realty in Berkeley who not only ran a very busy real estate concern, but squeezed me into her schedule so that I could utilize their photo collection; to Jeri Ewart, Kay Finney and the staff of the South Berkeley Public Library who loaned many photos to be used in the book and to the people of South Berkeley who donated

"A long-wished harbor cannot smile to the sailor more sweetly than Berkeley did to me, the first time I saw it."

—Robert Duponey, *Berkeley Reporter*, December 1906

their personal family photos for use in the Library's exhibit—I hope we increased your enjoyment of your contributions; to Irene Stachura and Mary Jo Pugh of the San Francisco Maritime National Historical Park for their interest and willingness and ability to help; to Carolyn Kemp of Alta Bates for photos of old Berkeley hospitals; to the Contra Costa Historical Society for their generosity and help with the photograph of John Muir; to Jeff Norman for his generous and talented efforts in editing and feedback; to Lisa Schulz for her professionalism and standards in her design firm, Elysium Design, whose work speaks for itself; to Bob Hawley, who at his Ross Valley Bookstore and Oyez Press has offered an oasis of western U.S. history against those who might forget, for his friendship and help; to Melissa Schwarz for her suggestions and feedback; to Stephanie Manning of the Berkeley Architectural Heritage Association who is everywhere there is Berkeley history to save, decade after decade; to Gray Brechin for his enthusiastic response to the manuscript and encouragement; to Patricia Holt for her time to meet with me, read the manuscript and email on the book's behalf; to all the folks at Copy Central (Nora, Rodney, Sheila, Rahman, Pico, Sharon, etc.) for their willingness to give a hand and a smile over the three-and-one-half years this project has been going on; to Marya Grambs for her enthusiasm and help with the initial project.

And to acknowledge support on the personal level: to my folks Milton and Mildred, my sister Maxeen, my brother-in-law Tom, my nephews Cody and Zac for all kinds of support; to Kyrie Valtair of whom I am very proud; to the Marymors for listening to my stories so often; to the Mascaro family for their 34 years of friendship; to Bernie Strauss for his friendship sticking by me for 30 years; to Bob Loreaux for his honesty and friendship of 20 years; to the Wheelers for 20 years of being right there; to all the Serotas and Bradins for being the Serotas and Bradins; to El Collie for sharing her amazing dreams with me; to Maggie Newsom, Peitsa Hirvonen, Amelia Ellis, Ron Smith, Walter Akubra Jackson, Earnest Katler, Janet Barriball, the McLais', the Wobb family, Dan Wilcox, Kay Hartshorn, Pam Streitfeld for her love of history and people, Joanna Taylor, Phil and Margo Thompson, Emilio Duenas, the Rooneys, the Penunuri-Browns, Carmen DeArcé, the Chen family, Suzanne Stanford and the Pup for their steadfast support.

"Everything here appealed to my heart; the proud barrenness of the hills and the dreamy swing of the eucalyptus trees, the happy silence everywhere and the happy quiet. And above all, that Bay of San Francisco, which greets me every morning with all its light and all its idle curves."

—Robert Duponey, *Berkeley Reporter*, December 1906